ADVAITA VEDANTA

ADVAITA VEDANTA

Being the Self

Prabhuji

Advaita Vedanta
Being the Self
by Prabhuji

First edition

Printed in Round Top, New York, United States

Published by Prabhuji Mission
Website: prabhuji.net

Avadhutashram
PO Box 900
Cairo, NY, 12413
USA

Painting on the cover by Prabhuji:
"I am that I am"
Acrylic on canvas, New York
Canvas size: 24" x 24"

Library of Congress Control Number: 2020903502
ISBN-13: 978-1-945894-20-6

Contents

Words from the author 3
Preface 7
Introduction 11

Chapter 1 What is Vedanta? 17
Orthodox and heterodox schools 17
Meaning of the term Vedanta 20
What is Vedanta? 22
Whom is Vedanta intended for? 25
What does Vedanta talk about? 26
Brahma-vidyā or "the wisdom of the Self" 27
Yoga-vidyā or "the wisdom of the yoga" 29

Chapter 2 Knowledge and wisdom 33
Knowledge and ignorance 33
Understanding 36
Integrative and differentiated knowledge 38
Knowledge and wisdom 39

Chapter 3 *Ātma-vicāraṇa* or "self-inquiry" 43

Chapter 4 The sacred literature 55
The Vedas 57
Sections of each Veda 65
Tri-vidyā or "three kinds of knowledge" 67
Vedāṅgas and *Upāṅgas* 69
The threefold Vedantic canon 71
The Upanishads 72
Prakaraṇa-granthas 78

Chapter 5 Brahman 79
Saguṇa-brahman 83
Nirguṇa-brahman 85
Brahman is *sac-cid-ānanda* 89
Sat – Brahman is existence 90
Cit – Brahman is consciousness 91
Ānanda – Brahman is bliss 92
The manifested and the unmanifested 93

Chapter 6 Illusion or *māyā* 97

Chapter 7 God (Īśvara) and the soul (*jīva*) 111

Chapter 8 The world or *jagat* 119
Levels of reality 121
Mithyā or "non-real" 125
The five factors of the objective universe 126
Substrate (*adhiṣṭāna*), appearance (*āropita*), and superimposition (*adhyāsa*) 129

Chapter 9 The causality of Vedanta or *vivarta-vāda* 133

Chapter 10 Creation according to Advaita 145

Chapter 11 A scientific view of our perception of the world 157

Chapter 12 The purposes of human beings or *puruṣārthas* 165
The purposes of human beings 167
Artha or "wealth, security" 168
Kāma or "pleasure" 170
Dharma or "ethics or righteousness" 175
Mokṣa or "liberation" 180

Chapter 13 The five afflictions or *kleśas* 185
Ignorance or *avidyā* 186
Egoism or *asmitā* 197
Attraction and repulsion, or *rāga* and *dveṣa* 198
Abhiniveśa or "clinging to life" 201
The Vedantic view 203

Chapter 14 *Sādhana-catuṣṭaya* 209
1. *Viveka* or "discernment" 214
2. *Vairāgya* or "dispassion, detachment" 218
3. *Ṣaṭ-sampat* or "the treasure of the six virtues" 221
3.1. *Śama* or "serenity" 222
3.2. *Dama* or "control over the senses" 223
3.3. *Uparati* or "renunciation of worldly desires" 225
3.4. *Titikṣā* or "tolerance" 226
3.5. *Śraddhā* or "trust, faith" 229
3.6. *Samādhāna* or "attention to the Self" 231
4. *Mumukṣutvā* or "the aspiration for liberation" 232

Chapter 15 The disciplines on the path of self-discovery 237
1. *Śravaṇa* or "listening" 239
2. *Manana* or "reflection" 241
3. *Nididhyāsana* or "Vedantic meditation" 242
Ātma-sākṣātkāra or "direct perception of the Self" 243

Chapter 16 Vedantic epistemology 247
Āroha-panthā or "the ascending method" 248
Avaroha-panthā or "the descending method" 252
Pramāṇas or "the means of acquiring knowledge" 252

Chapter 17 Consciousness 257

Chapter 18 Liberation or *mukti* 265
Jīvan-mukta or "the one liberated in life" 268
Mumukṣu or "the ideal aspirant" 273
Truth is not a means 275
The motivation of the seeker 275

Epilogue 277
The acceptance of solitude 277
Only reality is 280

Appendix:
The life and work of Śrī Śaṅkarācārya 285
About Prabhuji 337
About the Prabhuji Mission 351
About the Avadhutashram 353
The Retroprogressive Path 355
Prabhuji today 357

ॐ अज्ञानतिमिरान्धस्य ज्ञानाञ्जनशलाकया ।
चक्षुरुन्मीलितं येन तस्मै श्रीगुरवे नमः ॥

oṁ ajñāna-timirāndhasya
jñānāñjana-śalākayā
cakṣur unmīlitaṁ yena
tasmai śrī-gurave namaḥ

Salutations unto that holy Guru who, applying the ointment [medicine] of [spiritual] knowledge, removes the darkness of ignorance of the blinded ones [unenlightened] and opens their eyes.

This book is dedicated, with deep gratitude and eternal respect, to the holy lotus feet of my beloved masters His Divine Grace Avadhūta Śrī Brahmānanda Bābājī Mahārāja (Guru Mahārāja) and His Divine Grace Bhakti-kavi Atulānanda Ācārya Mahārāja (Gurudeva).

Words from the Author

The story of my life is nothing more than a long journey, from what I believed myself to be to what I truly am. It is an authentic inner and outer pilgrimage. It is a tale of transcending what is personal and universal, partial and total, illusory and real, apparent and true. My life is a flight beyond what is temporary and eternal, darkness and light, humanity and divinity. This story is not public but profoundly private and intimate.

Only what begins, ends; only what starts, finishes. One who lives in the present is neither born nor dies, because what has no beginning has no end.

I am a disciple of a seer, an enlightened being, and somebody who is nobody. I was initiated in my spiritual childhood by the moonlight. A seagull who loved flying more than anything else in life inspired me. In love with the impossible, I crossed the universe obsessed with a star. I have walked infinite paths, following the footsteps of those who could see.

Like the ocean that longs for water, I sought my home within my own house.

I am a simple intermediary who shares his experience with others. I am not a guide, coach, teacher, instructor, educator, psychologist, enlightener, pedagogue, evangelist, rabbi, *posek halacha*, healer, therapist, satsangist, psychic, leader, medium, savior, or guru. I am only a traveler whom you can ask for directions. I will gladly show you a place where everything calms upon arrival, a place beyond the sun and the stars, beyond your desires and longings, beyond time and space, beyond concepts and conclusions, and beyond everything that you believe you are or imagine that you will be.

I am just a whim or perhaps a joke from the sky and the only mistake of my beloved spiritual masters.

Aware of the abyss that separates revelation and our works, we live in a frustrated attempt to faithfully express the mystery of the spirit.

I paint sighs, hopes, silences, aspirations, and melancholies, inner landscapes, and sunsets of the soul.

I am a painter of the indescribable, inexpressible, and indefinable of our depths. Or maybe I just write colors and paint words.

Since childhood, little windows of paper captivated my attention; through them, I visited places, met people, and made friends. Those tiny *maṇḍalas* were my true elementary school, high school, and college. Like skilled teachers, these *yantras* have guided me through contemplation, attention, concentration, observation, and meditation.

Like a physician studies the human body, or a lawyer studies laws, I have dedicated my entire life to the study of myself. I can say with certainty that I know what resides and lives in this heart.

It is not my intention to convince anyone of anything. I do not offer theology or philosophy, nor do I preach or teach, I simply think out loud. The echo of these words may lead you to the infinite space of peace, silence, love, existence, consciousness, and absolute bliss.

Do not search for me. Search for yourself. You do not need me or anyone else, because the only thing that really matters is you. What you yearn for lies within you, as what you are, here and now.

I am not a merchant of rehashed information, nor do I intend to do business with my spirituality. I do not teach beliefs or philosophies. I only speak about what I see and just share what I know.

Avoid fame, for true glory is not based on public opinion but on what you really are. What matters is not what others think of you, but your own appreciation of who you are.

Choose bliss over success, life over reputation, and wisdom over information. If you succeed, you will know not only admiration but also true envy. However, jealousy is mediocrity's tribute to talent and an open acceptance of one's own inferiority.

I advise you to fly freely and never be afraid of making mistakes. Learn the art of transforming your mistakes into lessons. Never blame others for your faults: remember that taking complete responsibility for your life is a sign of maturity. When you fly, you learn that what matters is not touching the sky but the courage to spread your wings. The higher you rise, the smaller and less significant the world looks. As you walk, sooner or later you will understand that every search begins and ends in you.

Your unconditional well-wisher,
Prabhuji

Preface

nāsad āsīn no sad āsīt tadānīm
nāsīd rajo no vyomā paro yat
kim āvarīvaḥ kuha kasya śarmann
ambhaḥ kim āsīd gahanam gabhīram

> Then there was neither existence nor nonexistence. There was no ethereal space nor any celestial sphere beyond. What covered it? Where? Under whose protection? Was there water, deep and unfathomable?
>
> (*Ṛg Veda*, 10.129.1)

The search for reality has been a passion for many people since the very beginning of humanity. The legacy of this passion are the great monuments of scripture like the Bible, Quran, Zend Advesta, Dhammapada, Tao Te Ching, and so on. Pilate asks in the gospel of John (18:38): "What is truth?" This question has sparked debates among theologians, philosophers, logicians, and scholars.

Absolute Truth is immutable and completely indifferent to changes in time, space, and circumstances.

Advaita Vedanta, or "non-dual Vedanta," calls it *Brahman*. Reality is constant and not subject to modifications. Obviously, if something changes overnight it cannot be accepted as real. We may dream that we are a butterfly, a fish, or Superman, but upon waking, we regain our previous identity. Since dreams are temporary, we differentiate them from everyday reality.

In light of this, can the world we perceive be considered real? Advaita postulates that what we perceive through the senses is illusory because it is subject to constant change. In other words, no temporary phenomenon can be considered real.

We can see that the hands of a clock rotate because the clock face stays still. Similarly, the perception of every movement requires both a changing element and an invariable one. The world of names and forms is changeable and illusory; reality is the stable base. The *Vedānta Sūtra* emphatically states *athāto brahma jijñāsā* or "now we will inquire into Brahman, or 'the Absolute'" and suggests exploring the world's permanent background, that is, the unchanging foundation of the entire universe.

Any search for reality that is based only on logic is fruitless, since the mind is capable of arguing in favor of any truth, as the Sophists used to do. However, sincere seekers, sensing the transcendental, ask themselves the same question as Miguel de Unamuno in his book *The Tragic Sense of Life*, "Is only what is rational true? Could there be a reality that by its nature is inaccessible to reason and perhaps even opposed to it?"

As long as we are unable to transcend the mental level, which is saturated with ideas, concepts, conclusions, and rational hypotheses, we will go on developing mere philosophical theories. A weak quest for Truth will only create new doctrines. The fruit of a half-hearted longing for reality is yet another philosophy. But a sincere and honest thirst for Truth can lead to a revelatory vision of reality that transcends thinking.

The mind is memory. It is the warehouse of our past, and therefore, it is an inadequate tool to search for the unknown. Thought, as an instrument of the past, far from aspiring to reality only dreams of its own projections. It is incapable of finding Truth or even looking for it: it does not seek the unknown but the opposite of what it knows.

In the words of Alejandro Jodorowsky, "the Seekers of Truth, realizing that it was impossible to find it, became Seekers of Lies. As they found lies and eliminated them, they gradually faded away. When the Seekers disappeared completely, the Truth shone forth."

Most spiritual seekers create a mental concept of enlightenment based on books and lectures. In the pursuit of enlightenment, they do not aspire to a state of pure consciousness but to their own version of it. However, any effort to achieve enlightenment is superfluous, because consciousness already is: we already are what we aspire to be.

When this search is born of a genuine existential need for discovery, it will continue until it caresses authenticity. Only a vital, serious, and sincere search can end in the light of what is, as it is.

Introduction

Jñāna literally means "knowledge, wisdom, understanding, or cognition," and refers to existential knowledge. The Greeks called this revealing power *epiginosko* (ἐπιγινώσκω). The word *yoga* means "union." Thus, *jñāna-yoga* is a path that aims to realize the essential unity of the part and the Whole through knowledge. It is one of the four classical yogic methods of development. It leads to the dissolution of ignorance and to the revelation that the world is an illusory projection and our true nature is Brahman.

Jñāna-yoga is closely related to Advaita, the branch of Vedanta that recognizes a single reality behind this universe of names and forms. This yogic system is the practical aspect of Vedanta. According to *jñāna*, the Self (Ātman) resides in every place and in every being.

This path of wisdom leads you to the discovery that the center of your existence is not only yours, but the center of all that exists; it is the Self, or consciousness. It suggests restructuring the Western concept of consciousness. From our dualist and relativist perspective, we believe consciousness to be a capacity or faculty that we possess. In fact, from the perspective of the Absolute, it is consciousness that possesses us. Consciousness does not belong to us; we belong to it. Consciousness precedes us because as minds, we occupy a subsequent step in the process of cosmic manifestation.

Jñāna-yoga is considered a destructive path, since it destroys our habitual cognitive state of subject–object. It encourages us to question the source of our existence. Its basic teaching is that our true nature is divine; it is the ultimate reality that lies in the depths of every living being.

Although *jñāna-yoga* is the path of wisdom par excellence, it should be clarified that this is not knowledge that is known by a knower; rather, it is wisdom that eliminates all distinctions between knowledge, the known, and the knower. *Jñāna* is not the result of thinking but of becoming aware of reality.

Many think that embarking on an inner search is selfish. However, examining our own consciousness is a universal investigation and not a personal one. As we observe, the walls that demarcate our supposed individuality collapse and all differences evaporate. Clearly, what we intuit is beyond the mental domain and cannot be defined. However, we should not get frustrated by this inability to verbalize it, since we may be looking precisely for the unspeakable.

Jñāna-yoga aspires to *aparokṣānubhava,* or "the direct experience of our own authenticity": to realize Ātman as the absolute reality, or Brahman.

The *Kaṭha Upanishad* states:

nāyam ātmā pravacanena labhyo
na medhayā na bahunā śrutena
yam evaiṣa vṛṇute tena labhyaḥ
tasyaiṣa ātmā vivṛṇute tanūm svām

> This Self cannot be attained by study of the scriptures, by intellectual perception, or by hearing about it frequently; those whom the Self chooses, by them alone is it attained. To them the Self reveals its true nature.
> (*Kaṭha Upanishad,* 1.2.23)

Jñāna-yoga does not aspire to intellectual knowledge, but instead of rejecting the mind, it uses it to achieve a broader evolutionary process. The intellect explores and examines its own functioning. More than a philosophical inquiry, Vedanta promotes self-investigation: a study of the cognitive act itself.

The study of the Upanishads is an important aspect of this path, but it is wrong to believe that erudition is enough to lead us to self-realization. Scriptures, the master's teachings, and *sādhana* aim to awaken the memory of the disciple. The ego is just forgetfulness or amnesia. This wisdom cannot be instilled the way it is at school because *jñāna-yoga* is not a process of studying but of remembering who we really are, our true nature.

Nowadays, we acquire knowledge much faster than wisdom. Our skills allow us to manufacture smartphones but our conversations lack depth. We assemble sophisticated computers but end up wasting our time playing games. We have made great progress on the surface but internally, we are stuck. Although we have matured superficially, we are psychologically and spiritually trapped in childhood.

When we were bored as children, we obsessively looked for ways to kill time. As adults, some turn to newspapers, the radio, television, and computers, while others find entertainment or distraction in spirituality. Many people have turned this pursuit for Truth into a fun shopping trip. They window shop for retreats, courses, teachers, books, and so on. If our spiritual life is simply another form of recreation, the search will be limited to empty words and will certainly keep us on the surface. If we use spiritual life as entertainment, we turn God into another diversion and enlightenment into a simple source of pleasure.

The mystery of the unknown cannot be pursued the same way as money, fame, or sex. The mind cannot seek what it does not know. It can only aspire to what it manages to project from its own content. If we try to think about God, we end up with a mental projection from our past. To think about the Truth is to deal with the cultural legacy of our society. The Truth does not accept objectification and, therefore, it cannot be sought. If it is found, it loses its vitality. In this life, consciousness is the only thing that, despite being indefinable, is impossible to ignore.

The Truth reveals itself when the search for it stops. When we stop chasing our mental projections of the Truth, we realize that we are enlightened. As Master Kokuan expresses it in *The Ten Bulls of Zen*:

> Mediocrity has disappeared. The mind is free of limitation. I do not seek any state of enlightenment; nor have I stayed where there is no enlightenment. As I do not stay in any state, eyes cannot see me. If hundreds of birds covered my path with flowers, such praise would be meaningless.

As an egoic entity, you are an illusion. An unreal being cannot aspire to be authentic. Truth can only be revealed in a moment free of what is known, of memory, of past. You cannot search, reach, achieve, or know the Truth: you can only be it. Suddenly, you become aware that you *are* what you aspire to. Clearly, you cannot find the Truth by searching for it, but without searching you will never find it.

Chapter 1

What is Vedanta?

Orthodox and heterodox schools

Hindu philosophy comprises orthodox schools (*āstika*), which are based on the Vedas, and heterodox schools (*nāstika*), which do not accept Vedic spiritual authority.

Sanātana-dharma, or Hinduism as it is called today, is a collective term for six orthodox schools, also called *ṣad-darśanas* or *ṣat-śāstras*. The *Haya-śīrṣa Pañcarātra* enumerates them:

gautamasya kaṇādasya
kapilasya patañjaleḥ
vyāsasya jaimineś cāpi
darśanāni ṣad eva hi

There are in fact six *darśanas*: that of Gautama (*Nyāya*), Kaṇāda (*Vaiśeṣika*), Kapila (*Sāṅkhya*),

Patañjali (*Yoga*), Vyāsa (*Uttara-mīmāṁsā*) and Jaimini (*Pūrva-mīmāṁsā*).

(*Haya-śīrṣa Pañcarātra*)

- *Nyāya*, founded by Gautama Ṛṣi, explores the sources of knowledge.
- *Vaiśeṣika*, founded by Kaṇāda Ṛṣi, is an empirical system of atomism.
- *Sāṁkhya*, founded by Kapila Muni, is a system that postulates the duality of consciousness and matter.
- Yoga, founded by Patañjali Maharṣi, is a school that emphasizes concentration, contemplation, and meditation.
- *Pūrva-mīmāṁsā*, founded by Jaimini, explains the mantras of the *Ṛg Veda* that are chanted during fire sacrifices. This system does not support mysticism or asceticism.
- *Uttara-mīmāṁsā* or Vedanta, founded by either Bādarāyaṇa or Vyāsa, mainly teaches the wisdom revealed in the *Āraṇyakas* (Books of the Forest) and Upanishads. Vedanta philosophy includes three major schools: Mādhavācārya's dualism (*Dvaita*), Rāmānujācārya's qualified monism (*Viśiṣṭādvaita*), and Śaṅkarācārya's monism (Advaita), which is the school this book discusses in depth.

The first four philosophical systems accept the authority of the Vedas, but they do not derive their philosophical principles from these scriptures. On the other hand, the last two are textually based on the Vedas.

akṣapādaḥ kaṇādaś ca
kapilo jaiminis tathā
vyāsaḥ patañjaliś caite
vaidikāḥ sūtra-kārakāḥ

bṛhaspaty ārhatau buddho
veda-mārga-virodhinaḥ
ete 'dhikāritāṁ vīkṣya
sarve śāstra-pravartakāḥ

Akṣapāda (or Gautama), Kaṇāda, Kapila, Jaimini, Vyāsa, and Patañjali are all authors of philosophic *sūtras* and believe in the Vedas. Bṛhaspati, Ārhata (Jina), and Buddha are all opposed to the religious path of the Vedas. In view of the varying fitness of individuals, they all have become proponents of authoritative systems of religion and philosophy.
(Śaṅkarācārya, *Sarva-siddhānta-saṅgraha,* 1.23–24)

The *nāstika* schools are:

- *Cārvāka*, which is a system of materialist thought that accepts the existence of free will.
- Buddhism.
- Jainism.
- *Ājīvika*, which is a materialist philosophy that denies the existence of free will.

Meaning of the term Vedanta

Etymologically, the term *vedānta* is composed of the words *veda* (knowledge, wisdom) and *anta* (end, conclusion). Vedanta has two meanings:

1. The highest spiritual knowledge or the culmination of wisdom.
2. The part of the Vedas that was written last, since Vedanta is based on the Upanishads, the last section of the Vedas.

In the *Muktikā Upanishad*, we find this term used with both meanings. Hanumān asks Lord Rāma about his nature or state and the means for liberation. He replies:

sādhu pṛṣṭaṁ mahā-bāho
vadāmi śṛṇu tattvataḥ
vedānte supratiṣṭho 'haṁ
vedāntaṁ samupāśraya

vedāntāḥ ke raghu-śreṣṭha
vartante kutra te vada
hanūmañ chṛṇu vakṣyāmi
vedānta-sthitim añjasā

niśvāsa-bhūtā me viṣṇor
vedā jātāḥ suvistarāḥ
tileṣu tailavad vede
vedāntaḥ supratiṣṭhitaḥ

rāma vedāḥ kati vidhās
teṣāṁ śākhāś ca rāghava
tāsūpaniṣadāḥ kāḥ syuḥ
kṛpayā vada tattvataḥ

"Good question." I shall tell you: "I am well established in Vedanta." [Hanumān asked] "O best among the Raghus, please tell me, what are the Vedantas and where are they?" [Rāma replied] "The Vedas in all their great extent are my breath, Vedanta is well established in them, like oil in sesame." "O Rāma, please tell me how many are the Vedas and how many branches do they have? Of these, what are the Upanishads?"
(*Muktikā Upanishad*, 1.7–10)

Another name for Vedanta is *Uttara-mīmāṁsā*, or "one that surpasses *mīmāṁsā*," which distinguishes it from the old *mīmāṁsā* doctrine. To differentiate the new Vedanta, the retronym *Pūrva-mīmāṁsā* was coined, which means "previous, earlier, or old *mīmāṁsā*."

Śaṅkarācārya defines Vedanta in relation to the *Uttara-mimāṁsa* in his overview of India's philosophical schools, called *Sarva-siddhānta-saṅgraha*:

bhavaty uttara-mīmāmsā
tvaṣṭādhyāyī dvidhā ca sā
devatā-jñāna-kāṇḍābhyām
vyāsa-sūtra dvayos samam

pūrvādhyāya-catuṣkeṇa
mantra-vācyātra devatā
saṅkarṣaṇoditā taddhi
devatā-kāṇḍam ucyate

bhāṣya caturbhir adhyāyair
bhagavat-pāda-nirmitam
cakre vivaraṇa tasya
tad vedānta pracakṣate

> The *Uttara-mīmāṁsā* consists of eight chapters and is divided into two sections, *devatā-kāṇḍa* (the deities section) and *jñāna-kāṇḍa* (the wisdom section). Both sections have *sūtras* composed by Vyāsa. In the first four chapters, the deities mentioned in the (Vedic) mantras are described by Śaṅkarṣṇa (Vyāsa), therefore, it is called *Devatā-kāṇḍa.* A four-chapter commentary was later composed by Bhagavatpāda (Vyāsa). His explanation of this wisdom is called *Vedānta.*
> (*Sarva-siddhānta-saṅgraha,* 1.20–22)

What is Vedanta?

Western Indology scholars treat Vedanta as a philosophy, a school of thought, or a theology. This book does not present an academic perspective on Vedanta, but the view that the Vedantic tradition has about itself. The Vedanta defines itself as a means of knowledge, or *pramāṇa*, which offers a method revealed by a non-human source to experience our authentic divine nature.

> *vedanto nāmopaniṣat-pramāṇaṁ tad upakārīṇi śārīraka-sūtrādīni.*
>
> Vedanta is the means of knowledge (*pramāṇa*) of the Upanishads. The *Śāriraka Sūtra* and other books help to correctly expound its meaning.
>
> (Śrī Sadānanda Yogindra Sarasvatī, *Vedānta-sāra*, 3)

Vedanta is a *sampradāya*, or "a tradition of oral teachings," passed on through the chain of disciplic succession (*evaṁ paramparā-prāptam*, Bhagavad Gita, 4.2).

Hinduism does not have an authority figure like the pope in Catholicism. Different lineages interpret the scriptures according to their own perspective. Originally, families sent their children to live with gurus, who imparted spiritual education. Disciples used to live in the *guru-kula*, the house of the master, for at least twelve years, from childhood to their teens. The study program at the ashram included worship, hatha yoga, Sanskrit, music, sacred scriptures, and essential values such as respect, truthfulness, compassion, non-violence, and so on. This education was comprehensive and touched on many aspects of life. Learning alongside a master connects theoretical and intellectual teaching with the gestation of the disciple.

These days, most people do not have time to dedicate themselves to proper spiritual training. The study of Vedanta, or spiritual life in general, has become more of a pastime or a hobby. When Vedanta is taught through books or online lectures, the teachings are simplified in order to reach a larger audience that would otherwise not have access to this knowledge. Anyone who has not directly and personally worked with a spiritual master will be unable to understand why Vedanta cannot be learned only from a screen. As it is beautifully instructed in the *Muṇḍaka Upanishad*:

parīkṣya lokān karma-citān brāhmaṇo
nirveda-māyān nāsty akṛtaḥ kṛtena
tad vijñānārthaṁ sa gurum evābhigacchet
samitpāṇiḥ śrotriyaṁ brahma-niṣṭham

> Let a *Brāhmaṇa* having examined the worlds produced by karma be free from desires, thinking, "there is nothing eternal produced by karma"; and in order to acquire the knowledge of the eternal, let him, sacrificial fuel in hand, approach a guru alone, who is well-versed in the Vedas and situated in Brahman.
>
> (*Muṇḍaka Upanishad*, 1.12)

Clearly, Vedanta is not a popular philosophy aimed at the masses, because it is not only theoretical but also practical. The theory may be learned from a book but the practical aspect can only be grasped by living with a realized spiritual master who belongs to a line of disciplic succession. The process of learning develops within the framework of a personal relationship between master and disciple. It is no coincidence that the word *upaniṣad* means "to sit by the master's side."

Whom is Vedanta intended for?

vivekino viraktasya
śamādi guṇa-śālinaḥ
mumukṣor eva hi brahma-
jijñāsā-yogyatā matā

> Only a person of discrimination and dispassion, who possesses calmness and the allied virtues and is longing for liberation, is considered qualified to inquire after Brahman.
>
> (*Viveka-cūḍāmaṇi*, 17)

Vedanta is intended for seekers of Truth—for those who want to know their own reality and the reality of everything. Only those who aspire to liberation, or *mokṣa*, are qualified for Vedanta. Liberation from what? Liberation from limiting conditioning, in other words, from the mind. It takes a high spiritual level to aspire only to liberation from conditioning. In Sanskrit, such an advanced being is called a *mumukṣu*, a word that derives from the root *muc*, or "to liberate." Besides a desire for liberation, a *mumukṣu* must have the qualities required to assimilate the teachings. Some of these qualities, underdeveloped in most people, are dispassion, detachment, firm commitment to liberation, mental stability, and so on. The scriptures detail the qualifications that are needed to undertake this retroprogressive path.

What does Vedanta talk about?

The renowned Vedantic master Sadānanda Yogīndra Sarasvatī explained the subject matter of Vedanta in the beginning of his book *Vedānta-sāra*:

> *viṣayaḥ— jīva-brahmaikyaṁ śuddha-caitanyaṁ prameyaṁ tatra eva vedāntānāṁ tātparyāt.*
>
> The subject [of Vedanta] is to prove the identity of the individual self and Brahman, which is of the nature of pure conciousness and is to be realized. For, indeed, this is the meaning of the Vedanta texts.
>
> (*Vedānta-sāra*, 27)

> *prayojanaṁ tu— tad aikya-prameya-gatājñāna-nivrittiḥ sva-svarūpānandāvāptiś ca "tarati śokam ātma-vit"(Cha. U., 7.1.3) ity ādi-śruteḥ "brahma-vid brahma iva bhavati" (Muṇḍ. U., 3.2.9) ity ādi-śruteś ca.*
>
> The necessity [of the study of Vedanta] is the dispelling of ignorance relating to that identity which is to be realised, as well as

> the attainment of bliss resulting from the realisation of one's own Self. As in such *Śruti* passages: "The knower of Self overcomes grief" (*Chāndogya Upanishad*, 7.1.3), "One who knows Brahman becomes Brahman" (*Muṇḍaka Upanishad*, 3.2.9).
>
> (*Vedānta-sāra*, 29)

Vedanta deals with two central topics: *Brahma-vidyā* and *yoga-vidyā*.

Brahma-vidyā or "the wisdom of the Self"

tasmai sa vidvān-upasannāya samyak
praśānta-cittāya śamānvitāya
yenākṣaraṁ puruṣaṁ veda satyaṁ
provāca tāṁ tattvato brahma-vidyām

> To those who have thus approached, whose hearts are well subdued and who have control over their senses, let them truly be taught the *Brahma-vidyā* by which the true immortal Puruṣa is known.
>
> (*Muṇḍaka Upanishad*, 13)

Vidyā means "knowledge" and Brahma, or Brahman, is the essence and foundation of everything and everyone. Brahman is a Sanskrit term that comes from the root *bṛh*, "to expand or disseminate." Etymologically, Brahman means "expansion or dissemination." This word indicates that Brahman is omnipresent and transcends all limitations of space, time, and causality. Brahman is infinite; it is not limited by space; it is eternal since it transcends time; it is immutable since it is beyond causality.

We cannot attain *brahma-vidyā*, or "the wisdom of the Self," only from mental effort or intellectual study. *Jñāna-yoga* is much more than a theory, philosophy, doctrine, or system of logical and deductive knowledge: it is an existential vision. It is not a matter of understanding or knowing something, but being it. This is one of the most important messages. Lord Kṛṣṇa states:

sarvasya cāhaṁ hṛdi sanniviṣṭo
mattaḥ smṛtir jñānam apohanaṁ ca
vedaiś ca sarvair aham eva vedyo
vedānta-kṛd veda-vid eva cāham

> I am found in everyone's heart. I am the source of remembrance, wisdom, and forgetfulness. It is I who must be known through the Vedas. Indeed, I am the compiler of Vedanta and the knower of the Vedas.
>
> (Bhagavad Gita, 15.15)

In saying this, Lord Kṛṣṇa is informing us "It is I [the Self] who must be known through the Vedas." *Jñāna-yoga* is exactly this: to perceive our true and authentic "I": the infinite Self. To experience it is to realize God.

In this verse of the Gita, Kṛṣṇa declares himself to be the origin of remembering. Just as ignorance is forgetfulness, the wisdom that Hinduism refers to is remembrance. This is confirmed by the *Atharva Veda*:

punar ehi vācas-pate
devena manasā saha
vasoṣpate ni ramaya
mayyevāstu mayi śrutam

> O Lord of speech! Be so kind as to return with divine intelligence; instill it in me, O Lord of all blessings, so that your wisdom can dwell within me.
>
> (*Atharva Veda*, 1.1.2)

The wisdom of *jñāna-yoga* consists of remembering oneself. Only then will we realize that heaven and hell are nothing more than states of remembering or forgetting oneself.

sa yo ha vai tat paramaṁ brahma veda
brahmaiva bhavati nāsyābrahma-vit kule bhavati
tarati śokaṁ tarati pāpmānaṁ guhā-
granthibhyo vimukto 'mṛto bhavati

> He who knows that highest Brahman becomes even Brahman; and none who does not know Brahman will be born in his line. The knower of Brahman goes beyond grief, and virtue and vice; he breaks free from the knot of the heart and finally becomes immortal.
>
> (*Muṇḍaka Upanishad*, 3.2.9)

Yoga-vidyā or "the wisdom of the yoga"

While it is true that *Brahma-vidyā* is the essence of Vedanta, comprehending it would be impossible without the support of *yoga-vidyā*. This topic is discussed extensively in the scriptures and it is essential to understand it clearly.

Yoga-vidyā is a way to prepare ourselves to digest Vedantic truths. It involves developing certain attitudes, behaviors, and the right view of the fruits of our actions and of everything that happens to us in life. *Yoga-vidyā* is a preparatory and purifying lifestyle that supports our evolution and development on the path of knowing Brahman. Nevertheless, it is not a technique or practice disconnected from the Vedic revelation and perspective.

In his book *Aparokṣānubhūti*, Śaṅkarācārya details *yoga-vidyā* practices as a means to realize *Brahma-vidyā*. He describes the importance of these preparatory practices with the following words:

tri-pañcāṅgān yato vakṣye
pūrvoktasyaiva siddhaye
taiś ca sarvaiḥ sadā kāryaṁ
nididhyāsanam eva tu

nityābhyāsād-ṛte prāptir
na bhavet sac-cid-ātmanaḥ
tasmād brahma nididhyāsej
jijñāsuḥ śreyase ciram

Now, to attain the aforesaid [knowledge], I shall expound the fifteen steps one should

> always practice at all times to facilitate profound meditation. The Ātman that is absolute existence and knowledge cannot be realized without constant practice. So, one seeking knowledge should long meditate upon Brahman to attain the desired aspiration.
>
> (*Aparokṣānubhūti*, 100–101)

To really get to know someone, we should pay more attention to their actions than to their words. *Brahma-vidyā* and *yoga-vidyā* must be mutually supportive and harmonious. *Brahma-vidyā* will lose its effectiveness if we are not pure enough to retain it. We will listen to very nice explanations, but we will be unable to grasp them, much less apply them to our lives. In the West today, an incomplete *yoga-vidyā* is practiced, while the sought-after evolution can only be achieved by incorporating true *Brahma-vidyā*.

Chapter 2

Knowledge and wisdom

Jñāna and *ajñāna* or "knowledge" and "ignorance"

Jñāna is a Sanskrit term that means "knowledge"

Jñāna—also pronounced *gñāna*—comes from the verbal root *jña*, which means "to know, grasp, perceive, understand, or comprehend." If we add the prefix *a*, meaning "not," we get the term *ajñāna*, which means "ignorance or lack of knowledge." Calling ignorance "non-knowledge" is like defining darkness as "non-light." Like darkness, ignorance does not have its own existence but is the absence of the light of wisdom.

Jñāna is to know oneself as Brahman and to realize one's own reality as a transcendental being beyond time and space.

Jñāna is existential in nature since it is renouncing to what we heard about ourselves and knowing ourselves without any intermediary. Rather than providing information, explanations, and answers, this path inspires us to inquire. It urges us to doubt and impels us to investigate ourselves and our own essence.

Ajñāna means that we believe ourselves to be the doers of what is happening to us. It is a misconception, a false identification with the physical body, the mind, the senses, *prāṇa*, and in general, with illusory agency. Acting on an erroneous idea about ourselves clearly cannot lead us to a happy life.

Due to *ajñāna*, the mind tries to define whatever it perceives: it divides the indivisible and creates the fantasy called *māyā*. Illusion is the false appearance of multiplicity, the perception of diversity in what in fact is the One without a second.

In the Bhagavad Gita, Kṛṣṇa clearly explains that *jñāna* is discernment between the *kṣetra*, or "the field," which is our peripheral aspect, and *kṣetra-jña*, or "the knower of the field," which is the central core of our existence.

kṣetra-jñaṁ cāpi māṁ viddhi
sarva-kṣetreṣu bhārata
kṣetra-kṣetra-jñayor jñānaṁ
yat taj jñānaṁ mataṁ mama

> O son of Bharata! Know that I am the knower of the field in each and every field. I consider wisdom to be knowledge of both the field and the knower of the field.
>
> (Bhagavad Gita, 13.3)

Kṛṣṇa goes on to emphasize that the authentic sage, one who has truly gone beyond the duality of this relative world, knows the difference between the two:

kṣetra-kṣetra-jñayor evam
antaraṁ jñāna-cakṣuṣā
bhūta-prakṛti-mokṣaṁ ca
ye vidur yānti te param

> Those who know, through the eye of wisdom, the difference between the field and its knower, and those who differentiate liberation from material nature (*prakṛti*) reach the Supreme.
> (Bhagavad Gita, 13.35)

The Upanishads also speak of the awakening of our intuitive eye, which is necessary to approach "that."

na saṁdṛśe tiṣṭhati rūpam asya
na cakṣuṣā paśyati kaścanainam
hṛdā manīṣa manasā 'bhiklṛpto
ya etad vidur amṛtās te bhavanti

> The cosmic Self (Puruṣa) is not an object of our vision. No one can see it with their own eyes [or perceive it through any other sensory organ]. It reveals itself in the heart, only when the mind is pure and constantly thinks of it. Having realized it properly, one becomes immortal.
> (*Kaṭha Upanishad*, 2.3–9)

Similarly, the philosopher Richard of Saint Victor referred to three eyes: the eye of the flesh (*cogitatio*), the eye of intelligence (*meditatio*), and the eye of the soul (*contemplatio*).

The Bible refers to spiritual eyes capable of perceiving the Divine or the transcendental when it speaks of God opening the eyes of Hagar (Genesis 21:14–19), the Prophet Balaam (Numbers 22:21–28 and 22:31), and Elisha's servant (2 Kings 6:15–17). The New Testament describes how the eyes of Jesus' disciples were blinded by disbelief as they traveled to Emmaus (Luke 24: 13–16, 29–31). In his prayer for the church (Ephesians 1:17–19), Saint Paul prays for the eyes of his spiritual brothers and sisters' hearts to be enlightened so they may know God.

Understanding

Both understanding and existence are self-luminous, or *svataḥ-prakāśatva*: we exist knowing and we know that we exist. The understanding of one's existence is innate to every human being. In the universe, everything has a certain level of understanding, a natural and spontaneous sense of existence. Knowledge and understanding are signs of consciousness and they emanate from the depths of existence itself. Regardless of our developmental level, we all can understand even though we were never taught how to do it. Understanding at its most basic and essential level is that of our own existence.

The power to understand consciousness is not a mental activity because it precedes reasoning. Moreover, only when thought ceases, does understanding emerge as an act of consciousness: it begins exactly where mental activity ends.

It is a great mistake to believe that thinking more improves understanding. Quite the contrary: clear understanding takes place in the absence of thought. As Patañjali states in his *Yoga Sūtra* (1.2), *yogaś-citta-vṛtti-nirodhaḥ*, or "yoga is the cessation of all mental activity."

Although it seems to us that understanding is the result of thinking, Vedanta explains that it is not conditioned by a previous mental or emotional process and it has no causality. The understanding of consciousness does not even depend on the one who understands.

Human beings have the capacity to understand but only in relation to their own history and stored experiences. Human knowledge is tied to a collection of information. As egos, we are what we remember hearing about ourselves.

We relate understanding to a supposedly personal or individual consciousness. However, the egoic phenomenon exists only in memory. Although we believe in the existence of the conscious individual, there is in fact no entity or subject that can be attributed to consciousness.

This "I" apprehends pieces of information that depend on certain conditions. These conditions are relative because they have their own causes. True understanding is free from causal relativity; it is unlimited, and therefore, it is impossible to understand with a conditioned ego.

The consciousness that Vedanta refers to lies at the root of everything and everyone. It is not intelligent but it is intelligence itself, which establishes an unalterable order. Although consciousness cannot be seen, it sees whoever tries to see it. It is self-luminous because it can be known even though it lacks causality.

Only consciousness can know and understand itself. Nothing beyond it can understand it. The understanding of consciousness emerges along with the evaporation of personal consciousness. The limited egoic phenomenon is incapable of understanding the unlimited: only the unlimited can be the recipient of the unlimited. Meditation allows consciousness to be recognized.

Integrative and differentiated knowledge

According to Buddhism, there are two kinds of knowledge: *prajñā* and *vijñāna*. *Prajñā* is transcendental wisdom at the level of consciousness. *Vijñāna* is differentiated or relative information that distinguishes a subject from an object. Although *prajñā* lies at the base of every *vijñāna*, *vijñāna* is not aware of *prajñā* and considers it unnecessary. However, *vijñāna* does not in any way provide imperishable or stable knowledge.

Gnosis is the Greek noun most used to denote knowledge. *Ginosko* indicates more detailed knowledge. Finally, *epiginosko* refers to transcendental wisdom, a term found in the New Testament.

> For I can testify about them that they are zealous for God, but their zeal is not based

on knowledge (ἐπίγνωσιν or *epiginosko*).
(Romans, 10:2)

The nature of consciousness is integrative. Vedanta is not interested in scientific investigations of reality. For Vedanta, both observed reality and the observing subject are transient. In fact, there is no stable entity capable of differentiating permanent knowledge. Knowledge exists, but it is not differentiable. Knowledge itself is consciousness and, therefore, any part of it is equally conscious. The nature of consciousness and its knowledge is undifferentiated. The integrating nature of consciousness impedes a differentiation of knowledge.

Consciousness is the basis and foundation of reality; it is "what is" and it does not depend on a cause outside of itself to exist. It is its own reason. Since it has no cause, its knowledge is not the result of a process of reasoning. It is the origin and source of knowledge: it knows and understands without causation. Its understanding does not derive from a sequence of thoughts. It is totally autonomous since it does not depend on any other agent to exist, nor does it emerge from a mental or emotional process.

Knowledge and wisdom

Knowledge and wisdom seem similar but are completely different. It is important that seekers clearly recognize the difference between them.

Knowledge comes by learning from what we read and hear; it belongs to the mental domain. Wisdom comes from learning from what happens to us; it belongs to the realm of the spirit.

Knowledge proceeds from other people; wisdom always blossoms from and within one's own Self.

Knowledge originates from the external, from outside, from the surface; wisdom is born in the depths of our existence.

Knowledge touches the mind; wisdom touches us.

Knowledge changes our way of thinking; wisdom leads us to a complete metamorphosis.

Knowledge is information: a library or a computer has information but not wisdom; wisdom entails transformation.

Knowledge is conveyed from professor to student; wisdom belongs to the sphere of master and disciple.

Knowledge helps to conceal our ignorance; wisdom makes us conscious of our ignorance.

With knowledge, we believe that we know. With wisdom, we really know.

Knowledge offers us answers; wisdom inspires us to search for them.

Knowledge is a matter of words; wisdom is a matter of association, of silent communion.

Knowledge is reached through techniques, methods, and solutions; wisdom makes us conscious of the fact that there are no solutions because we ourselves are the problem.

Knowledge can be transferred even if the one who delivers it has never seen or experienced what is being taught. A blind person can easily give a lecture on painting. Wisdom, on the other hand, is a sign of the realization of God.

Knowledge is about many things; wisdom is knowing oneself.

Knowledge is useful, but only to operate in this world of names and forms. We need it when we move on the surface, but as we go deeper, we discover how useless it is. It can even become our most serious inner problem.

While knowledge may be a great help to know what meditation is, it can be a great obstacle when one actually tries to meditate.

In the Bhagavad Gita, we read:

daṇḍo damayatām asmi
nītir asmi jigīṣatām
maunaṁ caivāsmi guhyānāṁ
jñānaṁ jñānavatām aham

> Among punishers, I am the scepter; among seekers of victory, I am the art of governing; among secrets, I am silence; I am the wisdom of the wise.
>
> (Bhagavad Gita, 10.38)

Knowledge expresses itself as civilization and culture, while wisdom flows from the realization of our authentic nature as *sac-cid-ānanda*, or "absolute existence, consciousness, and bliss." Life and death merge in the infinite, eternal existence (*sat*); knowledge, the knower, and the known dissolve in an ocean of pure and absolute consciousness (*cit*); and love, the lover, and the beloved disappear in the supreme bliss (*ānanda*).

Chapter 3

Ātma-vicāraṇa or "self-inquiry"

Vicāraṇa is investigation and *ātma-vicāraṇa* is the specific inquiry into the Self. Consequently, it can also be translated as self-examination or self-inquiry.

ko 'haṁ katham idaṁ jātaṁ
ko vai kartā 'sya vidyate
upādānaṁ kim astīha
vicāraḥ so 'yam īdṛśaḥ

nāhaṁ bhūta-gaṇo deho
nāhaṁ cākṣa-gaṇas tathā
etad vilakṣaṇaḥ kaścid
vicāraḥ so 'yam īdṛśaḥ

Who am I? How was this [world] created? Who is its creator? What material is it made of? This is the way of that *vicāra* (inquiry). I am neither the body, a combination of the [five] elements [of matter], nor am I an aggregate of the senses; I am something different. This is the way of this *vicāra*.

(*Aparokṣānubhūti*, 12–13)

saṅghāto vāsmi bhūtānāṁ
karaṇānāṁ tathaiva ca
vyastaṁ vānyatamo vāsmi ko
vāsmīti vicārayet

vyastaṁ nāhaṁ samastaṁ vā
bhūtam indriyam eva vā
jñeyatvāt karaṇatvāc ca
jñātānyo 'smād ghaṭādi-vat

One should discern thus: Who am I? Am I a combination of the elements or the senses, or am I any one of them separately? I am not any one of the separate elements nor their aggregate; similarly, I am not any one of the senses nor their aggregate; for they are objects and instruments of knowledge such as jars and axes, respectively. The knower is different from all these.

(Śaṅkarācārya, *Upadeśa-sāhasrī*, 15.19–20)

The word "I" is perhaps the most used word in our daily lives: "I want," "I do not want," "I think," "I believe," "I am this or that," and so on. However, it is extremely difficult to respond to the question, "Who or what am I?" In our initial attempts, we become aware of the fact that our knowledge about what we are is extremely limited, if not negligible or even zero. In other words, it does not take us long to reach the conclusion that we do not have the slightest idea who we are.

"I am Michael," "I am John," "I am Mary," "I am Jacqueline" are answers that offer some information about our name, but not about what we really are.

"I am a professor," "doctor," "secretary" are answers that refer to our activities and careers, but not what we really are.

"I am Chilean," "Russian," "Chinese" are responses that refer to a geographical area where our physical body appeared, but they do not tell us anything about what we really are.

Our name, nationality, and body are ours, but they are not who we are.

The ego is the result of the masses. Society produces the ego to control, dominate, manipulate, and deprive us of liberty.

It is important to understand that the ego—or what we believe ourselves to be—is a foreign idea about ourselves that we have adopted as our own.

Those who have hypnotized us have made us believe we are what they think we are, and as a result, we have accepted foreign conclusions about our identity.

The I-idea is the basis of all ideas; the thought "I" is the supporting pillar that upholds the whole mental phenomenon. If the thought "I" disappears, no other thought can exist, as it will lack any basis. When the illusory identification with the idea "I" ceases, the continuous wandering of the mind and the activity that accompanies it also ceases. Eventually, the dual subject–object experience will also fade away, giving rise to the reality of the non-dual supreme Self.

"Who am I?" is not just a question we ask ourselves about ourselves, but an expression of the most elevated and noble rebellion.

That question restores our dignity and accepts us as the sole authority about ourselves and who we are. Self-inquiry is the essential and basic teaching of *jñāna-yoga*. From the very beginning, the *Vedānta Sūtra* urges us to inquire into the nature of Brahman:

Oṁ athāto brahma-jijñāsā

Oṁ, now, one must inquire into Brahman.
(*Vedānta Sūtra,* 1.1.1)

Brahma-jñāna, or "the wisdom of Brahman," is the wisdom of the Self: it is the only thing that can really liberate us from misery and illusion.

According to the explanation given by Ṛbhu to Nidāgha in the *Varāha Upanishad*, *vicāraṇa* is the second of the seven states (*bhūmikās*) in the process of developing wisdom.

jñāna-bhūmiḥ śubhecchā syāt
prathamā samudīritā
vicāraṇā dvitīyā tu
tṛtīyā tanu-mānasā

sattvāpattiś caturthī syāt
tato 'saṁsakti nāmikā

padārtha-bhāvanā ṣaṣṭī
saptamī turyagā smṛtā

The first stage in developing *jñāna* is *śubheccha* (good desire), the second is *vicāraṇā* (inquiry), the third is *tanu-mānasa* (pertaining to the body and mind), the fourth is *sattvāpatti* (attainment of *sattva*), the fifth is *asaṁsakti* (non-attachment), the sixth is *padārtha-bhāvanā* (analysis of objects), and the seventh is *turyagā* (fourth or final stage).

(*Varāha Upanishad*, 4.1–2)

In the *Yoga-vasiṣṭha* ("*Nirvāṇa-prakaraṇa*," 120.2), Manu teaches King Ikṣvāku the seven stages of yoga. His list is different from Ṛbhu's, but he also includes inquiry, or *vicāraṇa*, as the second stage.

The *Aparokṣānubhūti* of Śaṅkarācārya says:

notpadyate vinā jñānaṁ
vicāreṇānya-sādhanaiḥ
yathā padārtha-bhānaṁ hi
prakāśena vinā kvacit

Wisdom does not occur through practice (*sādhana*) without investigation (*vicāraṇa*), just as one cannot perceive objects without light.

(*Aparokṣānubhūti*, 11)

Many tend to connect *ātma-vicāraṇa* to the great master and Hindu saint, Śrī Bhagavān Rāmaṇa

Maharṣi of Tiruvanmalai. However, the origins of *ātma-vicāraṇa* go back to the glorious days of the Upanishads, as affirmed in the *Kaṭha Upanishad*:

taṁ durdarśaṁ gūḍham anupraviṣṭaṁ
guhāhitaṁ gahvareṣṭaṁ purāṇam
adyātma-yogādhigamena devaṁ
matvā dhīro harṣa-śokau jahāti

> Knowing that divinity (*deva*), which is difficult to perceive, which has entered a hidden place, which resides in the cave of the heart, which resides in the deepest place, through mastery of meditation [inquiry], the steadfast renounces happiness and sadness.
> (*Kaṭha Upanishad*, 1.2.12)

In the Bhagavad Gita we find similar guidance and direction:

śanaiḥ śanair uparamed
buddhyā dhṛti-gṛhītayā
ātma-saṁsthaṁ manaḥ kṛtvā
na kiñcid api cintayet

> With a firm mind, one should gradually become quiet, and placing the mind in the Self, one should not think of anything at all.
> (Bhagavad Gita, 6.25)

yato yato niścalati
manaś cañcalam asthiram
tatas tato niyamyaitad
ātmany eva vaśaṁ nayet

When the unstable and fickle mind is diverted, one must bring it under the dominion of the Self.

(Bhagavad Gita, 6.26)

We should not think that self-inquiry is a mere verbal exercise, because *ātma-vicāraṇa* actually injects a yogi with the strength of insatiable curiosity. Many mundane things awaken our curiosity such a shout in the street or the whispers of the neighbors. However, self-inquiry instills within us a curiosity, with a life-and-death urgency, to directly perceive and experience the presence that we are.

The wave can only know the sea by disappearing. We are waves in an infinite ocean of consciousness.

Ātma-vicāraṇa reaches the height of its expression with the question, "Who am I?" This is highly significant because for the first time we relinquish other people, neighbors, and everything external as sources of information about who we are.

Asking ourselves, "Who am I?" means rejecting the answers of others. We have assimilated their conclusions to the point that all our knowledge comes from them.

Persistence in self-inquiry through the question "Who am I?" prevents thoughts from emerging and maintains the mind in its source.

It is a destructive process in the sense that it makes use of negation: *neti-neti*, or "not this, not that." This process goes on negating whatever is illusory and false in us until all we are left with is what we really are: pure consciousness, *sac-cid-ānanda*. In dismissing what we are not, we strip ourselves of all false identification. We negate what lives to discover life. We negate what exists to reveal existence. We negate what we are in order to be... the Self.

> *athāta ādeśo neti neti na hy etasmād iti nety anyat param asty atha nāma dheya satyasya satyam iti.*
>
> Then, therefore, the instruction is *neti neti* or "not this, not this." There is no other instruction more excellent than *neti*, or "not this"; it is called the truth of truths.
>
> (*Bṛhad-āraṇyaka Upanishad*, 2.3.6)

> *niṣidhya nikhilopādhīn*
> *neti netīti vākyataḥ*
> *vidyādaikyaṁ mahā-vākyair*
> *jīvātma-paramātmanoḥ*
>
> Through a process of negating conditioning (*upādhis*) with the help of the scriptural statement 'it is not this, it is not this,' the oneness of the individual soul and the supreme soul should be realized, as indicated by the *mahā-vākyas*.
>
> (*Ātma-bodha*, 30)

Although the light of consciousness illuminates everything, in our cognitive state of duality we cannot conceive of a consciousness that is not related to objects. *Neti-neti*, or the negation of the objective, leads to the experience of pure consciousness, which is the Self in the absence of objects. Kṛṣṇa, absolute, or transcendental consciousness are some of the names for the state in which consciousness is conscious of itself.

Though *jñāna-yoga* is the pinnacle of religion, it contains certain skepticism, since it requires doubt, not faith. It aims at searching and discovering rather than believing.

Neti-neti is a process as destructive in its negation as skepticism is in its doubt. While reason leads the philosopher to understand "I think, therefore I am," self-inquiry brings the *jñāna-yogī* to the existential realization of the Self. The sole answer the mind can reach is *cogito, ergo sum*, or "I think, therefore I am," while the response of the *ṛṣi* is "I am, therefore I am." The mind and its logic cannot lead René Descartes to make this leap from the mind to the transcendental.

tat tvam asy ādi vākyena
svātmā hi pratipāditaḥ
neti neti śrutir brūyād
anṛtaṁ pāñca-bhautikam

With phrases such as "you are that," our own Self is affirmed. About that which is untrue and composed of the five elements, the *Śruti* (scripture) says, "Not this, not this."

(*Avadhūta Gīta*, 1.25)

The *jñāna-yogī* renounces all doubt to remain with a single question: "Who am I?" It is the arrow of inquiry that points directly at the nature of the inquirer. In the search for ourselves, there is no place for faith. In other words, there is no need to believe in something or someone.

While the question about what we are is born in the intellect, the answer is found in the silence of meditation. It is existential; it is not something to describe but to be. The correct response consists of simply being what one is. There is no need to transform oneself into something else, but only to be what we are, what we have always been, and what we cannot stop being. For a religion like Hinduism, in which God is not a belief but an experience, not a faith in something or someone but an experience of the Whole, the response is the Truth.

Atma-vicāraṇa does not stem from the Self, but from the mind. The "I" in the ego's question is none other than the ego itself. However, this question is like acid capable of dissolving the one who asks it and it exposes the Self.

Although "who am I?" is a thought, it is capable of dissolving all other thoughts, until it finally dissolves itself. This question is an acid that burns up all illusions and all that is nonexistent, leaving only what is true and authentic.

bhātīty ukte jagat-sarvaṁ
bhānaṁ brahmaiva kevalam
marubhūmau jalaṁ sarvaṁ
marubhūmātram eva tat

jagat-trayam idam sarvaṁ
cin-mātraṁ sva-vicārataḥ

If it is said that the universe shines, then it is Brahman alone that shines. [The mirage of] all the water in an oasis is really nothing but the oasis itself. Through inquiry of one's Self, the three worlds [above, below, and middle] are revealed as only of the nature of consciousness (*cit*).

(*Varāha Upanishad,* 2.72)

CHAPTER 4

The sacred literature

The first step on this path is to study Vedantic literature. Intellectual effort is indispensable in the initial stages because it provides a solid foundation. Reasoning must only be used to understand the sacred scriptures and not for empty mental speculations. This reasoning is called *śruty-anugṛhīta tarka*, or "logical reasoning that is consistent with the revelation." Vedantic teachings do not expand our store of knowledge but are like acid that destroys the mental complex.

> *śruty anugṛhīta eva hy atra tarko 'nubhavāṅga-tvenāśrīyate.*
>
> But such deceitful and dry logic does not apply here, only logic in consonance with the revealed scriptures should be used, since it contributes to realization.
>
> (Śaṅkarācārya, *Brahma Sūtra Bhāṣya*, 2.1.6)

On the basis of Upanishadic teachings, *jñānīs* use the mind to inquire, investigate, and embark on the fascinating search for themselves. They purify their intellect, or *buddhi*, by questioning their own reality, source, and origin. As we read in the sacred *Ṛg Veda*:

> *apaśyāma hiraṇyayaṁ. dhībhiś cana manasā svebhir akṣabhiḥ somasya svebhir akṣabhiḥ.*
>
> We have seen the brilliant radiance through the eyes of contemplation and intellect.
>
> (*Ṛg Veda*, 1.139.2)

The *Muṇḍaka Upanishad* describes the Vedic literature in the following way:

> *tatrāparā, ṛg-vedo yajur-vedaḥ sāma-vedo 'tharva-vedaḥ śikṣā kalpo vyākaraṇaṁ niruktaṁ chando jyotiṣam iti atha parā, yayā tad akśaram adhigamyate.*
>
> Lower knowledge constitutes of the four Vedas: the *Ṛg*, the *Yajur*, the *Sāma*, and the *Atharva* [and] the six *Vedāṅgas*: phonetics, rituals, grammar, etymology, metrics, and astrology. Now, the higher knowledge is that which leads to immortality [or that which goes beyond the literal meaning].
>
> (*Muṇḍaka Upanishad*, 1.1.5)

The way of *jñāna-yoga* is an invitation to lift the veil of illusion. As they walk this path, aspirants find within themselves what they have sought for so long.

The Vedas

Vedanta originates in the Vedas. The Sanskrit term *veda* comes from the root *vid*, which means "knowledge." The treasure of Vedic knowledge is both material and spiritual. It does not stem from a limited mind, so it is called *apauruṣeya*, or "not coming from humans."

chandāṁsi yajñāḥ kratavo vratāni
bhūtaṁ bhavyaṁ yac ca vedā vadanti
asmān māyī sṛjate viśvam etat
tasmiṁś cānyo māyayā san-niruddhaḥ

> The sacred Vedas, the offerings, the sacrifices, the penances, the past, the future, and all that the Vedas declare have been produced from the *māyīn* (source of *māyā,* i.e., Brahman). Brahman projects the universe through the power of its *māyā.* Again, in this universe Brahman as the *jīva* is entangled through *māyā.*
>
> (*Śvetāśvatara Upanishad*, 4.9)

In the *Mahābhārata,* Bhīṣma reaffirms this statement:

tapasvino dhṛti-mataḥ
śruti-vijñāna-cakṣuṣaḥ

sarvam ārṣaṁ hi manyante
vyāhṛtaṁ viditātmanaḥ

tasyaivaṁ gata-tṛṣṇasya
vijvarasya nirāśiṣaḥ
kā vivakṣāsti vedeṣu
nirārambhasya sarvaśaḥ

> Persons devoted to penances, intelligent, and who have the *Śrutis* and knowledge for their eyes regard the injunctions of the Vedas, which have been declared through and compiled by the *ṛṣis*, to be the words of the Divine. What can anybody say with respect to the contents of the Vedas when these happen to be the words of the supreme Being itself, who is completely freed from desire, who does not have the fever of envy and aversion, who is addicted to nothing, and who experiences no exertion?
> (*Mahābhārata*, "*Śānti-pārva*," 260.10–11)

Many scholars try to estimate the age of the Vedas. Some consider them to be 2500 years old, others 5000, and still others venture a guess of 8000 years. However, the Vedas were transmitted orally from master to disciple long before they were written down. The reality is that the Vedas are eternal and have no historical origin.

The *Śrīmad-devī-bhāgavatam* tells us that in the beginning, there was only one sacred Veda, which was then divided by Vyāsa-deva:

dvāpare dvāpare viṣṇur
vyāsa-rūpeṇa sarvadā
vedam ekaṁ sa bahudhā
kurute hita-kāmyayā

In every Dvāpara-yuga, Viṣṇu in the form of Vyāsa, wishing to benefit [the world], always divides the single Veda into many.
(*Śrīmad-devī-bhāgavatam*, 1.3.19)

The *Mahābhārata* explains that the four disciples of Śrī Vyāsadeva asked him to establish the Vedas through them. Vyāsa granted their wish and divided the Veda into four, so each one could descend to earth to teach a part of this wisdom.

catvāras te vayaṁ śiṣyā
guru-putraś ca pañcamaḥ
iha vedāḥ pratiṣṭherann
eṣa naḥ kāṅkṣito varaḥ

We are four disciples and the fifth is the son of our guru; let the Vedas be established in us; this is our desire.
(*Mahābhārata*, "*Śānti-parva*," 327.38)

In the *Bhāgavata Purāṇa*, it is described in more detail:

cātur-hotraṁ karma śuddhaṁ
prajānāṁ vīkṣya vaidikam
vyadadhād yajña-santatyai
vedam ekaṁ catur-vidham

Seeing that the Vedic sacrifices performed by the four priests had a purifying effect on human beings, he divided the single Veda into four so the sacrifices would continue.

(*Bhāgavata Purāṇa*, 1.4.19)

ṛg-yajus-sāmātharvākhyā
vedāś catvāra uddhṛtāḥ
itihāsa-purāṇaṁ ca
pañcamo veda ucyate

The four divisions of the original sources of knowledge, the four Vedas, namely *Ṛg*, *Yajur*, *Sāma*, and *Atharva*, were made separately. The historical facts and authentic stories mentioned in the *Purāṇas* are called the fifth Veda.

(*Bhāgavata Purāṇa*, 1.4.20)

tatra ṛg-veda-dharaḥ pailaḥ
sāmago jaiminiḥ kaviḥ
vaiśampāyana evaiko
niṣṇāto yajuṣām uta

After the Vedas were divided into four parts, Paila Ṛṣi became the compiler of the *Ṛg Veda*, Jaimini the compiler of the *Sāma Veda*, and Vaiśampāyana alone became glorified by the *Yajur Veda*.

(*Bhāgavata Purāṇa*, 1.4.21)

atharvāṅgirasām āsīt
sumantur dāruṇo muniḥ
itihāsa-purāṇānāṁ
pitā me romaharṣaṇaḥ

Sumantu Muni Aṅgirā, who was very devotedly engaged, was entrusted with the *Atharva Veda*. And my father, Romaharṣaṇa, was entrusted with the *Purāṇas* and historical records.

(*Bhāgavata Purāṇa*, 1.4.22)

ta eta ṛṣayo vedaṁ
svaṁ svaṁ vyasyann anekadhā
śiṣyaiḥ praśiṣyais tac-chiṣyair
vedās te śākhino 'bhavan

All these wise scholars, in turn, transmitted the Vedas entrusted to them to many disciples, disciples of their disciples, and disciples of the disciples of their disciples, and thus the respective branches of the followers of the Vedas came into being.

(*Bhāgavata Purāṇa*, 1.4.23)

The following verse says that the Vedas and the rest of the *śāstras* emanated from the four mouths of Brahmā:

maitreya uvāca-
ṛg-yajuḥ-sāmātharvākhyān
vedān pūrvādibhir mukhaiḥ

śāstram ijyāṁ stuti-stomaṁ
prāyaś-cittaṁ vyadhāt kramāt

Maitreya said: 'Lord Brahmā brought out the *Ṛg*, *Yajur*, *Sāma*, and *Atharva Veda*, from his mouths facing east, south, west, and north, respectively. In the same way, he gradually produced the scriptures which had not been pronounced before (*śāstra*), priestly rituals (*ijyā*), the subject matters of recitation (*stuti-stoma*), and transcendental activities (*prāyaś-citta*).

(*Bhāgavata Purāṇa*, 3.12.37)

āyur-vedaṁ dhanur-vedaṁ
gāndharvaṁ vedam ātmanaḥ
sthāpatyaṁ cāsṛjad vedaṁ
kramāt pūrvādibhir mukhaiḥ

Starting from the front face, in this order, he also created from his four mouths the *Āyur Veda* (medicine), *Dhanur Veda* (the art of war), *Gāndharva Veda* (the art of music), and *Sthāpatya Veda* (the art of architecture).

(*Bhāgavata Purāṇa*, 3.12.38)

itihāsa-purāṇāni
pañcamaṁ vedam īśvaraḥ
sarvebhya eva vaktrebhyaḥ
sasṛje sarva-darśanaḥ

> Then the all-seeing Lord created the fifth Veda, the *Itihāsas*, and the *Purāṇas* and all *darśanas* from all his mouths.
>
> (*Bhāgavata Purāṇa*, 3.12.39)

Each section of the Vedas emphasizes different subjects:

1. The *Ṛg Veda*, or "the Veda of mantras," is the principal Veda. It deals mainly with glorifying *devas* and the powers of cosmic manifestation. It is divided into ten books (*maṇḍalas*) containing a total of 1028 hymns (*sūktas*), made of 10580 mantras. A Vedic priest who specializes in chanting these hymns is called a *hotṛ*. The main deities of the *Ṛg Veda* are Indra, Agni, Soma, Mitra, Varuṇa, Uṣas, Savitṛ, Viṣṇu, Rudra, Pūṣan, Bṛhaspati, Pṛthivī, Sūrya, Vāyu, Āpas, Parjanya, Vāc, the *maruts*, the *ādityas*, the *viśva-devas*, and the *ṛbhus*.
2. The *Yajur Veda*, or "the Veda of sacrifice." This Veda's name comes from the Sanskrit word *yajus*, or "sacrifice." It deals with liturgy and provides instructions for Vedic ceremonies. A Vedic priest who recites these verses is called an *adhvaryu*. The *Yajur Veda* contains two *Saṁhitās*, or "collections of verses," which include hymns for rituals: *Śukla Yajur Veda* (white *Yajur Veda*) and the *Kṛṣṇa Yajur Veda* (black *Yajur Veda*); the latter also has comments in prose and detailed instructions. There are 1975 mantras written in

poetic and prose forms, divided into 40 chapters: the first 39 have hymns, poems, and mantras for important worship ceremonies and rituals. The last chapter deals with transcendental knowledge. This final chapter of the *Yajur Veda* is the *Īśāvāsya Upanishad* and it is associated with the sage Vājasaneya (Yājñavalkya). It is also called *Vājasaneyi-samhitā* because it is the only Upanishad in the *samhitā* portion of the *Śukla Yajur Veda.*

3. The *Sama Veda*, or "the Veda of chants." This Veda's name comes from the word *sāman*, which means "a metric hymn." It consists primarily of devotional chants divided into 27 cantos. The *Sama Veda* contains a compilation of 1875 hymns that serve as the prayer book for the priest that performs sacrifices, who is called the *udgātṛ*. It is similar to and uses various stanzas from the *Ṛg Veda*, especially in its eighth and ninth *maṇḍalas*.
4. The *Atharva Veda*, or "the Veda of Atharvan," is named after Atharvan, the ancient Vedic sage who compiled most of this Veda. Other portions are attributed to the *ṛṣi* Aṅgiras. It consists of 731 *sūktas*. This text does not represent the religion of priests, but rather the religion of the people. It covers diverse topics that are highly practical and pertain to the home, including a large collection of approximately six thousand mantras whose vibrations are specifically intended to preserve good health and prolong life.

Sections of each Veda

Each Veda has four sections:

1. *Mantra Saṁhitās*: These are collections of *stotras*, or "hymns," and metric mantras recited during sacrificial rites. They are of paramount importance because the efficacy and success of sacrificial rites depend on their correct recitation. The *Ṛg Veda Saṁhitā* is the largest and oldest of the *Mantra Saṁhitās*.
2. *Brāhmaṇas*: This is the sacrificial section of the Vedas. It has detailed information, commentaries, important clarifications, and profound explanations of the many sacrifices, or *yajñas*, and their meanings. Later, great *ṛṣis* such as Manu, Nārada, and Yājñavalkya gathered the kernels of knowledge in the *Brāhmaṇas* and systematically elaborated on them, giving rise to the *sūtras*. In the *sūtras*, we find the first methodical guide to Vedic sacrifices and home worship. For example, the *Śrauta Sūtra* offers guidance on conducting Vedic fire sacrifices such as *agni-hotra*, *darśa-pūrṇa-māsa*, *cātur-māsya*, *paśu-yāga*, *aśva-medha*, *rāja-sūya*, and *vāja-peya*. The *Gṛhya Sūtra* offers instructions to *Sanātana-dharma* followers on how to perform ceremonies and family rituals at home. There is an intimate connection between the *Gṛhya Sūtra* and the *Dharma Sūtra*. The latter offers explanations about *varṇāśrama-dharma*, which determine the

duties and rules of conduct of each individual as an integral part of the Vedic society.

3. *Āraṇyakas*: This part of the Vedas is concerned with worship. *Araṇya* means "forest," so the meaning of *āraṇyaka* is "composed in the forest." These texts delve into the wisdom of the *Brāhmaṇas* and include important details on meditation, yoga, and the esoteric aspect of the rituals. These treatises are intended to prepare one for a life of detachment.
4. Upanishads: These texts are dedicated to *jñāna*. The word *upaniṣad*, composed of the prefix *upa* (close), the prefix *ni* (beneath), and the verb *sad*, (to be seated), is generally translated as "to be seated close, beneath, or at the feet (of the spiritual master)." However, the verb *sad* also has other meanings that can give different connotations to the word *upaniṣad*. If we translate *sad* as "to destroy" or "to dissolve," then *upaniṣad* means "that which eliminates the darkness of ignorance." If we translate *sad* as "to loosen," then *upaniṣad* means "that which loosens (the knots of doubt, misunderstanding, and illogical inference)." Finally, *sad* can also mean "to set into motion," indicating that the Upanishads activate the wisdom of the seeker. The Upanishads are the philosophical section and final conclusion of the Vedas.

Tri-vidyā or "three kinds of knowledge"

The Veda is also subdivided into three parts according to the type of wisdom they convey. This classification is called *tri-vidyā*, or "three kinds of knowledge":

1. *Karma-kāṇḍa*, also known as *Veda-pūrva*, is the knowledge about actions that provide benefits. It is found in the *Mantra Saṁhitās* and *Brāhmaṇas*. This section is very long because it deals with desires and the means to satisfy them. It covers rituals, sacrifices, and mantras. *Veda-pūrva* is concerned with:

- *Dharma*: Religious ethics.
- *Kāma*: Religious activities and rituals to obtain pleasure.
- *Artha*: Activities necessary for security.

The *Muṇḍaka Upanishad* explains this section:

> *tad etat satyaṁ mantreṣu karmāṇi kavayo yāny apaśyāṁs tāni tretāyām bahudhā santatāni. tāny ācaratha niyataṁ satya-kāmā eṣa vaḥ panthāḥ sukṛtasya loke.*

> Know That to be the Truth: various karmas are enjoined in the mantras which were realized by the wise *ṛṣis*. In the *Tretā-yuga*, these karmas were in fashion and practiced by many. Even if these karmas are practiced now, one can certainly acquire the desired object.

> This is your legitimate way of attaining any heavenly world one desires.
>
> (*Muṇḍaka Upanishad*, 1.2.1)

2. *Upāsanā-kāṇḍa*: This section is found in the *Āraṇyakas* and explains the esoteric aspect of the rituals. If we compare the Vedas to the human body, the *karma-kāṇḍa* section would be the extremities and the *upāsanā-kāṇḍa* section would be the heart, because it is intended to help focus attention on the Supreme and cultivate devotion to God.

The *Muṇḍaka Upanishad* describes this portion of the Vedas in this way:

tapaḥ śraddhe ye hy upavasanty araṇye
śāntā vidvāṁso bhaikṣya-caryāṁ carantaḥ
sūrya-dvāreṇa te virajāḥ prayānti
yatrāmṛtaḥ sa puruṣo hy avyayātmā

> Those who perform penance with faith while living in the forest (solitude), with control over their senses, such learned ones, living the simple life of mendicants, to the solar world of light they go, their merits and demerits are consumed, where the immortal and non-decaying supreme Puruṣa (God with form) dwells.
>
> (*Muṇḍaka Upanishad*, 1.2.11)

3. *Jñāna-kāṇḍa*, also known as Vedanta, is a smaller section that only deals with the desire for liberation, or

mokṣa. This wisdom is imparted in the Upanishads. While *karma-kāṇḍa* teaches how to satisfy desires through actions without violating *dharma*, *jñāna-kāṇḍa* is directed at the desire for liberation through wisdom instead of actions.

The *Muṇḍaka Upanishad* also refers to the Vedanta portion of the Vedas in the following way:

divyo hy amūrtaḥ puruṣaḥ
sa bāhyābhyantaro hy ajaḥ
aprāṇo hy amanāḥ śubhro
hy akṣarāt parataḥ paraḥ

> The divine Self is formless, indeed; both within and without. Unborn, pure, and preceding both life and mind. Verily, it is higher even than the indestructible [causal], despite how high it is!
>
> (*Muṇḍaka Upanishad*, 2.1.2)

Vedāṅgas and *Upāṅgas*

aṅgopāṅgopavedā syur
vedasyaivopakārakā
dharmārtha-kāma-mokṣāṇām
aśrayā syuś catur-daśa

vedāṅgāni ṣad etāni
śikṣā vyākaraṇa tathā
nirukta jyautiṣa kalpaś
chando vicitirity api

> The auxiliary limbs (*aṅgas* of the Vedas), the secondary limbs (*Upāṅgas*), and the supplementary Vedas (*Upavedas*) are all helpful to the Vedas themselves. They are the sources of knowledge on duty (dharma), wealth (*artha*), desire (*kāma*), and final liberation (*mokṣa*). There are fourteen of them.
> (Śaṅkarācārya, *Sarva-siddānta-saṅgraha,* 1.2–3)

In order to understand the Vedas, students should learn Sanskrit. Spiritual aspirants cannot rely on translations of the scriptures since they are often not true to the original. Some writings, for example, were translated from Sanskrit to German or French and then to English or Spanish, which can distort the original message. Vedanta students should also be acquainted with the six auxiliary disciplines presented in the *vedāṅgas*:

1. Phonetics (*śikṣā*): Pronunciation in Sanskrit is particularly important since mantras lose their effectiveness and energetic power if they are pronounced improperly.
2. Grammar (*vyākaraṇa*): This is essential in order to understand the scriptures.
3. Prosody (*chandas*): This is a branch of linguistics that formally analyzes and represents various elements of speech, such as accent, tone, and intonation.
4. Etymology (*nirukta*): This deals with the origins of words.
5. Astrology and astronomy (*jyotiṣa*): According

to the Vedic tradition, our life is governed by the movements of the planets. Astrology helps us determine auspicious dates and hours for weddings, rituals, and so on, based on the position of the planets.

6. Ritualism (*kalpa*): This includes the knowledge of ceremonies and purifying rituals, which are important for aspirants' development.

The *Upāṅgas* are complementary texts that include:

1. Analysis.
2. Logic.
3. Puranic literature, which is divided into *Itihāsas* and *Mahā-purāṇas*. The best known *Itihāsas* are the *Mahābhārata* and the *Rāmāyaṇa*.
4. *Dharma-śāstras*: Treatises on laws and moral regulations.

The threefold Vedantic canon

Prasthāna-trayī, or "three sources," is the body of authoritative scriptures of the Vedantic schools. These are three types of texts: *Śruti*, *Smṛti*, and *Nyāya*. Every student of Vedanta is expected to become familiar with these three branches of knowledge.

1. *Śruti-prasthāna*: *Śruti* comes from the Sanskrit root *śru*, which means "hearing." It is the wisdom revealed to ancient seers through meditation. The divine revelation was heard by the *ṛṣis*, so we refer to it as

"what was heard." The knowledge called *śruti* is the revelation whose origin is not human, and therefore, it is called *apauruṣeyā*. It is perfect knowledge free of the limitations and imperfections of the human intellect. It refers specifically to the four original Vedas including the Upanishads, about which Śaṅkarācārya wrote elaborate commentaries.

2. *Smṛti-prasthāna*: The word *smṛti* means "what is remembered." The *smṛti* teaches the transcendental experiences of the sages of yore. While the *śruti* occupies the main place in the Vedic hierarchy, the *smṛti* takes a secondary position, with the exception of the Bhagavad Gita. Even though the Bhagavad Gita is a *smṛti*, it is accepted as a *śruti* because it comes from Kṛṣṇa. It is also called the *sādhana-prasthāna*, or the "practical source."

3. *Nyāya-prasthāna*: The term *nyāya* means "logic." The *Vedānta Sūtra*, also called *Brahma Sūtra*, systematizes the wisdom contained in the Upanishads and the *smṛti*. It is an extensive and complex scripture that expounds Upanishadic knowledge in a logical and organized way.

The Upanishads

The Upanishads do not resemble any Western philosophical texts, from the times of ancient Greece to the present. Instead of ideas or philosophical conclusions, Vedantic texts relate inner spiritual experience. Upanishads are not to be learned but to be heard in the silence of meditation. The Upanishadic message goes beyond the domain of philosophy. It does not encourage philosophical reflection or faith in myths or dogmas. Mental manipulations will not help us to assimilate these authentic revelations, only silence will.

While the knowledge offered by the *karma-kāṇḍa* section is a means, what the *jñāna-kāṇḍa* offers is the end itself. In order to obtain what we lack, we need to learn the means to achieve it. Knowledge differs from the goal. But if we desire to know our reality, or to realize our own true nature, knowledge will clearly be an end in itself.

The Upanishads were mostly written as poetic verses or dialogues between a master and a disciple. The word *upaniṣad* (sitting near or at the feet of the master) suggests an intimate process of teaching. The meaning of this term was extended to imply secret teachings imparted by gurus to disciples.

According to tradition, it is a collection of 108 sacred texts—although this number can reach nearly 150—comprising invaluable authoritative testimony received directly from the Vedic sages of antiquity. While these texts refer to the same topics, they view them from a variety of perspectives.

śrī-rāma uvāca-
ṛg-vedādi-vibhāgena
vedāś catvārair itāḥ
teṣāṁ śākhā hy anekāḥ
syus tāsūpaniṣadas tathā

ṛg-vedasya tu śākhāḥ syur
ekaviṁśati-saṅkhyakāḥ

navādhika-śataṁ śākhā
yajuṣo mārutātmaja

sahasra-saṅkhyayā jātāḥ
śākhāḥ sāmnaḥ parantapa
atharvaṇasya śākhāḥ syuḥ
pañcāśad-bhedato hare

ekaikasyāstu śākhāyā
ekaikopaniṣan matā
tāsām ekām ṛcaṁ yaś ca
paṭhate bhaktito mayi

Lord Rāma said: there are four Vedas, *Ṛg Veda* and so on; many branches and Upanishads exist within them. *Ṛg Veda* has 21 branches and *Yajur* has 109. *Sāma* has 1000 and *Atharva* has 50. Each branch has one Upanishad. Even by reading one verse of them with devotion, one reaches a state of union with me, which is difficult even for sages to attain.
(*Mukti Upanishad*, 11–14)

The Upanishads conclude the series that begins with the four collections of *Saṁhitas*: *Rig*, *Yajur*, *Sama*, and *Atharva*. These four literary groups comprise the Vedic revelation called *śruti*, or "what was heard." After the Upanishads, the Vedic literature ceases to be called *śruti* and is named *smṛti*, or "what is remembered." In a way, the sacred literature of India up to the Upanishads can be considered pure revelation, while later texts are more rooted in tradition.

The following 108 Upanishads are generally accepted by Vedic tradition:

The ten Upanishads of the *Ṛg Veda*:
Main Upanishad: *Aitareya Upanishad.*

- *Vedanta Upanishads*: *Ātma-bodha Upanishad, Kauṣītaki-brāhmaṇa Upanishad,* and *Mudgala Upanishad.*
- *Sannyāsa Upanishads*: *Nirvāṇa Upanishad.*
- *Yoga Upanishads*: *Nāda-bindu Upanishad.*
- *Vaiṣṇava Upanishads*: none.
- *Śaiva Upanishads*: *Akṣa-mālika Upanishad.*
- *Śākta Upanishads*: *Tri-pura Upanishad, Bahvṛca Upanishad,* and *Saubhāgya-lakṣmī Upanishad.*

The 19 Upanishads of the *Śukla Yajur Veda*:
Main Upanishads: *Īśāvāsya Upanishad* and *Bṛhad-āraṇyaka Upanishad.*

- *Vedanta Upanishads*: *Adhyātma Upanishad, Nirālamba Upanishad, Paiṅgala Upanishad, Mantrika Upanishad, Muktikā Upanishad,* and *Subāla Upanishad.*
- *Sannyāsa Upanishads*: *Advaya-tāraka Upanishad, Jābāla Upanishad, Turīyātīta Upanishad, Parama-haṁsa Upanishad, Bhikṣuka Upanishad, Yājña-valkya Upanishad,* and *Śāṭyāyanī Upanishad.*
- *Yoga Upanishads*: *Tri-śikhi-brāhmaṇa Upanishad, Maṇḍala-brāhmaṇa Upanishad,* and *Haṁsa Upanishad.*

- *Vaiṣṇava Upanishads*: *Tāra-sāra Upanishad.*
- *Śaiva Upanishads*: none.
- *Śākta Upanishads*: none.

The 32 Upanishads of the *Kṛṣṇa Yajur Veda*:
Main Upanishads: *Kaṭha Upanishad* and *Taittirīya Upanishad.*

- *Vedanta Upanishads*: *Akṣi Upanishad, Ekākṣara Upanishad, Garbha Upanishad, Prāṇāgni-hotra Upanishad, Śvetāśvatara Upanishad, Śārīraka Upanishad, Śuka-rahasya Upanishad, Skanda Upanishad,* and *Sarva-sāra Upanishad.*
- *Sannyāsa Upanishads*: *Kaṭha-rudra Upanishad* and *Brahma Upanishad.*
- *Yoga Upanishads*: *Amṛta-bindu Upanishad, Amṛta-nāda Upanishad, Kṣurikā Upanishad, Tejo-bindu Upanishad, Dhyāna-bindu Upanishad, Brahma-vidya Upanishad, Yoga-kuṇḍalī Upanishad, Yoga-tattva Upanishad, Yoga-śikha Upanishad, Varāha Upanishad,* and *Avadhūta Upanishad.*
- *Vaiṣṇava Upanishads*: *Kali-santaraṇa Upanishad* and *Mahā-nārāyaṇa Upanishad.*
- *Śaiva Upanishads*: *Kālāgni-rudra Upanishad, Kaivalya Upanishad, Dakṣinā-mūrti Upanishad, Pañca-brahma Upanishad,* and *Rudra-hṛdaya Upanishad.*
- *Śākta Upanishads*: *Sarasvatī-rahasya Upanishad.*

The 16 Upanishads of the *Sāma Veda*:
Main Upanishads: *Kena Upanishad* and *Chāndogya Upanishad.*

- *Vedanta Upanishads*: *Mahā Upanishad, Maitrāyaṇīya Upanishad, Vajra-sūcikā Upanishad,* and *Sāvitrī Upanishad.*
- *Sannyāsa Upanishads*: *Āruṇeya Upanishad, Kuṇḍikā Upanishad, Maitreyyi Upanishad,* and *Sannyāsa Upanishad.*
- *Yoga Upanishads*: *Darśana Upanishad* (*Jābāla-darśana Upanishad*) and *Yoga-cūḍāmaṇi Upanishad.*
- *Vaiṣṇava Upanishads*: *Avyakta Upanishad* and *Vāsudeva Upanishad.*
- *Śaiva Upanishads*: *Jābāli Upanishad* and *Rudrākṣa-jābāla Upanishad.*
- *Śākta Upanishads*: none.

The 31 Upanishads of the *Atharva Veda*:
Main Upanishads: *Praśna Upanishad, Māṇḍūkya Upanishad,* and *Muṇḍaka Upanishad.*

- *Vedanta Upanishads*: *Ātma Upanishad* and *Sūrya Upanishad.*
- *Sannyāsa Upanishads*: *Nārada-parivrājaka Upanishad, Parabrahma Upanishad,* and *Parama-haṁsa-parivrājaka Upanishad.*
- *Yoga Upanishads*: *Pāśupata-brahma Upanishad, Mahā-vākya Upanishad,* and *Śāṇḍilya Upanishad.*
- *Vaiṣṇava Upanishads*: *Kṛṣṇa Upanishad, Garuḍa Upanishad, Gopāla-tāpinī Upanishad, Tripād-vibhūti-mahā-nārāyaṇa Upanishad, Dattātreya Upanishad, Nṛsiṁha-tāpanī Upanishad, Rāma-tāpanīya Upanishad, Rāma-rahasya Upanishad,* and *Hayagrīva Upanishad.*

- *Śaiva Upanishads*: *Atharva-śikha Upanishad*, *Atharva-śira Upanishad*, *Gaṇapati Upanishad*, and *Bṛhaj-jābāla Upanishad.*
- *Śākta Upanishads*: *Annapūrṇa Upanishad*, *Tripurā-tāpinī Upanishad*, *Devī Upanishad*, *Bhāvana Upanishad*, and *Sītā Upanishad.*

Prakaraṇa-granthas

In addition to the *śāstras*, which are concerned with ultimate reality, or Brahman, there is another category of books called *Prakaraṇa-granthas* that explain the terminology used in the *śāstras*. The *Prakaraṇas* are short texts with simple explanations of the basic subjects of Vedanta. They intended for beginners who are not yet familiar with the Upanishads or the Bhagavad Gita. The best known *Prakaraṇa-granthas* are:

- *Viveka-cūḍāmaṇi*
- *Upadeśa-sāhasrī*
- *Ātma-bodha*
- *Aparokṣānubhūti*
- *Daśa-ślokī*
- *Śata-ślokī*
- *Vākya-vṛtti*
- *Pañcī-karaṇam*
- *Prabodha-sudhākara*
- *Tattva-bodha*
- *Vedānta-sāra*
- *Pañca-daśī*

Chapter 5

Brahman

tiryag ūrdvam adhaḥ pūrṇaṁ
sac-cid-ānandam advayam
anantaṁ nityam ekaṁ yat
tad brahmety avadhārayet

Realize "that" to be Brahman, which is absolute existence, knowledge, and bliss (*sac-cid-ānanda*), which is non-dual, infinite, eternal, one, which pervades all the quarters: above and below, and all that exists in between.

(*Ātma-bodha*, 56)

According to the revelation of the Vedantic *ṛṣis*, underneath the universe of names and forms lies a single reality called Brahman. This is the singular nature in the depths of this world of multiplicity. Brahman is neither matter nor energy, since these exist only within the limits of time and space. It can only be considered to be pure consciousness.

Brahman is neither dependent on nor relative to anything or anyone.

The *Taittirīya Upanishad* refers to Brahman in the following way:

satyaṁ jñānam anantaṁ brahma

> Brahman is [of the nature of] pure existence (*satyam*), omniscience (*jñānam*), and infinity (*anantaṁ*).
>
> (*Taittirīya Upanishad*, 2.1.1)

The Advaita Vedanta states that Brahman is the only reality (*brahma satyaṁ*) and that the world has a temporary existence (*jagan mithyā*).

brahma satyaṁ jagan mithyā
jīvo brahmaiva nāparaḥ

> Brahman is real. The universe is false. The *jīva* is Brahman itself: it is not different from Brahman.
>
> (Śaṅkarācārya, *Brahma-jñānāvalī-mālā*, 20a)

This statement is rooted in the *Nirālambha Upanishad*:

tapa iti ca brahma satyaṁ jagan-mithyety aparokṣa-jñānāgninā brahmādy aiśvaryāśā siddha-saṅkalpa-bīja-santāpaṁ tapaḥ.

> What is *tapas*? *Tapas* is the act of burning—through the fire of direct cognition of the

> knowledge that Brahman is the truth and the universe is false—the seed of the deep-rooted desire to attain the powers of Brahman, and so on.
>
> (*Nirālamba Upanishad*, 35)

This premise is supported by the Upanishads:

sad eva somyedam arga āsīd ekam evādvitīyam

> My dear Śvetaketu, in the beginning, before the creation of this universe (*idam arga*), all that existed was the reality (*sat*) of Brahman, the One without a second (*ekam evādvitīyam*).
>
> (*Chāndogya Upanishad*, 6.2.1)

According to the sages of the Upanishads, Brahman has two aspects: *saguṇa* and *nirguṇa*. Saguṇa, or Apara-brahman, is Brahman conditioned by the *upādhis* of *māyā*, or "limiting agents of illusion." *Nirguṇa* is Brahman devoid of any quality or attribute and is also called Para-brahman, or "supreme Brahman."

The *Kaṭha Upanishad* clearly describes both aspects of Brahman:

agnir yathaiko bhuvanaṁ praviṣṭo
rūpaṁ rūpaṁ pratirūpo babhūva
ekas tathā sarva-bhūtāntarātmā
rūpaṁ rūpaṁ pratirūpo bahiś ca

> Just as fire is one but upon entering the world, it assumes different shapes depending

on the object it consumes, thus also the non-dual Self, which dwells in all beings, assumes the shape of every creature it enters.

(*Kaṭha Upanishad*, 2.2.9)

vyāyur yathaiko bhuvanaṁ praviṣṭo
rūpaṁ rūpaṁ pratirūpo babhūva
ekas tathā sarva-bhūtāntarātmā
rūpaṁ rūpaṁ pratirūpo bahiś ca

Just as air is one but assumes different shapes when it enters different objects, the non-dual Self takes the shape of every creature it enters.

(*Kaṭha Upanishad*, 2.2.10)

sūryo yathā sarva-lokasya cakṣuḥ
na lipyate cākṣuṣair bāhya-doṣaiḥ
ekas tathā sarva-bhūtāntarātmā
na lipyate loka-duḥkhena bāhyaḥ

Just as the sun, which is the eye of the world, is not tainted by eye stigmas or external things that it reveals, thus also the Self, which dwells in all beings, is not tainted by the misery of the world. For the Self transcends everything!

(*Kaṭha Upanishad*, 2.2.11)

Saguṇa-brahman

The Upanishads describe both the transcendent and immanent aspects of Brahman. Brahman assumes the *upādhis* of *māyā* and manifests as the universe and its creator. From the relative point of view, Brahman is omnipresent. In its immanent aspect, Brahman not only resides in the universe but also becomes it. However, despite becoming the universe, Brahman does not completely transform into it, because its essential nature remains transcendent. The *Śvetāśvatara Upanishad* refers to Brahman as the one that permeates everything:

tileṣu tailaṁ dadhinīva sarpir
āpaḥ srotaḥ svaraṇīṣu cāgniḥ
evam ātmā 'tmani gṛhyate 'sau sat
yenainaṁ tapasāyo 'nupaśyati

> Like oil in sesame seeds, like butter in curds, like water in underground streams, like fire [hidden] in wood, the Self is perceived within oneself through truth and concentration.
> (*Śvetāśvatara Upanishad*, 2.15)

According to the Upanishadic revelation, Brahman existed in the beginning and then created the universe out of itself. Brahman pervades the universe. There is no second principle that provides materials for creation. Creation comes from Brahman like a web emanates from a spider or like the sparks that fly from a fire.

Brahman is both the material and the efficient cause of the universe. It is the essence of everything. Everything depends on it.

sarvaṁ khalv idaṁ brahma
taj jalān iti śānta upāsīta

> Brahman is the origin, the end, and the maintenance of all [this universe]. One should therefore quietly meditate on Brahman.
>
> (*Chāndogya Upanishad*, 3.14.1)

The *Chāndogya Upanishad* mentions the term *taj-jalān* in this verse, a secret name used to worship Brahman. Taj-jalān is composed of the words *taj-ja* (the creator of this), *taj-la* (the destroyer of this), and *tad-an* (the breath of this). According to Śaṅkara's commentary (*Bhāṣya*), the name Taj-jalān summarizes Brahman's attributes as creator, preserver, and destroyer of the universe.

> *kathaṁ sarvasya brahmatvam? ityata āha—taj-jalān iti; tasmād brahmaṇo jātaṁ tejo-'vannādi-krameṇa sarvam, atas taj-jam; tathā tena iva janana-krameṇa pratilomatayā tasminn eva brahmaṇi līyate tad-ātmatayā śliṣyata iti tal-lam, tathā tasminn eva sthiti-kāle 'n iti prāṇiti ceṣṭata iti. evaṁ brahmātmatayā triṣu kāleṣv aviśiṣṭaṁ tad vayyatir ekeṇāg murahaṇāt.*

> But how can the character of Brahman belong to everyone? It is explained as

Taj-jalān: beginning, ending, and continuing in it. Everything, beginning with light, food, and so on, is born out of Brahman, hence *taj-ja*, or "beginning in it." Similarly, in reverse order of birth, everything dissolves into Brahman (and becomes identical to it): hence *tal-la*, or "ending in it." In the same manner, during existence, everything lives and moves in it; hence *tad-an*, or "continuing or breathing in it." Thus, at all three times (creation, maintenance, and dissolution) this universe remains one with Brahman and is never known to be separate from it.

(Śaṅkarācārya, *Chāndogya Upanishad Bhāṣya*, 3.14.1)

Nirguṇa-brahman

The Sanskrit word *guṇa* means "quality" and *nir* means "without"; *nirguṇa* means "devoid of all qualities." Qualities lie in what they qualify, therefore, they create a qualifier–qualified relationship on the dual platform.

Brahman does not allow for such a relationship, because Brahman is all that actually exists. Transcending all qualities or limitations, Brahman is the One without a second. Since the Absolute does not have any attributes, it is called Nirguṇa-brahman.

eko devaḥ sarva-bhūteṣu gūḍhaḥ
sarva-vyāpī sarva-bhūtāntarātmā

karmādhyakṣa sarva-bhūtādhivāsaḥ
sākṣī cetā kevalo nirguṇaś ca

> The non-dual and resplendent Lord is hidden in all beings. All-pervading, the innermost Self of all creatures, the impeller to actions, abiding in all things, it is the witness, the animator and the Absolute, free from *guṇas*.
>
> (*Śvetāśvatara Upanishad*, 6.11)

Because no qualities or attributes can be given to it, Nirguṇa-brahman is indescribable with language. It is impossible to objectify or define in words, not because it is complicated, but because it precedes verbal definitions. The only way to describe it is through a method called *neti neti*, or "not this, not this," which is the negation of empirical attributes, definitions, and relationships. Since it is undefinable and inconceivable, only negative statements are legitimate affirmations about the Absolute, which is devoid of qualities.

This relative world is a reality made up of pairs of opposites. If we know what cold is, it is because we have experienced heat; if we recognize pain, it is because we know pleasure; if we feel joy, certainly we have suffered. Each of these examples is a pair of opposites: it is impossible to know one and ignore the other since they are interrelated.

If someone had been locked in a lit room since birth, they would not know what darkness is, nor would they know what light is.

Our knowledge of the phenomenal world is based on pairs of opposites. Any word or expression used in this dual world is necessarily relative. We only understand the existence of something in relation to its opposite. Therefore, it is impossible for the human mind to conceive of Brahman as the only existing reality. To refer to Brahman as absolute or infinite is a mere attempt to verbalize what cannot be defined with words.

Through our mind, we understand the word *infinite* only by contrasting it with the word *finite*.

The finite mind cannot conceive ideas such as eternity or infinity, because if it could define infinity, infinity would no longer be infinite. Any "infinity" that can be mentally defined is necessarily limited, for any definition implies a limitation. Any limit would create a secondary reality outside of that limit, and there cannot be two infinities.

Terms like *infinite* or *eternal* are adjectives, that is to say, words used to describe objects or people. All objects and people are limited by space and time, but Brahman transcends all such limitations. Therefore, no adjective is suitable for Brahman. Masters have only used words to facilitate intellectual understanding. The Upanishads repeatedly attribute irreconcilable qualities to Brahman to show that it is completely different from all that is known through the mind and the senses.

> *taj janita-vāsanā-rūpaṁ ca sarva-jñaṁ sarva-śakti sopakhyaṁ bhavati. kriyā-kāraka-phalātmakaṁ ca sarva-vyavahārāspadam. tad eva brahma*

> *vigata-sarvopādhi-viśeṣam samyag darśana-viṣayaṁ, ajam ajaram amṛtam abhayam, vāṅ manasayor apy aviṣayam advaitatvāt 'neti neti' iti nirdiśyate.*
>
> Brahman, omniscient and omnipotent, is conditioned with the nature of impressions arising out of the elements. It consists of actions, their factors and results and constitutes the basis of all activities. That very same Brahman, devoid of all limiting adjunct, it is the object of right perception. It is unborn, non-decaying, immortal, fearless, and unattainable even by speech and mind. Being non-dual, it is predicated in such words as "not this, not this."
>
> (Śaṅkarācārya, *Bṛhad-āraṇyaka Upanishad Bhāṣya*, 2.3.1)

Only once the reality that is limited by space, time, and causality is transcended, Brahman is experienced as the One without a second. Brahman has no form. Forms and names exist within the context of time and space. God is the foundation of the reality of *nāma-rūpa,* or "names and forms," and resides at the root of everything and everyone. Although God transcends space and time, he is the basis of both and he is aware of everything simultaneously. As indicated in the *Bṛhad-āraṇyaka Upanishad* (4.4.19): *neha nānāsti kiñ cana*, or "there is no form apart from the non-dual absolute Truth."

Brahman is indivisible. According to Vedanta, there are three kinds of distinctions:

1. *Sajātīya-bheda*: Distinctions between objects of the same nature.
2. *Vijātīya-bheda*: Distinctions between objects of a different nature.
3. *Svagata-bheda*: Distinctions between different parts of the same object.

> *sajātīya-vijātīya-svagata-bheda-rahitā anubhūtiḥ sattā.*
>
> The state which is devoid of distinctions as regards of its own parts, its own nature, as well as other natures.
>
> (Śaṅkarācārya, *Viṣṇu-sahāsra-nāma Bhāṣya*, *śloka* 75)

Being the only reality, Brahman does not possess the two first classes of distinctions. Being amorphous, it lacks parts and, therefore, it does not have *svagata-bheda* either. Brahman is immutable, and any division would imply a change.

Brahman is *sac-cid-ānanda*

Brahman is *sac-cid-ānanda*, or "existence (*sat*), consciousness (*cid*), and bliss (*ānanda*)."

> *nitya-śuddha-cidānanda-*
> *sat-tāmātro 'ham avyayaḥ*
> *nitya-buddha-viśuddhaika*
> *sac-cid-ānandam asmy aham*

> I am nothing else but *sat* (existence), *ānanda* (bliss), and unconditioned and pure *cit* (consciousness). I am the *sac-cid-ānanda* that is eternal, enlightened, and pure.
>
> (*Tejo-bindu Upanishad*, 2.11)

Sat – Brahman is existence

yataḥ sarvāṇi bhūtāni
pratibhānti sthitāni ca
yatraivopaśamaṁ yānti
tasmai satyātmane namae

> Salutations to who is reality itself, from whom all beings proceed, by whom they are manifest, upon whom they depend, and in whom they become extinct in the end.
>
> (*Yoga-vāsiṣṭha*, "*Vairāgya-prakaraṇa*," 1.1.1)

Brahman does not exist, but it is existence itself, or *sat*. The sages of Vedanta define reality in terms of perpetuity. If something is subject to change or if its manifestation is temporary, they do not consider it to be real. We cannot clearly define an entity that at some moment is a cat, then a chicken, then an elephant, and finally turns into a turtle. We cannot consider an entity real if we see it for a second and then it vanishes. For example, the reality of a dream appears for a time and then vanishes forever: it is an illusion because it has a beginning and an end. What is real exists yesterday, today, and tomorrow. Only what is immutable can be considered real. Therefore, since it is absolute immutability, Brahman is the only reality. Brahman is the screen on which the game of life (*līlā*) is projected. Everything we see in the movie exists because the screen is present. Brahman is *adhiṣṭhāna*, or "the substratum," that lies behind the relative reality of names and forms.

Cit – Brahman is consciousness

jñātājñānaṁ tathā jñeyaṁ
draṣṭā darśana dṛśyabhūḥ
kartā hetuḥ kriyā yasmāt
tasmai jñātmane namaḥ

> He is the knower, knowledge, and all that is to be known. He is the seer, the act of seeing, and all that is to be seen. He is the actor, the cause, and the effect. Therefore, salutations to him, who is knowledge itself.
>
> (*Yoga-vāsiṣṭha*, "*Vairāgya-prakaraṇa*," 1.1.2)

Brahman is consciousness itself (*cit*). Every entity in creation that seems conscious borrows its awareness from Brahman, which is the only source of consciousness. If you look superficially, the body or the mind of a person seem to be aware. However, the body cannot experience anything if it is disconnected from the mind. On the other hand, an anaesthetized mind loses consciousness and contact with the surroundings. This shows that awareness does not constitute an integral part of the mind, because otherwise it would be impossible to separate one from the other. The fact that the body can be present yet lack awareness proves that it is not the origin of consciousness. Brahman is not only the source and origin of consciousness: it is consciousness itself.

Ānanda – Brahman is bliss

phuranti śīkarā yasmād
ānandasyāmbare 'vanau
sarveṣāṁ jīvanaṁ tasmai
brahmānandātmane namaḥ

> Salutations to him who is supreme bliss itself. From whom the dews of delight flow, as water springs from a fountain, both in heaven and earth, and who is the life of everything.
> (*Yoga-vāsiṣṭha, "Vairāgya-prakaraṇa,"* 1.1.3)

Brahman is *ānanda*, or "absolute bliss." It should not be confused with happiness, which comes from sensory perception. Happiness belongs to the relative platform of time, space, and causality.

We relate our enjoyment to objects or people. We live striving to reach and obtain them as if there were happiness within them. However, if we look inside jewelry, dollar bills, cigarettes, beer, and cars in a laboratory, we will find no happiness. When we enjoy a painting or a song, we experience it in the depths of our heart. Therefore, bliss does not belong to the dual platform but to our inner depths. Happiness is relative because it has an opposite: sadness. But *ānanda* is absolute since it transcends both happiness and distress. The essence of what we are, or Brahman, is bliss.

The manifested and the unmanifested

Through the senses, we observe the relative reality of names and forms, which is made of a superficial layer of coarse matter that covers innumerable and increasingly subtle layers, to the innermost depths of the universe.

Matter, energy, and spirit cannot be considered separate and disconnected, but different states of consciousness. They can be compared to the states of water: ice, liquid, and steam.

For many years, physicists have focused their research on the subtlest planes of matter, with the idea that if they discovered the subtlest form of energy, our objective reality could be explained as different manifestations of this primordial form of energy.

Reality—the unmanifested Self—lies at the core of the world of names and forms as the very root of the manifested. The manifested is not opposed to the unmanifested, instead it is the unmanifested expressing itself.

Creation, or all that we are able to perceive through the senses, is nothing more than an expression of this pure existence, of this transcendental domain. The one Self is the essential plane that is expressed as diversity, the One making itself many, unity manifesting as multiplicity.

Life is abstract, and all that is alive is life's physical expression. Existence is subtle, and all that exists is a rough manifestation of existence. The Self is the unmanifested and the manifestation of the Self is all there is.

The Self, or Brahman, is life or existence, the source and origin of all that is, was, and will be, as stated in both the *Vedānta Sūtra* (1.1.2) and the *Bhāgavata Purāṇa* (1.1.1):

oṁ janmādy asya yataḥ

> *Oṁ.* (Brahman) is that from which proceeds the creation, preservation, and destruction of this manifestation.
>
> (*Vedānta Sūtra*, 1.1.2)

The body is nothing more than the superficial aspect of our reality. The more we go within ourselves, the more we acquire consciousness of the Self, the essence that we really are. *Jñāna-yoga* aspires to direct experience of the very foundation of existence, or the subjective basis of the objective world. This realization enriches all aspects of our life. For this reason, *jñāna-yoga* does not view the Self as something to reach or obtain through a specific practice. Rather, it is a discovery, a revelation of our authentic nature, that is, what we really are.

rāja-vidyā rāja-guhyaṁ
pavitram idam uttamam
pratyakṣāvagamaṁ dharmyaṁ
su-sukhaṁ kartum avyayam

> This is the king of all wisdom and the supreme mystery. It is pure and excellent.

> It can be directly experienced, and it is in accordance with *dharma*, imperishable and easily performed.
>
> (Bhagavad Gita, 9.2)

Ignorance can lead many to the false conclusion that *jñānīs* are self-absorbed and disconnected from the world and society. However, nothing could be further from the truth. To the extent that one awakens to the Whole as the essence of what one is, one becomes aware that diversity is only the manifestation of unity. Hence, the realization of the Self does not separate us from others or situate us above them; instead it creates intimacy and closeness with everything and everyone.

Chapter 6

Illusion or *māyā*

Throughout history, explaining the relationship between God and the universe has been a great challenge for philosophers and theologians alike: how can an unlimited and absolutely pure God create a limited and impure world? Gauḍapāda, the spiritual master of Śaṅkara, emphasizes in several of his treatises (*kārikās*) that Brahman becomes a differentiated multiplicity only due to *māyā*. *Māyā* projects the relative and dual world onto the supreme Brahman, which is unborn, eternal, and undifferentiated.

kalpayaty ātman-ātmānam
ātmā devaḥ svamāyayā
sa eva budhyate bhedān
iti vedānta-niścayaa

The shining Ātman imagines itself by itself through its *māyā*; it is this alone that gives entities consciousness; this is the conclusion of the Vedanta (Upanishads).

(*Gauḍapādīya Kārikā*, 2.12)

prāṇādibhir anantaiś ca
bhāvair etair vikalpitaḥ
māyaiṣā tasya devasya
yayā saṁmohitaḥ svayam

[Ātman] is imagined to be life (*prāṇa*) and innumerable other entities. This is the *māyā* of the shining one [Ātman] by which it itself has been deluded.

(*Gauḍapādīya Kārikā*, 2.19)

The *māyā* principle is a fundamental pillar of Advaita Vedanta. The term *māyā* began to evolve in the *Ṛg Veda* period and Śaṅkara gave it the particular meaning it has today. His view was so different from the rest of the philosophical schools that his detractors called his system *māyā-vāda*. In his commentaries on the *Vedānta Sūtra*, Śaṅkara refers to *māyā* as illusion, or the false perception of multiplicity.

eka eva parameśvaraḥ kuṭastha-nityo vijñāna-dhātur avidyayā māyayā māyāvi vad anekadhā vibhāvyate nānyo vijñāna-dhātur astīti.

The eternal Lord is but one, immutable, eternal, whose substance is consciousness, and who, by means of *avidyā* (nescience), which is called *māyā*, manifests itself in

various ways, just as a magician appears in different shapes through magical powers.
(Śaṅkarācārya, *Brahma Sūtra Bhāṣya*, 1.3.19)

The world as we perceive it does not have an independent and absolute existence. Its reality is empirical and remains only as long as we perceive it through the senses. If we had different senses, our environment would seem completely different.

Being immutable and One without a second, Brahman transcends the mind. Confused by ignorance, the mind perceives multiplicity in the objective world because *māyā* is superimposed upon Brahman. It is impossible to attain true knowledge of Brahman through an impure mind that is limited by concepts such as time, space, and causality. This apparent universe will remain until we transcend *māyā* with the help of knowledge. When Brahman is realized, *māyā* vanishes.

Śaṅkara refers to the principle that is responsible for the projection of the phenomenal universe in various ways: *māyā* (illusion), *avidyā* (ignorance), *ajñāna* (lack of knowledge), and *avyakta* (unmanifested). In his book *Viveka-cūḍāmaṇi*, he describes the nature of *māyā* as follows:

san nāpyasan nāpy ubhayātmikā no
bhinnāpy ubhayātmikā no
sāṅgāpy anaṅgāpy ubhayātmikā no
mahādbhutā anirvacanīya-rūpā

If you ask about its form, it cannot be expressed: it is indescribable. It is not real

> or unreal, neither is it a mixture of the two. Is it different from the Ātman? It is not separate or independent. It is not part of the Ātman, neither can it be said to be not part of the Ātman. It is not the body. It is most wonderful and beyond description.
>
> (*Viveka-cūḍāmaṇi*, 109)

The paradoxical principle of *māyā* can be explained from two perspectives: empirical (*vyāvahārika*) and transcendental (*pāramārthika*). The former is meant for those who are blinded by *avidyā* and try to understand Brahman through the mind. The latter is for the enlightened who have fully experienced their authentic nature.

> *evaṁ paramārthāyāṁ sarva-vyavahārābhavaṁ vadanti vedāntāḥ sarve.*
>
> Thus, all the Vedanta texts declare the cessation of all worldly phenomenal dealings (*vyavahārā-bhāva*) of one who has reached the highest state of reality (*paramārtha*).
>
> (Śaṅkarācārya, *Brahma Sūtra Bhāṣya*, 2.1.14)

> *evaṁ nirūpitānāṁ pramāṇānāṁ prāmāṇyaṁ dvi-vidham— vyāvahārika-tattvāvedakatvaṁ pāramārthika-tattvāvedakatvañ ceti.*
>
> The validity of the means of knowledge that has been described in the above manner is

> of two kinds, that of conventional reality and absolute reality.
> (Dharmarāja Adhvarīndra, *Vedānta-paribhāṣā*, chapter 7)

From the empirical perspective, the nature of *māyā* is inconceivable and inexplicable, or *anirvacanīya*, which stands for *sattvena asattvena va anirvacanīya* or 'cannot be described as real or unreal', since *māyā* is neither real nor unreal.

- *Māyā* is not real: If *māyā* were real, it would imply that something exists outside of Brahman. *Māyā* is temporary and disappears with the awakening of consciousness.
- *Māyā* is not unreal: If *māyā* were unreal, its effects would not be perceived even as long as human ignorance lasts.
- *Māyā* is not simultaneously real and unreal: If *māyā* were real and unreal at the same time, this would be a contradiction.

Human knowledge lies within the boundaries of illusion. Our mental perception is limited by time, space, and causality. Therefore, it is impossible to know *māyā*. In fact, *māyā* has no real existence but only an empirical one. Its reality is not absolute but relative to our mind and senses. The relative world of names and forms is illusory, so there is no point in asking how it was created.

Knowing something requires a distance between the knower and the known. We cannot know *māyā*, because it is not separate from the knower. *Māyā* is not a power outside of us: as egoic phenomena, we are *māyā*. Our egoic existence is intrinsically illusory and, therefore, *māyā* remains inconceivable and inexplicable.

Writings by Śaṅkara and his followers describe the characteristics of *māyā* from the empirical perspective. In his commentary on the *Vedānta Sūtra*, Śaṅkara states that all empirical activity in the relative world is nothing more than *adhyāsa*, or "superimposition," of the non-Self onto the Self (*pratyag-ātmany api anātmādhyāsa*). *Avyakta* (unmanifested), or *māyā*, constitutes the projecting principle of *prakṛti* (the primordial matter) that gives limiting qualities to both Īśvara (God) and the *jīvas* (souls). Its nature is relative and its effects exist only in appearance. It should be noted that the term *māyā* denotes the limiting attributes of God, while *avidyā* (ignorance) refers to the limiting attributes of the *jīva*. The sages explain that the origin of *adhyāsa* (superimposition) is *avidyā* (ignorance). Therefore, although *māyā* lacks a beginning in space and time, it can be eradicated through knowledge (*vidyā*) of Brahman.

> *vidyāyāṁ hi satyām udite savitari śārvaraṁ iva tamaḥ praṇāśam upagacchati avidyā.*
>
> When knowledge dawns, necience perishes like the darkness of the night when the sun rises.
>
> (Śaṅkarācārya, *Bhagavad Gītā Bhāṣya*, 2.69)

From the transcendental perspective, *māyā* does not exist. All intellectual inquiries about it require empirical concepts. For those who have realized their true nature as Brahman, *māyā* has no reality and the relationship between *māyā* and Brahman is absurd. Enlightened beings are aware that there is no differentiation, duality, or limitation. They know that neither *māyā* nor the objective universe exist, in other words, only Brahman is.

As Śaṅkara says in his commentary on the *Vedānta Sūtra*:

> *tasmād antyena pramāṇena pratipadita ātmaikatve samastasya prāciīnasya bheda-vyavahārasya bādhitatvān nānekātmaka brahma-kalpanāvakāśo 'sti.*
>
> Therefore, in the wake of the unity of the Self, as imparted by the final proof of valid knowledge, there would be no means of imagining Brahman as consisting of various elements, since all the old activities that involve differences have been annihilated.
>
> (Śaṅkarācārya, *Brahma Sūtra Bhāṣya*, 2.1.14)

Moreover, in his *Aparokṣānubhūti* he says:

> *sadaivātmā viśuddho 'sti*
> *hy aśuddho bhāti vai sadā*
> *yathaiva dvi-vidhā rajjur*
> *jñānino 'jñānino 'niśam*

> Ātman, though ever pure to a wise person, always appears to be impure to an ignorant person, just as a rope always appears to be two different things to a knowing person and an ignorant one.
>
> (*Aparokṣānubhūti*, 68)

Although Brahman appears to be the universe, its absolute purity is not affected in the least by the limitations of the relative world. A well-known Vedantic parable says that if we walk in the garden at nightfall, we can confuse a rope for a snake; however, the illusionary qualities attributed to the rope do not affect it in the least. Although we confuse it for a snake, the original nature of the rope remains unchanged. In the same way, clay can be shaped into a jug or a pot, but its existence as clay does not change. Gold remains immutable even if it takes the form of rings, earrings, lockets, or bracelets. Brahman may become objective reality through *māyā* but it does not undergo any change. It remains the One without a second, or *ekam evādvitīyam*.

> *yad adhyāsas tat-kṛtena doṣeṇa guṇena vā 'ṇumātreṇāpi sa na saṁbadhyate.*

> Such being the case, the thing on which the superimposition takes place is not in the least affected by the evil or good caused by the superimposition.
>
> (Śaṅkarācārya, *Brahma Sūtra Bhāṣya*, "*Adhyāsa-prakaraṇa*")

As explained above, Brahman is truth, knowledge, infinity, and purity, whereas the objective world is illusion, ignorance, finitude, and impurity.

ātmā jñāna-mayaḥ puṇyo
deho māṁsa-mayo 'śuciḥ
tayor aikyaṁ prapaśyanti
kim ajñānam ataḥ param

> Ātman is all consciousness and holiness while the body is all flesh and impure yet the people see these two as one. What else can be called ignorance but this?
>
> (*Aparokṣānubhūti*, 19)

So, we might ask, how can a pure and infinite Brahman be the source of an impure and limited reality? Reason cannot accept that eternity is the origin of temporality. The objectification of the undifferentiated breaks down our logic. If Brahman is the origin of the objective universe, the limitations present in the effect should have been in the cause. Qualitatively, the effect cannot be different from its cause. The deficiencies of creation should originate in the creator. But according to the non-dual teachings of Advaita Vedanta, Brahman is not the cause or origin of the objective universe.

From the empirical perspective, neither Brahman nor *māyā* can be the sole cause of the world: both combine together into a single cause. *Māyā* is the cause of the mutable and inert elements, while Brahman is the cause of the manifestation and the principles of reality. As this verse states:

māyāṁ tu prakṛtiṁ vidyān
māyinaṁ ca maheśvaram
tasyāvayava-bhūtais tu
vyāptam sarvam idam jagat

> Know that nature is *māyā* and that the supreme Lord is the reality of *māyā*. In fact, this universe is impregnated by objects that are the Lord's own effects.
>
> (*Śvetāśvatara Upanishad*, 4.10)

If we compare this verse to the Vedantic parable of the rope and the snake, the rope would be Brahman and the snake would be the objective world and the individual souls. Through superimposition, Brahman gives reality to a nonexistent world. As this verse says, it is Brahman itself who becomes the objects that constitute the phenomenal world. Being their cause, it is the essence of all things, as water is the essence of the bubbles and waves of the ocean. Thus, the Upanishad reveals that our souls and the world are unreal, since only Brahman really is.

Māyā has two energies: one conceals and the other projects. With the first energy called *āvaraṇa-śakti*, *māyā* covers the authentic nature of Brahman as pure consciousness (*caitanya*). With the second energy called *vikṣepa-śakti*, *māyā* projects the dual reality onto Brahman. This process is similar to dreaming: first it is necessary to ignore the reality of the waking state and then the dream can be projected.

śakti-dvayaṁ hi māyāyā
vikṣepāvṛti-rūpakaṁ
vikṣepa-śaktir liṅgādi
brahmāṇḍāntaṁ jagat-sṛjet

> Undoubtably, there are two *śaktis* (powers) to *māyā*: the projecting (*vikṣepa*) and the veiling (*āvṛti*). The projecting power creates everything, from the subtle body to the gross universe.
>
> (Śaṅkarācārya, *Dṛg-dṛśya-viveka*, 13)

antar dṛg-dṛṣyayor bhedaṁ
bahiś ca brahma-sargayoḥ
āvṛṇoty aparā śaktis
sā saṁsārasya kāraṇam

> The other power [of *māyā*] conceals the distinction between the perceiver and perceived objects, which are cognized within the body as well as outside one's own body in the distinction between Brahman and the phenomenal universe. This power (*śakti*) is the cause of the phenomenal universe.
>
> (*Dṛg-dṛśya-viveka*, 15)

To the wise, the whole relative universe is nothing but a dream. They are not influenced by the concealing power of *māyā*. We can cover the eyes of an observer, but we cannot hide the sun. Similarly, *māyā* does not hide absolute reality but only obstructs the faculty of knowledge and, therefore, our perception of reality.

Let us suppose that I dream that I am chased by a tiger. Although the tiger is unreal and does not exist in my waking state, it is not completely false either, because the emotions it arouses in me are real. The tiger could be considered false only if it had not appeared in my dream. Similarly, this objective universe is not absolutely false but exists only in appearance for those who live asleep. Only when we wake up do we become aware that the dream is not real. While we remain in the objective reality of ignorance, this world must be accepted as real for all practical purposes. We will become aware it is not real only by waking up to the ultimate reality.

According to Vedanta, the objective universe is unreal but it appears real to those in a state of dual consciousness. In the state of supreme consciousness, the world vanishes. Therefore, the appearance we currently perceive through the senses is unreal. As long as our ignorance remains, what is dual and relative will seem real to us. But when we experience our nature as Brahman, this temporal universe vanishes as if it had never existed. Objective diversity dissolves and only Brahman remains. Just like when we say "touch wood!", chairs and tables disappear and all we see is wood. Only by situating ourselves in our authentic nature will we no longer mistake a snake for a rope. Then we will know that only Brahman exists and nothing is real apart from it. In that state, Brahman is realized in all its splendor and purity.

rajju-rūpe parijñāte
sarpa-khaṇḍaṁ na tiṣṭhati
adhiṣṭhāne tathā jñāte
prapañcaḥ śūnyatāṁ gataḥ

When the real nature of the rope is known, the appearance of the snake no longer persists; hence when the substratum is known, the phenomenal world disappears completely.

(*Aparokṣānubhūti*, 96)

rūpa-varṇādikam sarvam
vihāya paramārtha-vit
paripūrṇa-cid-ānanda
svarūpeṇāvatiṣṭhate

One who has realized the Supreme discards all identification with objects of names and forms. Thereafter one dwells as an embodiment of the infinite, consciousness, and bliss. One becomes the Self.

(*Ātma-bodha*, 40)

Chapter 7

God (Īśvara) and the soul (*jīva*)

avidyopādhiḥ san ātmā jīva ity ucyate
māyopādhiḥ san īśvara ity ucyate

> Awareness (*ātma*) conditioned by nescience (*avidyā*) is known as soul (*jīva*). Awareness conditioned by illusion (*māyā*) is known as Īśvara.
>
> (Śaṅkarācārya, *Tattva-bodha*, 9.3–4)

In devotional terminology, the word *īśvara* means "Lord." Its theological meaning is "the supreme Self" or "the supreme Lord." *Īśa* means "possessor" and derives from the root *īś*, or "to possess or control." The term appears for the first time in the *Manu Smṛti*. The *Śvetāśvatara Upanishad* uses the word *īśa* to refer to Rudra. Shaivism made *īśa* part of one of Śiva's names: Māheśvara, or "the great Lord." In Shaktism, the feminine term Īśvarī refers to the Divine Mother of the Universe. In Vedanta, Īśvara refers to Brahman as perceived from the dual and relative platform of illusion, or *māyā*.

Brahman is the absolute reality devoid of qualities, or *nirguṇa*. Since it transcends the human intellect, it is indescribable and inconceivable. Its nature is purity, consciousness, and freedom; it is absolutely immutable and not affected by phenomenal limitations. Brahman constitutes the transcendental principle of pure consciousness and although it is the basis and essence of the phenomenal world, it is not tainted by the world. Its nature surpasses determinism and the distinctions between the knower, knowledge, and the known. Since Nirguṇa-brahman is transcendental (*pāramārthika*) and not phenomenal (*vyāvahārika*), it does not perform the functions of a personal God. The Upanishads do not refer to *nirguṇa* as an object of devotion but of meditation, or *upāsanā*.

Obviously, what is unqualified, transcendental, and immutable cannot be the cause of a changeable, qualified, and phenomenal reality. Therefore, the Lord, sovereign, and creator of the universe is Saguṇa-brahman, or qualified Brahman. The second aphorism of the *Vedānta Sūtra* states that Brahman is the origin of the cosmic manifestation. As the aspect of Brahman committed to the empirical reality, Īśvara is in charge of causality and is an object of devotion for conditioned souls on the dual plane.

At this point, we need to understand the meaning of the terms *svarūpa-lakṣaṇa* and *taṭastha-lakṣaṇa*. *Svarūpa-lakṣaṇa* is the intrinsic quality of something that is always present. *Taṭastha-lakṣaṇa* is an incidental attribute that is sometimes present and sometimes not. The former is the essential definition while the latter refers to the characteristics that differentiate an object from others, even though these characteristics do not last as long as what they define, for example, the smell of an object.

Dharmarāja Adhvarīndra explains this in his *Vedānta-paribhāṣā*:

> *tatra lakṣaṇaṁ dvi-vidham— svarūpa-lakṣaṇaṁ taṭastha-lakṣaṇañ ceti. tatra svarūpam eva lakṣaṇaṁ svarūpa-lakṣaṇam.*
>
> Now, characteristics are of two kinds: essential and secondary. Of these, essential characteristics (*svarūpa*) consist in the very nature (*svarūpa*) of a thing.
>
> *taṭastha-lakṣaṇaṁ nāma yāval lakṣya-kāla-manavasthi tatve sati yad vyāvartakaṁ tad eva.*
>
> A secondary characteristic is that which, although lasting less than its possessor, yet differentiates it from other things.
>
> (*Vedānta-paribhāṣā*, chapter 7)

According to the *Vedānta-paribhāṣā*, the *svarūpa-lakṣaṇas* of Brahman are its intrinsic attributes mentioned in the Upanishads: *satyam* (truth), *jñānam* (consciousness), *anantam* (limitlessness), and so on. Since they are integral parts of its nature, they are Brahman itself. The *taṭastha-lakṣaṇa* of Brahman is to be the creator, preserver, and destroyer of the universe.

Causality and agency of the phenomenal universe are only temporary aspects of Brahman caused by illusion. If Brahman were the creator, this would mean that it has the desire to create an effect. Clearly, desire is not an essential feature of Brahman but of its qualified aspect Īśvara, or God.

> *satyādikaṁ brahma-svarūpa-lakṣaṇam "satyaṁ jñānam anantaṁ brahma", "ānando brahmeti vyajānāt" ity ādi śruteḥ.*
>
> Truth, and so on are the essential characteristics (*svarūpa-lakṣaṇas*) of Brahman, which is stated by such *Śruti* quotations as "Brahman is Truth, knowledge, and infinitude" (*Taittirīya Upanishad*, 2.1) and "He knew that bliss was Brahman" (*Taittirīya Upanishad*, 3.6).
>
> (*Vedānta-paribhāṣā,* chapter 7)

The Upanishads describe Apara-brahman or Saguṇa-brahman as an infinite reality that gives birth to, maintains, and destroys the universe. These descriptions are efforts to characterize an omniscient and omnipotent reality that is beyond understanding. Brahman can express itself with a multiplicity of names and forms without an external cause. Such names and forms, lacking an ontological status independent of Brahman, have characteristics that differ from the nature of Brahman. In Advaita metaphysics, *māyā* is responsible for the inconceivable transformation of the

One into many without the One diminishing or losing its unity.

Īśvara is the only aspect of absolute reality that the human intellect can comprehend. Human beings can relate to the Absolute in relative terms because Īśvara, as well as its creation, lies within the limits of phenomenal reality, or *vyāvahārika*. From an absolute point of view, both Īśvara and souls belong to the realm of *māyā*. While *jīvas* are unaware of their essence, Īśvara is aware of his nature because he is not subject to *āvaraṇa-śakti*, or "the illusory power of *māyā*." Īśvara is the divine Self: creator, sustainer, and destroyer of the universe. He is omnipotent, omniscient, the controller of all energies, and what is conscious in everything, living or inert. He is the personification of Brahman and resides in the mind, heart, and body of every individuality. He is the enjoyer of all delights, the father of all that exists, the friend of all beings, and the lover of all creatures. He is the source and refuge for everyone, the ultimate object of devotion, the supreme Individuality, the Whole, and equality in difference.

Īśvara and the individual souls are manifestations that originate in Brahman and are conditioned by *māyā* and *avidyā*, respectively. Just as the space inside a pot is not limited by the clay edges, the limiting agents of the *jīvas* and Īśvara do not alter the true nature of Brahman. The *upādhis* are limiting agents but they do not change the essential nature of the entity they limit, that is to say, they do not cause a qualitative change. The phenomenal existence of Īśvara, or *māyika*, does not differ at all from the essential existence of Brahman.

In their original state, both souls and the supreme Lord are the reality of the One without a second. When the soul returns to its original state and is situated in *pāramārthika* reality, it realizes itself as Brahman.

Īśvara has infinite wonderful qualities and lordship over everything and everyone. He is not subject to karma or reactions to past actions. Since he is free of the veiling power of *māyā*, he is fully aware at all times of his original identity as Brahman. The individual soul, or *jīvātman*, is covered by ignorance. Immersed in *saṁsāra*, or "the cycle of repeated births and deaths," it suffers the consequences of past actions. However, the differences between the individual soul and the Lord exist only in relative reality and not in absolute reality (*pāramārthika*), where both are Brahman. The difference between Īśvara and *jīva* is only in terms of limiting agents, or *upādhis*.

To accept the reality of the world means accepting God. *Avidyā* is the power that prevents individual souls from directly experiencing their reality, and *māyā* is the force that covers reality and projects the universe. Such powers would be meaningless without Īśvara, the controller of these powers.

If *māyā* had an independent ontological existence, there would be a separation between the two levels of Brahman: the higher Brahman (Nirguṇa-brahman) and the lower Brahman (Saguṇa-brahman). The higher Brahman is the Absolute devoid of attributes, immutable, transcendental to causality and to nomenclature and form. Being like this, it obviously cannot assume the role of the creator of a relative and dual universe. *Māyā* allows

Brahman to make the transition from unity to diversity, from impersonal absolute consciousness to the personal creator of the objective world. Universal causality requires a Brahman–*māyā* combination, which we call Saguṇa-brahman, Apara-brahman, or Īśvara. Īśvara interacts with the phenomenal universe and is defined by that relationship; therefore, it is considered inferior, or *apara*. This compromise with empirical reality, or *vyāvahārika*, places Apara-brahman in a secondary position with respect to Para-brahman. Saguṇa-brahman is not the Absolute as it is, but the highest appearance of Brahman within an apparent world. Nirguṇa-brahman, on the other hand, is the Absolute as it is and transcends cause and effect. If it were the cause, it would be relational and objective in nature; if it were an effect, it would be finite. Saguṇa-brahman is considered inferior because it has attributes and qualities, whereas Nirguṇa-brahman lacks distinctions between substance and attributes. Thus, it is clear that the conception of the Absolute as God belongs to a lower, relative, practical, and dual point of view, whereas Nirguṇa-brahman, devoid of attributes, belongs to a higher level. Saguṇa-brahman is Īśvara, or God, whose various expressions are worshipped by devotees of many religions.

Ultimately, the objective universe, with its apparent diversity, is a superimposition onto Brahman. Returning to the old Vedanta parable, the snake turns out to be just a rope. The qualities of the snake were superimposed onto the rope. Questions about the origin of names and forms can only be raised on the dual and relative plane. All mysteries lose meaning when empirical reality is transcended. Discovering that the snake is only a rope dissolves fear of it. It would be incongruent to attribute the origin of the snake to the rope or that of the world to Brahman. Causality needs explanations on the relative plane, but it is meaningless on the absolute plane. Brahman and Īśvara should not be understood as two different realities. Both are one and the same, but Īśvara's existence depends on our degree of acceptance of objective reality. If we accept the phenomenal universe as real, Īśvara becomes indispensable. When the finite and limited human mind turns toward the Absolute, Brahman is projected onto the mind as Īśvara. When *māyā* reflects the Absolute like a mirror, human beings see it as God.

Īśvara and *jīva* are mere superimpositions of *māyā* and *avidyā*, respectively, onto the only reality of the absolute Brahman. The phenomenal universe is both real and unreal: while you perceive it as separate from Brahman, it is illusory. When you perceive it as Brahman, you realize its reality. The world was not created the way a painter paints a picture or a writer writes a book. In both cases, the creation is independent of its creator. Paintings and books have an existence that is independent of the painter and the writer. The relationship between the universe and God is like the one between a karateka and a *kata* or a dancer and a dance: they remain unified as one and it is impossible to separate them.

CHAPTER 8

The world or *jagat*

tavāt satyaṁ jagad bhāti
śuktikā-rajataṁ yathā
yāvan na jñāyate brahma
sarvādhiṣṭānam advayam

The world (*jagat*) appears to be true (*satyam*) so long as Brahman, the substratum, the basis of all this creation, is not realized. It is like the illusion of silver in mother-of-pearl.

(*Ātma-bodha*, 7)

upādāne 'khilādhare
jaganti parameśvare
sarga-sthiti-layān yānti
budbudānīva vāriṇi

Like bubbles in the water, worlds rise, exist, and dissolve in the supreme Self, which is the material cause and the support of everything.

(*Ātma-bodha*, 8)

Although Advaita Vedanta offers several different theories of creation, it ultimately sees the universe as a limited expression of the infinite. In other words, it is a segmented appearance of the Absolute or a dual manifestation of the single reality that is all that is. Without denying the existence of the world, the Advaita Vedanta negates the world's reality and aspires to an existential realization of the Truth.

If we wake up in the middle of the night and see a crocodile in the corner of the room that disappears after a few moments, we will conclude that it was a hallucination. Likewise, we consider dreams unreal because they last for a while and then vanish when we wake up. But how substantial is the phenomenal universe? Although not accepted as real, it is not completely false. Then how does the Advaita Vedanta explain the diversity of worldly objects? Obviously, nothing and no one can be considered completely true within a changeable reality. Vedanta considers all temporal phenomenon neither real nor false.

To explain it more clearly, let's return to the well-known Advaitic analogy of the rope and the snake. While walking in the forest at dusk, we see a rope lying by the trail. Due to the dim light, we take it for a snake. It is our fear that prevents us from seeing the rope. When we finally perceive the rope, the snake disappears. Although the snake is only apparent, it is real as long as our fear does not allow us to see the rope. Only when we become aware of the absence of the snake does it completely cease to be real. The snake was never born and never died; it had no beginning in the annals of history. It did not come from the rope or disappear into it. It was the darkness that prevented us from seeing it was just a rope. Only when someone turns on a flashlight do we recognize our mistake and dispel our ignorance. In this way, with the right knowledge, we can perceive reality as it is.

Levels of reality

The monist Vedanta proposes three criteria of reality: real, non-real, and false. What is true always exists, and what is false never existed. The Truth is, was, and will never cease to be. As this verse states:

nāsato vidyate bhāvo
nābhāvo vidyate sataḥ
ubhayor api dṛṣṭo 'ntas
tv anayos tattva-darśibhiḥ

> The seers of the Truth have concluded that what is nonexistent does not endure and what is eternal does not change. This they have concluded by studying the nature of both.
> (Bhagavad Gita, 2.16)

Śaṅkara offers a brilliant explanation of the phenomenon of the world and its relation to ultimate reality. In his writings, he mentions three orders or levels of reality: absolute reality (*pāramārthika*), relative reality (*vyāvahārika*), and illusory reality (*prātibhāsika*), which he distinguishes from non-existence (*alīka*).

Dharmarāja Adhvarīndra eloquently encapsulates this principle:

> *yad vā tri-vidhaṁ sattvam-pāramārthikaṁ vyāvahārikaṁ pratibhāsikañ ceti. pāramārthikaṁ sattvaṁ brahmaṇaḥ, vyāvahārikaṁ sattvam ākāśādeḥ, prātibhāsikaṁ sattvaṁ śukti-rajatādeḥ.*
>
> [Or we may say] there are three kinds of existence: absolute, conventional, and illusory. Absolute existence belongs to Brahman, conventional existence to the ether, and so on, and illusory existence to the silver in nacre.
>
> (*Vedānta-paribhāṣā*, chapter 2)

Absolute reality or *pāramārthika-sattā:* This refers to Brahman, which is the only reality that exists; it is pure, immutable, and eternal. Objective phenomena are unreal superimpositions over the background of this absolute reality. From the point of view of *pāramārthika-sattā*, both relative and illusory reality are false. Differences between the two are only relevant to those who are still blinded by ignorance. Those who have realized transcendental consciousness perceive that plurality is a manifestation of a single reality. Plurality vanishes along with the disappearance of ignorance. *Pāramārthika* refers to the transcendental consciousness that perceives the absolute reality behind the objective diversity of names and forms. Just as an ordinary person knows that the moon reflected in the lake is not the real moon, a realized being perceives that objects are unreal. The wise ones look at the objective world like we look at a mirror: knowing that the reality they see is only a reflection.

Relative reality or *vyāvahārika-sattā*: This is the empirical, practical, relative, and temporal reality that is based on subject–object relationships. Śaṅkara reveals in his commentary on the *Vedānta Sūtra* that *vyāvahārika-sattā* comes from the mutual superimposition of the real and the unreal, or the Self and non–Self, caused by ignorance. Every existing phenomenon combines reality and unreality. Since *vyāvahārika-sattā* is based on time, space, and causality, it is constantly mutating. Its temporary nature differentiates it from absolute reality, which is eternal. Even though the objective world is only an empirical reality, in practical life we should relate to the world as if it were real.

Illusory reality or *prātibhāsika-sattā*: *Prātibhāsika* is only an appearance of *vyāvahārika*. It refers to the apparent reality of the illusory phenomena, such as hallucinations, mirages, dreams, and so on. This reality is accepted as real as long as the illusion lasts, but this ends when one becomes conscious of empirical reality (*vyāvahārika*). These illusions originate in *avidyā*, or "ignorance," and they vanish as soon as one recognizes the real basis that gave rise to the appearances. The illusion dissipates only through the knowledge of essence, or *adhiṣṭhāna*.

Prātibhāsika is like the reflection of the moon in a calm and peaceful lake. Although it is only an appearance, the reflection may seem to be the moon itself. The reflection of the moon is perceptible, but the reflected moon is false.

It can be very beautiful, but it is not the real moon. In relation to its reflection, the moon is considered real.

Inexistence or *alīka*: This refers to absolute non-existence. The three levels of reality mentioned above are different from *alīka*. It is impossible to perceive *alīka* in the past, present, or future, for example, a son of a sterile woman.

For Śaṅkara, 0only absolute reality (*pāramārthika*) exists, whereas relative reality (*vyāvahārika*) is non-real, or *mithyā*. However, non-real existence (*vyāvahārika*) is different from illusionary reality (*prātibhāsika*) and of course of absolute non-existence (*alīka*). The objective universe is a non-real phenomenon (*mithyā*) but perceptible.

avācchinnaś cid-ābhāsas
tṛtīyaḥ svapna-kalpitaḥ
svijñeyas tri-vidho jīvas
tatrādyaḥ pāramārthikaḥ

> There are three conceptions of jīva (consciousness): one is limited by prāṇa (vital energy), one is present in the mind, and one is consciousness as imagined in dream [to have assumed the forms of man, etc.]. The first of these is true nature.
>
> (*Dṛg-dṛṣya-viveka*, 32)

Mithyā or "non-real"

Of the above levels, the *prātibhāsika* reality is surpassed by *vyāvahārika*, which in turn is transcended by *pāramārthika*. *Prātibhāsika* is a private reality, *vyāvahārika* is shared by all human beings, and *pāramārthika* belongs only to the enlightened. Only sages have the right to relate to the world as *mithyā*, or "non-real," not those who are still blinded by illusion.

What is real exists (*sat*) in the present, past, and future. What is unreal does not exist (*asat*) in the present, past, or future. What is non-real (*mithyā*) occupies an intermediate place between *sat* and *asat*: sometimes it exists and sometimes it does not.

> *sad-asad vilakṣaṇatvam mithyātvam.*
>
> *Mithyātva* (non-reality) is neither real nor unreal.
>
> (Madhusūdana Sarasvatī, *Advaita-siddhi*, *pariccheda* 1)

Walking in the dark, we take a rope for a snake. The snake is not real (*sat*) in the present, past, or the future. The snake is not unreal (*asat*) because it causes us fear. The snake is non-real (*mithyā*): it has existence for the frightened person, but it ceases to exist when ignorance vanishes.

Ignorant people perceive objects and accept distinction between them as real. They are attracted by some objects and repulsed by others. On the other hand, manifold reality has no meaning for enlightened beings with Advaitic experience: they know that is only due to the *upādhis*, or "limitations," that objects of the phenomenal world appear to be separate. They see everything and everyone without attraction or repulsion. Due to their transcendental vision, they see the essence of everything and do not love or hate anything in particular: nothing is *priya* or *apriya*.

In other words, enlightened beings do not pay attention to the diversity of this world but they are aware of the world's true identity. Neither do they ignore the existing objective variety, although they know that the differences are false, temporary, and illusory. The awakened ones move through the world respecting dual *vyāvahārika* reality but conscious of the transcendental *pāramārthika* reality.

The five factors of the objective universe

In the *Sarasvatī-rahasya Upanishad*, it is said that in the objective universe we can observe five factors:

1. Existence (*sat* or *asti*).
2. Consciousness (*cit* or *bhāti*).
3. Bliss (*ānanda* or *priya*).
4. Name (*nāma*).
5. Form (*rūpa*).

The first three belong to reality, while the last two belong to the objective world. *Nāma* and *rūpa* are illusory, while Brahman is *sac-cid-ānanda*.

asti bhāti priyaṁ rūpaṁ
nāma cety aṁśa pañcakam

ādya trayaṁ brahma-rūpaṁ
jagad-rūpaṁ tato dvayam
apekṣya nāma-rūpa-dve
sac-cidānanda tat paraḥ

There are five factors: being (*asti*), shining (*bhāti*), loving (*priya*), form (*rūpa*), and name (*nāma*). The first three are equivalent to *sat*, *cid*, and *ānanda* and pertain to Brahman. The other two make up the world.

(*Sarasvatī-rahasya Upanishad,* 23b-24)

Śaṅkara, in his *Dṛg-dṛṣya-viveka*, quotes this Upanishad and then continues:

kha-vāyvagni-jalorvīṣu
deva-tiryaṅ narādiṣu
abhinnāḥ sac-cid-ānandā
bhidyete rūpa-nāmanī

Existence (*sat*), consciousness (*cit*), and bliss (*ānanda*) are the same in space, air, fire, water, and earth as well as in celestial beings, animals, and humans. They only differ in name and form.

(*Dṛg-dṛṣya-viveka*, 21)

Apart from Brahman, the categories that make up the universe are name and form. If we eradicate them from an object, only Brahman remains, which is existence (*sat*), consciousness (*cit*), and bliss (*ānanda*).

Only names and forms are distinctive. The other three are shared by all things. What all objects in the world have in common is a single immutable nature that remains during all periods of time. Only the name and form can change or disappear.

Let us compare objects to rings and reality to gold. Gold jewelry can be melted and lose its form, but the gold always preserves its *asti*, *bhāti*, and *priya* qualities. Like gold, Brahman adopts a great diversity of forms. Supreme reality presents itself as trees, flowers, rivers, stars, human beings, and so on. These forms are temporary and subject to change. As long as we focus on the form of rings, earrings, or bracelets, we do not see the gold. As long as we focus on the gold, we overlook the jewels. A woman who goes to buy a jewel pays more attention to the form than the gold. On the other hand, the jeweler concentrates on the weight of the jewel, conscious at all times that it is made of gold. Within all types of jewelry lies the same single shared reality. Rings and earrings can be melted, but the gold remains. The form and the name are temporary and transient. Only the essential nature, or Brahman, remains.

Substrate (*adhiṣṭāna*), appearance (*āropita*), and superimposition (*adhyāsa*)

The phenomenal world is like the snake that is seen in place of the rope. Brahman takes the form of different objects in the universe. The objects are real in their Brahman aspect, because what is real never disappears. However, even though we can see the objects, they cannot be considered real; they are *mithyā* just like the snake that scares the confused person.

In his *Viveka-cuḍāmani*, Ādi Śaṅkara states:

ananyatvam adhiṣṭhānād
āropyasya nirīkṣitam
paṇḍitai rajju-sarpādau
vikalpo bhrānti-jīvanaḥ

> That which is superimposed upon something else is observed by the wise to be identical to the substratum, as a rope appears to be a snake. The apparent difference is solely due to delusion.
>
> (*Viveka-cuḍāmani*, 407)

This *mithyā* concept implies that the snake does not appear out of nowhere. Instead, an already existing rope is mistaken for a snake: the rope is the substrate (*adhiṣṭāna*) and the snake is the appearance (*āropita*). Obviously, in relation to the substrate, the appearance lacks reality. Being confused, we superimpose (*adhyāsa*) the snake on reality. Confused, we point to something and say "this is a snake" (*idam sarpam*). This, or *idam*, is the basis of misperception. In Vedanta, this is called *adhiṣṭāna*, the imposed snake is called *āpita*, and the superimposition is called *adhyāsa*.

Adhyāsa is an overlap of something that is and something that is not (*buddhiḥ tad tasmin* or *atasmiṁs-tad-buddhiḥ*). Someone with incorrect knowledge (*ajñāna*) perceives a snake (*āropita*) because it is superimposed (*adhyāsa*) on the rope (*adhiṣṭāna*). Correct knowledge (*samyak-jñāna*) can make the superimposition of the snake disappear and allow the perception of "this," its reality as rope.

> *āha— ko 'yam adhyāso nāmeti. ucyate— smṛti-rūpaḥ paratra pūrva-dṛṣṭāvabhāsaḥ.*
>
> It may be asked: What is meant by the term *adhyāsa* (superimposition)? The answer: like memory, it is just a reflection elsewhere of something seen earlier.
>
> (Śaṅkarācārya, *Brahma Sūtra Bhāṣya*, *"Adhyāsa-prakaraṇa"*)

The shared foundation (*adhiṣṭāna*) of all objects is Brahman, the ultimate reality. It is not perceived by ordinary people because of their *ajñāna*. Lacking discrimination, ordinary people confuse what is apparent with what is real. They keep striving for things that are temporary, as if all objects were real and eternal. However, objects are like reflections in a mirror. Behind the diversity of objects lies a single absolute reality, Brahman, which manifests as diversity. What is perceived through the senses is illusory but has its own source, or *adhiṣṭāna*. The snake disappears along with the emergence of true *jñāna*, but the rope remains. Something similar happens for potters, who do not see jars or plates but perceive them as clay.

Such a vision does not perceive separate or disconnected objects, but a single absolute reality. Ordinary mundane consciousness sees objective diversity as real. Knowledge of the true nature of objective reality will appear through the guidance of a spiritual master and study of the sacred scriptures. When knowledge manifests, the consciousness of the phenomenal world disappears and ultimate reality comes into view.

Chapter 9

The causality of Vedanta or *vivarta-vāda*

A cause-effect relationship exists between two objects when one is the origin of the other. We call the producing element cause and the produced one effect. The term cause is called in Sanskrit *kāraṇa*, *nidāna*, *hetu*, or *mūla*; and the term effect is translated as *kārya*, *phala*, *pariṇāma*, or *śuṅga*. Most theories of causation hold that the cause is distinct from its effect and precedes it. Other theories hold that the effect comes into existence when the cause ends, while there are others that postulate that the cause continues to exist in its effect. The subject of cause and effect holds a relevant place within all the different schools of Vedanta; it is much discussed in classical and medieval Vedantic literature and different views have been proposed.

According to the Upanishadic masters, in every productive process, the cause has three aspects: material, instrumental, and efficient. For example, if the vessel is the effect, the clay would be the material cause; the potter's wheel, the instrumental cause; and the potter, the efficient cause. When these causes combine, the vessel comes into existence in the phenomenal universe.

In the West, we see that Aristotle pointed to the prime motor as the final cause of motion, which moves everything without moving, reminiscent of Kṛṣṇa, the all attractive one especially in *Gauḍīya* Vaishnavism, or the lover moving the beloved.

Aristotle divides beings into natural and manufactured. Natural beings are those that have movement by or from themselves, while manufactured beings receive it from the outside. The characteristics of natural beings are their motion, development, and transformation as a function of an intrinsic force. *Physis* , or "nature," is the principle of movement and mutation. The notion of *physis* occupies a central place in Aristotelian thought, just as the concept of ideas was in Platonic thought.

The theory of the four causes developed by Aristotle had great influence on several philosophers in history. It is a theory focused on the understanding of motion, which is considered synonymous with change. The Aristotelian concept of cause is broader. What we understand by cause today is only what Aristotle referred to as efficient cause and final cause. According to the great Greek philosopher, cause is every principle of being, that which the existence of an entity depends on, in some way or other; every factor to which we have to resort to explain certain process.

According to Aristotle, cause is the factor on which a thing depends. Every change has a cause.

All knowledge will be knowledge of causes, because to know something will be to know the reasons for its existence or causes. Explaining nature, he refers to four kinds of causes: (1) the formal or what a thing is, (2) the material or that of which an object is made, (3) the efficient or that which has produced the thing, and (4) the final or that to which it tends or may become. The first two are intrinsic, because these principles reside in the entity itself. The other two are extrinsic, they explain the becoming: they are principles external to the entity.

(1) Formal cause is a change or movement brought about by the disposition, form, or appearance of the thing that changes or moves. This is the cause of something insofar as it determines that something making it to be what it is. It is the specific cause of the entity in question, that is, the cause proper to the species. It is the essence of the object or being.

(2) The material cause of a change or movement is the aspect of the change or movement that is determined by the material that composes the movement or changing things. For a table, it might be wood; for a statue, it might be bronze or marble.

(3) The efficient cause consists of agents other than the thing that mutates or moves, which interact to be an agency of the change or motion. It is the stimulus that triggers the process of development. It is the cause of what the thing is, the cause of the child being a person is the parents, or the table of being a table, is the carpenter.

(4) The final cause is about the end, goal, or objective toward which a being is directed. It consists of a change or movement for the sake of a thing to be what it is. It is the plan considered while it has not yet been incorporated into the thing; it is an aspiration of nature that has not yet been achieved. It is the perfection toward which the thing naturally tends to attain. As an example, we would say that for a seed is to become a tree.

To illustrate the four Aristotelian causes, we propose a practical example: let us imagine a sculpture. The material cause would be the marble from which the sculpture is made, the formal cause would be its form, the efficient cause would be the sculptor, and the final cause would be to decorate a room.

For their part, the Vedantic sages offer their respective explanations of the relationship between God as cause and creation as effect: God can be the transcendental cause of creation, its immanent cause, or both. We will briefly discuss some postulates about causality offered by different *darśanas*, or "philosophical schools."

***Asat-kārya-vāda* or "the theory of the non-existent effect" (*ārambha-vāda* or "the origin theory"):** The *nyāya-vaiśeṣika* school posits a theory of causality called *asat-kārya-vāda*. According to this school, every effect is a new product of a cause. The effect differs from the cause and it does not exist before being produced by the cause; otherwise, causality would lack all meaning. The cause takes place first and then the effect appears. According to this theory, Īśvara is the primordial cause of the universe and is different from his creation. Like a painting created by a painter or a vessel made by a potter, the universe is a creation made by the hands of God. The activities of God in the universe of names and forms are *sṛṣṭi*, *sthiti*, and *saṁhāra*, or "creation, maintenance, and absorption."

This theory faces many difficulties. The jeweler creates jewelry from gold, which is a material independent of the jeweler and exists prior to both the jewelry and the manufacturing process. What materials does God use to create and what is his relationship with them? God cannot create from the void, because this would conflict with the laws of the phenomenal universe.

***Sat-kārya-vāda* or "the theory of the existent effect":** The *Sāṅkhya* school proposes a totally different theory called *sat-kārya-vāda*, that says that the effect is not a new creation but preexists within the cause. The cause undergoes a total transformation after which it cannot go back, similar to the irreversible change of milk that has turned into curd. The theory of transformation, or *pariṇāma*, says that *prakṛti* (the primordial matter) is transformed into the universe. *Prakṛti*, also called *pradhāna*, is the first principle of the universe (*tattva*). It is the unconscious and unintelligent principle comprised of the three modes of nature, or *guṇas*: *sattva*, *rajas*, and *tamas*. This theory also raises questions. For example, how can something lacking intelligence, such as primordial matter, create the universe? It is impossible for *pradhāna*, as a non-intelligent principle, to modify itself in order to create the universe. Knowledge, which is sattvic, is essential to create the universe. However, in the original state of *prakṛti*, the *guṇas* are in perfect balance.

Without going into more detail, we will only say that proponents of these two theories attacked each other in long debates, which paved the way for the non-dual postulate called *vivarta-vāda*.

***Vivarta-vāda* or "the theory of modification":** The Vedantic proposition called *vivarta-vāda* is, in a way, a variant of the *sat-kārya-vāda* of the *sāṅkhya*, since it also states that the effect preexists its cause and is a manifestation of the cause. However, it postulates that the effect is not a new entity but a different expression of the cause. The Sanskrit term *vivarta* can be translated as "modification, alteration, or change of form." This Vedantic proposition explains that the cause of the objective world is Brahman and that creation is only an *apparent* mutation (*vikāra*) and by no means a modification of the immutable Brahman. The world is a superimposition, or *adhyāsa*, upon Brahman caused by ignorance. Only knowledge reveals the true nature of objects.

The sensory universe was not created; it is only an appearance of the ultimate reality under certain limiting conditions such as space and time. Advaita Vedanta rejects the theory of causality as inconsistent, because from the perspective of the timeless absolute platform, one event does not precede another.

The phenomenal world is nothing but Brahman manifesting itself in a multiplicity of names and forms. Along with the experience of the Self, all objects lose their distinctions and dissolve in the substratum of the world, which is the only reality.

Returning to the analogy of the rope and the snake, we could say that the snake existed prior to the rope, since it was the rope that was mistaken for a snake. For the confused traveler, the snake appeared, lasted for a while, and vanished on the rope, but in fact, only the rope exists. The snake was nothing but the rope, whose existence was hidden by ignorance, or *ajñāna*. According to *vivarta*, whatever appears differently does not cease to be what it really is: Brahman is one, even in diversity. In fact, the only thing that really exists is the rope, that is, Brahman devoid of *nāma* and *rūpa*. The phenomenal world is neither a creation nor a transformation of something; it is not real either, since its multiplicity vanishes along with enlightenment. However, we cannot reject its reality completely because it seems real when we perceive it through the senses.

The effect can return to its cause, that is, the snake can disappear into the rope. The objective universe is not creation, evolution, or transformation. Any creation theory implies substantiality, as well as the ultimate veracity of objective multiplicity. These theories affirm the existence of objects and the validity of names and forms. But for Advaita, only Brahman is real and true, devoid of form, name, action, and attributes. Brahman is eternal and immutable, or *nitya*. It is what is real, or *sat*, and what is true, or *satya*. As stated by Śaṅkara in his *Viveka-cūḍāmaṇi*:

nirvikalpakam analpam akṣaraṁ
yat kṣarākṣara-vilakṣaṇaṁ param
nityam avyaya-sukhaṁ nirañjanaṁ
brahma tat tvam asi bhāvayātmani

> That which is free from duality, that which is infinite and indestructible, that which is distinct from the universe and from *māyā*, supreme, eternal, that which is undying bliss and is untainted: this is the Brahman that you are. Meditate upon this within your own self.
>
> (*Viveka-cūḍāmaṇi*, 261)

By superimposing itself upon reality, *māyā* conceals it and presents it as the objective world of names and forms. This diversity vanishes with knowledge of Brahman. If what we are looking for is a cause of the universe in the conventional sense of the term, it would be the *vivarta* of Brahman, or "the apparent transformation of Brahman." The One is formless, devoid of qualities, and inactive but it appears to have diversity, form, qualities, and activity.

When worldly consciousness is overcome by Brahmanic consciousness, creation (*sṛṣṭi*), maintenance (*sthiti*), and dissolution (*saṁhāra*) of the universe are revealed as projections onto Brahman. Saguṇa-brahman is Īśvara, or God, who creates, maintains, and destroys the phenomenal universe at the end of each cycle. Since nothing exists apart from Brahman, Brahman is both the material and instrumental cause of the universe.

Saguṇa-brahman, or Īśvara, emerges from the relationship between Brahman and *māyā*. Īśvara creates the world from himself, remains in it, and finally removes it from himself. God remains in the universe as the universe, transcendental to it and simultaneously being its very essence. The relationship between God and the world is not one of causality. Only a theistic theory needs God as the creative cause of the universe. The diversity of the universe is an aspect of Brahman and not a creation. A creative act is not consistent with the inactive nature of Brahman.

The manifestation of the universe is only an appearance, or *vivarta*, due to the superimposition onto Brahman. Hence, efforts to describe the process of universal evolution are futile and meaningless. Since time, space, and causality are the result of a superimposition, it is obviously pointless to investigate what was before or how it started. Due to *avidyā*, the world of multiplicity seems to be a modification of Brahman. But the change is an illusion, just as the snake is not a modification of the rope.

According to non-dual Vedanta, the reality of the world is not independent of Brahman. Moreover, the phenomenal reality that we perceive through our senses is essentially Brahman.

The great Vedantic sage Ānandagiri, in his *ṭika* to the *Māṇḍūkya Kārikā Bhāṣya* of Śaṅkara, sheds light on the essence of the *vivarta-vāda* and its relation to the *pariṇāma* or *sat-kārya-vāda*:

The verse of the *Māṇḍūkya Kārikā* describes the syllable *Oṁ*:

sarvasya praṇavo hy ādir
madhyamantas tathaiva ca
evaṁ hi praṇavaṁ jñātvā
vyaśnute tad anantaram

Oṁ is verily the beginning, middle, and end of everything. Knowing *Oṁ* as such, one undoubtedly and immediately attains the supreme Reality.

(*Māṇḍūkya Kārikā,* 1.27)

Śaṅkara's commentary explains thus:

ādi-madhyāntā utpatti-sthiti-pralayāḥ sarvasyaiva māyā-hasti-rajju-sarpa-mṛgatṛṣṇikā-svapnādi vad utpadyamānasya viyadādi-prapañcasya yathā māyāvy ādayaḥ. evaṁ hi praṇavam ātmānaṁ māyāvy ādi sthānīyaṁ jñātvā tat kṣaṇād eva tad ātma-bhāvaṁ vyaśnuta ity arthaḥ.

Oṁ is the beginning, middle, and end of all; that is, everything originates from *Oṁ,* is sustained by it, and ultimately merges into it. As the magician, and so on [without undergoing any change in themselves] stand in relation to the illusory elephant, [the illusion of] snake-rope, the mirage and the dream, and so on, so also is the sacred syllable *Aum* to the manifested manifold such as *ākāśa* (ether), etc. The meaning is that one who knows that the *Aum,* Ātman, like the magician, etc., does not undergo any change, at once becomes unified with it.

Ānandagiri elaborates on Śaṅkara's explanation:

yad oṁkārasya pratyag ātmatvam āpannasya turīyasyāpūrvatvam anantaratvam ity ādi-viśeṣaṇam uktaṁ tatra hetum āha–sarvasyeti. yathokta-viśeṣaṇaṁ praṇavaṁ pratyañcaṁ pratipadya kṛtakṛtyo bhavatīty āha– evam hīti. sarvasyaivotpadya mānasyotpatti stiti layā yathokta-praṇavādhīnā bhavanti. atas tasyoktam viśeṣaṇaṁ yuktam ity arthaḥ. tatraḥ parīṇāma-vādaṁ vyāvartyaṁ vivarta-vādaṁ dyotayitum udāharati– māyeti. anekodāharaṇam utpadyamānasyāneka-vidhatva-bodhanārthaṁ praṇavasya pratyagātmatvaṁ prāptasyāvikṛtasyaiva sva-māyā-śakti-vaśāj jagadd hetutvam ity atra dṛṣṭāntam āha– yatheti. yathā māyāvī svagata-vikāra-mantareṇa māyā-hastyāder indra-jālasya svamāyāvaśād eva hetuḥ. yathā vā rajjvādauaḥ svagata-vikāra-virahiṇaḥ svājñānād eva sarpādi-hetavas tathā 'yam ātmā praṇavabhūto vyavahāra-daśāyāṁ sva-vidyayā sarvasya hetur bhavati. ato yuktaṁ tasya paramārthāvasthāyāṁ pūrvokta-viśeṣaṇavat tvām ity arthaḥ. dvitīyārdhaṁ vibhajate– evaṁ hīti. pūrvokta-viśeṣaṇa-saṁpannam iti yāvat. jñānasya mukti-hetoḥ sahāyāntarāpekṣā nāstīti sūcayati– tat kṣaṇād eveti. tad ātma bhāvam ity atra tac-chabdenāpūrvādi-viśeṣaṇaṁ paramārtha-vastu parāmṛśyate.

Oṁ — when a cause of the universe is sought, *Oṁ* is pointed out. This is in accordance with the *pariṇāma-vāda.* As the magician, and so on—This is from the standpoint of the *vivarta-vāda.* The magician, the rope, and the desert, appear to be an elephant, a snake, and a mirage, respectively, without actually undergoing any change. Similarly, *Oṁ* appears to become the entire manifested world without undergoing any change, from a relative point of view. But from the standpoint of the soundless *Oṁ,* there is no manifested manifold. It is not the cause of anything nor does it appear in any way other than its true nature. *Oṁ* is inferred as is a juggler (*māyāvi*) by those who see the fact of creation and explain it as *māyā.* But the idea of the juggler is also an illusion and it lasts as long as we look upon the manifold as *māyā.* It vanishes as soon as the illusion disappears. At once—*jñāna,* or 'knowledge,' is alone the cause of *mukti* which does not depend on anything else. The moment we know the real nature of *Oṁ,* we become unified with it.

Chapter 10

Creation according to Advaita

True to the spirit of Hinduism, Advaita Vedanta does not adhere to a single creation theory but proposes several. It does not discard any version or prefer one over the others. Instead, it argues that each theory is intended for aspirants of different levels. All of them describe the same phenomenon but explain it to beings with different degrees of subtlety. These explanations do not result in a conflict but are appropriate for each student's needs.

Although certain foods are beneficial and healthy, newborns will only be able to digest them when they reach a certain age. Similarly, dualist theories are for the basic stage of neophyte seekers. The subtler and more sophisticated theories are reserved for *sādhakas* who are more prepared to grasp them.

The teachings of Śaṅkarācārya are based on all the theories of creation. However, later Advaitic masters preferred one or another version. When only certain aspects of Śaṅkara's teachings are studied, his explanations seem to conflict with the statements of certain Upanishads or other masters. These confusions can be avoided if we understand that these statements are directed at seekers of different levels.

The theories proposed by Advaita can be summarized in three *vādas*, or "doctrines":

1. *Sṛṣṭi-dṛṣṭi-vāda* focuses on the perception of what was created.
2. *Dṛṣṭi-sṛṣṭi-vāda* suggests that perception and creation are simultaneous.
3. *Ajāti-vāda* argues that creation is not absolutely real.

Points of view such as *sṛṣṭi-dṛṣṭi-vāda* or *dṛṣṭi-sṛṣṭi-vāda* are tenable only from relative reality, or *vyāvahārika*. The *ajāti-vāda* view, elaborated by Gauḍapāda, becomes relevant only when we are situated in absolute reality, or *pāramārthika*. Advaitic masters have used one, two, or three *vādas* for students of different levels.

Sṛṣṭi-dṛṣṭi-vāda: *Sṛṣṭi* means "creation," and *dṛṣṭi* is translated as "perception." According to this doctrine, an object must first exist in order to be perceived, which clearly implies that creation (*sṛṣṭi*) precedes perception (*dṛṣṭi*). *Sṛṣṭi-dṛṣṭi-vāda* is meant for neophyte *sādhakas* who perceive the universe as something different from themselves, based on the premise that "I perceive the universe because it exists" and "I am something completely different from it."

At the beginning of the path, seekers perceive what is observed as different from themselves because they are completely unaware that they are the Self (Ātman). Because of this ignorance (*avidyā*), they ignore their authentic nature and perceive the world as a creation of God.

Every creation story, whether dualist or not, must necessarily assume the existence of a creator. Advaita believes the creator to be Brahman in the form of God, or Īśvara, and the creation is *māyā*, the power of God. It should be noted that on this point there is an essential difference between Advaita and the dualist *Sāṅkhya*. For the former, *māyā* does not exist independently of the Absolute, while for the latter *prakṛti* has its own existence. For non-dual Vedanta, the dissipation of *māyā* implies its reabsorption in the Absolute. Brahman is the only independent cause and *māyā* vanishes with the recognition of Brahman. The concept of Brahman as Īśvara with qualities is essential since it preserves the non-duality of the teachings. *Sṛṣṭi-dṛṣṭi-vāda* may include devotion, or bhakti, without affecting the non-dual essence of Advaita. It is a proposition that, while not ceasing to be Advaita, harmonizes with a personal relationship with Īśvara.

> *śruti-darśitena krameṇa parameśvara-sṛṣṭam ajñāta-sattā-yuktam eva viśvaṁ tat tad viṣaya-pramāṇāvataraṇe tasya dṛṣṭi-siddhir iti.*

> [The *sṛṣṭi-dṛṣṭi-vāda* says that] the world is created by God, as narrated in the *Śruti*, so the world exists even when it is not perceived. In short, it has *ajñāta-satta*, or unperceived

existence. Objects are known through the means of knowledge (*pramāṇās*), so they are not illusory (in the sense that the *Dṛṣṭi-sṛṣṭi-vāda* holds the illusionary).

(Śrī Appaya Dīkṣita, *Siddhānta-leśa-saṅgraha*, "*pariccheda* 2", "*dṛṣṭi-sṛṣṭi-nirūpaṇam*")

Dṛṣṭi-sṛṣṭi-vāda: This proposition suggests that cognition and creation are simultaneous. The world exists only when it is perceived by a perceiver. Emphasis is placed on the existence of the perceiver and perception; what is perceived is secondary. The world, or what is perceived, depends entirely on the existence of the perceiver and perception. Although the world is perceived, there is no perception of the perceiver, which is the Self.

The *dṛṣṭi-sṛṣṭi* does not define the creator in relation to creation, nor does it accept a multiplicity of souls. What is perceived is a dependent Brahman, while the perceiver or witness is the absolute Brahman. The objective universe is not independent of Brahman. Although the perceiver and the perceived are one and the same, the ignorant emphasize what is perceived. The perceiver has will, knowledge, and action, while the creative power is *māyā*, or "illusion." This view is expressed by Prakāśānanda Sarasvatī in his *Vedānta-siddhānta-muktāvalī*. There is a very similar view in the *Gauḍapādīya Kārikā*: the universe is a creation of souls in a cognitive act.

It is closely linked to the *eka-jīva-vāda*, which postulates that there is only one soul, which is identical to the Absolute. To understand the proposition of the *dṛṣṭi-sṛṣṭi-vāda*, we can compare it to a dream. When the experience of the waking state is veiled, the projection of dream reality begins. As everyone knows, the worlds that we experience in dreams are mental projections. When we wake up, we realize that whatever we experienced was not real. However, if someone pointed out this out during a dream, we would not accept it. If we were told that what we perceive does not exist but is only a mental projection, we would not believe it. In the same way, we do not believe that this objective world lacks substantiality. We do not accept the Vedantic statement that this universe of names and forms depends only on us and our observation. While we dream, the dream seems to be independent of us. In our current state of perception, it is impossible to see the unreality of this experience as long as our attention remains on mundane matters. It becomes possible to realize that the phenomenal world is a projection only after minimizing the importance we attribute to the world. Only then will we be able to observe and evaluate its reality.

> *paripūrṇaś cid-ātmā avidyayā avaccheda-pratibimba-bhāvo vinā 'pi prāpta-jīva-bhāvaḥ san ātmānam eva sarve āvaraṁ kalpayati. prāpteśvara-bhāvāt svasmād eva gaganādi-sṛṣṭiṁ kalpayati. …tathā krameṇa manuṣyādi-bhāvaṁ kalpayati. …ca svasminn eva sarva-prapañca-kalpakatvāt jīva-bhāvāpannaṁ brahma sarvopādānam iti dṛṣṭi-sṛṣṭi-vād iva āhur ity arthaḥ.*

The absolute Self becoming *jīva* due to nescience (*avidyā*) even without limitation

> (*avaccheda*) and reflection (*pratibimba*) imagines itself to be God. … And thus, becoming God it imagines the creation of the world consisting of the sky and so on from itself only. It gradually, imagines human being, etc. …Thus, Brahman, which has become *jīva*, is the material cause because it imagines the entire phenomena in itself only. This is the view of the *dṛṣṭi-sṛṣṭi-vādins*.
>
> (Acyutakṛṣṇānanda Tīrtha, commentary on *Siddhānta-leśa-saṅgraha*)

Ajāti-vāda: The word *ajāti-vāda* is composed of *a* (not), *jāti* (creation), and *vāda* (doctrine); it is translated as "the doctrine of non-creation." This proposition is the basis of Gauḍapāda's teachings. According to *ajāti-vāda*, creation is not an event that occurred at a particular moment. Hence it cannot be analyzed from a chronological point of view. According to these teachings, creation never really happened. Similarly, *māyā* also lacks a substantial reality; it is an illusion without real existence. The only absolute reality is Brahman. Being eternal and unborn, or *aja*, Brahman is immutable; therefore, it is not subject to changes such as birth, old age, or death. On the other hand, the reality of the world is only apparent; it is a superimposition upon reality. Advaita recognizes that the soul and Brahman share the same identity and invites us to seek the essence. As stated in the *Māṇḍūkya Kārikā* of Gauḍapāda:

na kaścij jāyate jīvaḥ
sambhavo 'sya na vidyate
etat tad uttamaṁ satyaṁ
yatra kiñcin na jāyate

No soul begins to exist. There is no cause that can produce it. The supreme Truth is that nothing is ever born.

(*Māṇḍūkya Kārikā*, 3.48)

We perceive the universe just as we perceive ourselves. As long as we consider ourselves to be something or someone independent, we cannot understand *ajāti-vāda*. Only by accepting that *māyā* is unreal and that Brahman is the absolute existence will we understand that creation never occurred: *māyā* is an epistemic but not an ontological reality; only Brahman really exists.

Many seekers explore what they perceive through their senses. However, they do not pay attention to the perceiver. The senses constantly remind them of the dual plane. Through sight, taste, touch, smell, and hearing they are dragged toward the outside world. Media and advertisements keep their attention occupied on the surface. However, instead of investigating the objective world, they should focus on the depths of subjectivity. This investigation should search for the perceiver. Such a contemplative introspection will lead us to discover the ontological unreality of *māyā*.

It should be noted that the realization of our true nature as Brahman is unrelated to states such as waking (*jāgrat*), dreaming while asleep (*svapna*), and deep sleep (*suṣupti*): it belongs only to *turīya*, or "the fourth state." Returning to *vyāvahārika*, or the platform of the phenomenal world, one arrives again at the states *jāgrat*, *svapna*, and *suṣupti*, but the knowledge acquired in the *turīya* state remains and the preliminary perception of *sṛṣṭi-dṛṣṭi* loses much of its meaning. The *Māṇḍūkya Upanishad* explains *turīya* in this way:

> *nāntaḥ prajñaṁ na bahiṣ prajñaṁ nobhayataḥ prajñaṁ na prajñā na ghanaṁ na prajñaṁ nāprajñam. adṛṣṭam avyavahāryam agrāhyam alakṣaṇaṁ acintyam avyapadeśyam ekātma-pratyaya-sāraṁ prapañcopaśamaṁ śāntaṁ śivam advaitaṁ caturthaṁ manyante sa ātmā sa vijñeyaḥ.*
>
> The fourth state (*turīya*), according to the sages, is neither internal nor external knowledge, nor a combination of both. It is not an indefinite mass of knowledge nor is it collective knowledge. It is a lack of knowledge. It is invisible, unrelated, inconceivable, not inferable, unimaginable, and indescribable. It is the essence of self-knowledge common to all states of consciousness. Everything phenomenal ceases in it. It is peace, it is bliss, it is non-dual. This is the Self; this is what has to be realized.
>
> (*Māṇḍūkya Upanishad*, 7)

Such verses from Upanishadic literature are especially relevant to understanding *ajāti-vāda*. This verse says that in the *turīya* state, true Brahmanic nature is realized and the objective universe is no longer perceived as separate from the observer. The "I" vanishes along with the supposed phenomenal universe outside of it and only the Self remains. The verse accurately describes *ajāti*. The term *prapañcopaśamam* refers to the unreality of the objective universe. It is the fusion of what is objective and subjectivity as a single reality. When the walls of the room fall, the boundary between the supposed interior space and the apparent exterior disappears. The "I" and the "you" evaporate; the awareness emerges that they were never separate. The *Bṛhad-āraṇyaka Upanishad* refers to the same idea in this passage:

> *[...] yatra vā asya sarvam ātmāivābhūt, tat kena kaṁ jighret, tat kena kaṁ paśyet, tat kena kaṁ śṛṇuyāt, tat kena kam abhivadet, tat kena kam manvīta, tat kena kaṁ vijānīyād yenedaṁ sarvaṁ vijānāti, taṁ kena vijānīyād, vijñātāram are kena vijānīyād iti.*
>
> [...] If everything is the Self of knowledge, what does that Self know, except its own being? Who sees the object of perception when it has itself become an integral part of the perception process itself? Everything is known by the knower, but who knows the knower? Hence, like I told you Maitreyī, it is not possible to have ordinary cognition, perception, reasoning, and understanding

in that absolute state, which is the supreme bliss of plenitude.

(*Bṛhad-āraṇyaka Upanishad*, 2.4.14, second part)

Any idea about the independent existence of an external universe is meaningless. According to the *Bṛhad-āraṇyaka Upanishad*, absolute reality implies the absence of all sensory activity, which entails a disintegration of the egoic phenomenon.

The Upanishad asks *vijñātāram are kena vijānīyād?* or "who knows the knower?" The question arises from the obvious understanding that the perceiver cannot be perceived through the senses. It is clear that the knower knows himself or herself without distinguishing the knower from the knowledge and what is known, since in the absolute state, the question about creation is not even asked.

It follows that upon realizing the identity of *ātman* and Brahman as one and the same, nothing begins or ceases to exist; only absolute existence remains. According to *ajāti-vāda*, when the objective world dissolves in Ātman, we can refer to *prapañca* (the expansion of the universe) as the non-created.

Generally, non-dual orthodox masters begin by explaining creation in terms of *sṛṣṭi-dṛṣṭi-vāda*. *Sṛṣṭi-dṛṣṭi* is accepted only in the sense of *vyāvahārika*, and it needs to be transcended to attain *mokṣa*. Then they explain the doctrine of the denial of erroneous superimposition, or *adhyāropa-apavāda*, which is closely linked to the *vyāvahārika* and *pāramārthika* ways of understanding reality. Only later do they present *ajāti-vāda*, which completely denies the chronological beginning of the universe. When we realize that *pāramārthika* is real, *ajāti* is accepted.

Other systems of Vedanta, as well as the majority of religions, present *sṛṣṭi-dṛṣṭi-vāda*. Only within the Advaita Vedanta teachings do we find the teachings of *dṛṣṭi-sṛṣṭi-vāda* and *ajāti-vāda*.

Many spiritual seekers are inclined to seek the Absolute as the essence of the objective world. However, Advaita considers this useless because *mukti*, or "liberation," is the realization of our true nature as Brahman. We should begin by investigating and exploring ourselves, since all enigmas are clarified when we realize Brahman. By analyzing a drop of water, we will discover the components of the entire ocean. There is no need to bring the entire ocean to the laboratory or analyze every wave: a small drop will suffice. Therefore, Advaita suggests directing our attention to the seeker. In the end, attention will be directed toward attention itself and consciousness will become aware of itself.

Chapter 11

A scientific view of our perception of the world

Many of us say "seeing is believing," as if what we perceive through the senses were absolute reality. Through sensory perception, we conceive the world around us as real. We try to possess objects and we become attached to people. However, what we call "world" or "universe" does not exist as we perceive it. We identify forms, colors, textures, and smells that, in reality, do not exist. The universe is not physical; its essence is pure consciousness.

The world is definitely not as we perceive it. The nerve endings in our sensory organs—the tongue, skin, nose, eyes, and ears—are capable of capturing external and internal stimuli and generating nerve impulses that translate as sensations. Each sensory receptor is in charge of detecting a different kind of physical energy such as light or sound waves. These stimuli are transformed into electrochemical signals, which are transmitted through the nervous system and finally arrive at the cerebral cortex. The cerebral cortex organizes the neural impulses. Different areas of the cortex are engaged in translating the sensory information into psychological experiences such as landscapes, faces, melodies, perfumes, textures, and so on.

It is worth remembering that brain activity is the same whether we look at something or imagine it. It is now possible to observe brain activity with radiolabeling: an atom in a chemical compound such as glucose is replaced by its radioactive isotope and then, the new compound is injected into the bloodstream. Then, positron emission tomography (PET) can be performed—an imaging technique that detects the radioactivity emitted by the radiolabeled atom. This makes it possible to produce a three-dimensional image that shows how specific tissues and organs are functioning. However, we will not find an image of a red rose within the brain, but only electrical and chemical activity between the neurons—nerve cells whose main property is the electrical excitability of their plasma membranes.

The intercellular contact between neurons that transmit nerve impulses is called synaptic transmission. This transmission begins with a chemical discharge that creates a shift in the electric potential of the transmitting or presynaptic cell. When this impulse reaches the end of the axon (the long nerve fiber that conducts nerve impulses away from the cell), the neuron releases chemicals called neurotransmitters into the synaptic gap (the small space between two nerve cells). These chemicals are responsible for either exciting or inhibiting the activity of the postsynaptic cell. Thus, when we see a red rose, our brain does not produce an image, but only electrical and chemical activity that is interpreted as an image.

The red color of a rose does not exist inside the brain. Nor does it exist outside of it. In reality, the colors we perceive do not exist. Avocados and grass are not green; the sea and the sky are not blue; human beings do not have different skin colors. Colors are not properties of objects or of light beams, instead they are mental interpretations of light that comes from the external world. Colors do not really exist in nature.

We feel pain when we are hit with a stone, yet we know that pain does not reside in stones. In the same way, we see colors when light hits our retinas, but colors do not belong to objects. Like pain, colors only exist in the mind.

Isaac Newton explored the nature of colors. In a dark room, he decomposed a sunbeam with a prism. He found that white light is made up of a spectrum of colored rays. Visible light is electromagnetic radiation that is perceptible to the human eye and can be seen by the sense of sight. According to their pigments, objects reflect or absorb different wavelengths of light. We consider an object to be white when it reflects all visible wavelengths and to be black when it absorbs all of them. Thus, colors are perceptions of light rays with different wavelengths after they have been reflected off objects and reach our retinas. The ability of the human eye to differentiate between colors is based on the sensitivity of receptors in the retina to different wavelengths of light. Therefore, colors do not exist but are interpretations of different wavelengths of light by our brain; light itself has no color. Color is not a feature of the perceived world, but rather of our perception of the world.

The universe is not colorful: colors are generated by our brain. There are only colorless electromagnetic waves that travel through space and reach our eyes.

Brain abnormalities can distort the perception of colors. People suffering from chronic migraine often see different colors when they have headaches. Their condition causes changes in the area of the brain that is in charge of visual processing, altering the behavior of the neurons responsible for processing electromagnetic waves and converting them into colors. Since we all share the same genetic patterns, almost all humans perceive colors in a similar way.

Our red rose, besides not existing inside the brain, does not exist outside of it either. The solid reality that we see, touch, smell, and hear is not as real as it seems. What we perceive is not reality as such but the result of how our brain interprets nerve impulses.

For example, let us examine sight. First, it is important to differentiate between sight and vision: the former is one of the senses and the latter is our ability to interpret what we see. The eyes see but vision occurs in the brain.

The process of vision is divided into four phases: perception, transformation, transmission, and interpretation.

1. Perception: Light enters the eye through the cornea and passes first through the pupil, then a fluid called the aqueous humor, a crystalline lens, and a clear gel-like vitreous body.
2. Transformation: The light then reaches the retina where sensory cells known as cones and rods are activated and transform light into nerve impulses.
3. Transmission: Nerve impulses are routed through the optic nerve to the cerebral cortex.
4. Interpretation: In the cerebral cortex, the process of recognition and interpretation of impulses occurs.

We do not see objects that are supposedly in front of us. What we perceive are only interpretations or the internal decoding of nerve impulses. Those messages lead us to assume that the red rose is there, although nobody in the world can prove it. In other words, through the process of vision we can only assume that a particular object is in front of us. To perceive reality would be to apprehend what happens at this moment. If we perceive something that happened in the past, it may not be real now. The process of vision, although it is fast, takes some time and is not immediate; therefore, what is observed does not belong to the present reality. The only thing that can be perceived directly in the present is consciousness, or our authenticity, because there is no distance or process of perception that separates us from it.

If we explore the objective world, we will discover that the supposedly red rose is mostly composed of emptiness. If we look at it more closely, we will find molecules, atoms, and a quantum world of subatomic particles, but mainly, we will see empty space.

To understand the proportions, let us imagine that we enlarge the nucleus of an atom to the size of a basketball. The nearest electron would be orbiting at a distance of several kilometers. The rest of the atom is nothing more than emptiness. Similarly, if a carbon atom had the dimensions of a two-hundred-acre golf course, the nucleus would be roughly the size of one of the holes. The empty space within atoms is so great that if all empty space were removed from the atoms in a human body, it would be reduced to the size of one grain of salt. If we did the same with all of humanity, the volume of all humans on the planet would be reduced to the size of an apple.

If we explore the sense of touch, perhaps more than one of us would be surprised to learn that nobody has ever touched solid matter. When we lean against a wall, we are prevented from passing through it by the electromagnetic repulsion of electrons around atoms that make up solids. Our hands are also made up of atoms with electron clouds. Electric fields are very intense because they consist of millions of atoms. When touching any object, its electrons prevent the electrons in our fingers from taking their place and replacing them in the atoms. That is why nobody has ever touched solid matter: we do not walk on the floor; we levitate. As both the electrons of objects and those of our bodies are negatively charged, they repel each other, and this impedes us from getting any closer, actually touching an object, or passing through it.

There are different states of matter aggregation, which depend on the degree of force that joins or aggregates particles in an object, body, or substance. In some kinds of matter such as metals or rocks, particles are strongly united. In liquids such as water, vinegar, or oil, particles are weakly united. In gases, particles are scattered. Since the link between particles in liquids is weaker, our body is able to break them apart and our bodies are able to move through water. If the cohesion coefficient of the object's surface is greater than that of our fingers, the object will not become distorted but our skin will experience compression and electrical resistance, which transforms into mechanical resistance.

Touch sensations are transmitted by various receptors to the cerebral cortex, specifically the area located behind the fissure of Rolando (a fold in the cerebral cortex that separates the parietal lobe from the frontal lobe). Solid matter, in fact, does not exist. In an analysis of the external world, we will inevitably arrive at the conclusion that the only reality we know is that which is formed in our brain as it interprets the billions of sensory signals it receives every moment.

The world, which seems to be solid matter, is actually nothing but discontinuity. All the objects that we observe through our senses are made up of atoms, which, in turn, consist of subatomic particles that emerge in one place and disappear in another. These particles vibrate, appearing and disappearing, in one-trillionth of a second, in what we call a "quantum leap," becoming a vibrating flow with empty spaces. Discontinuity is the very foundation of the universe as well as the essence of everything.

We do not experience the world as it is but as it seems to us. Instead of perceiving reality, we interpret it. Most conflicts between human beings derive from different ways of interpreting the perceived world. However, consciousness is completely transcendental to such interpretations and remains unaffected by them.

Assessing whether chairs and tables are real misses the essence of the Vedantic message. The old masters do not maintain that mountains and seas do not exist, but that what is really illusory is the world created by the mind. You yourself have made up the imaginary world in which you move. Both you and your world are products of your mental activity. Your thoughts create you as an egoic phenomenon. The bipolar world of anxiety and calmness, expectations and disappointments, and happiness and misfortune, is fictitious. But the greatest fictitious creation is yourself, or the thought creating a thinker. As long as you continue to project your mental activity, reality will keep functioning like a screen. Reality remains hidden behind the illusory world that you project on it. As long as the mind is not transcended, reality remains hidden. Vedantic teachings say that meditation is the path to stop creating worlds devoid of substance and made up only of ideas, concepts, and conclusions. Blame no one, take responsibility, and change your reality, simply by changing your attitude.

Chapter 12

The purposes of human beings or *puruṣārthas*

As consciousness conceals itself, the universe unfolds. The sole consciousness can only hide by appearing to be a multiplicity. The human being is the cosmic point where consciousness starts a process of involution and turns back in on itself.

Consciousness is an asset shared by humans and animals; however, only *Homo sapiens* has self-consciousness and the ability to choose. Unlike animals, we can change ourselves and adapt the world to our own choices. Animals are like leaves that float down the river, carried by the current; human beings are like motor boats that can steer in different directions, even against the current.

Animals are motivated by instinct; they do not suffer from the dilemmas and conflicts that human beings confront. Beasts cannot oppose the nature of their physical body. They can attack and eat one another without any guilt because they do not question the morality of their own actions. Dogs, cats, and pigs only react according to their preprogrammed nature. On the contrary, human beings, conscious of themselves, can evaluate what the most beneficial option and use discretion. They can resist their desires and inclinations and, for example, stop eating meat to avoid causing suffering to other creatures.

Animal reactions are predictable because they come from instinct, but human beings can break away from instinct and choose the best way to react. Beasts are fully conditioned, while humans can overcome conditioning to such an extent that at some point in their evolution they can embark on the discovery of reality. For this reason, some have called human beings religious animals.

Both animals and human beings are physically limited. Embedded in a physical environment, animals' ability to respond is extremely elementary. On the other hand, human beings can transcend physical reality and access mental worlds through art, literature, philosophy, cinema, and so on. According to Vedanta, both animals and human beings have the basic needs of eating, sleeping, defending themselves, and reproducing. However, since humans are self-conscious, they can discriminate and reach conclusions about themselves. When they perceive themselves through their limited minds and senses, they see themselves as imperfect and incomplete beings. They feel inadequate, dissatisfied, and limited. The natural reaction to this incompleteness is to desire plenitude. Therefore, every desire is motivated by the aspiration to complete ourselves, which drags us into a lifestyle completely based on this ambition. Depending on their developmental level, people choose different purposes or goals in life that can be divided into four main categories, or *puruṣārthas*.

The purposes of human beings

Puruṣa can mean both "God" and "human being," while *artha* means "aim, goal, or objective." *Puruṣārtha* thus means "the object of human pursuit" or "the goal of human beings" and refers to the four goals or aims of human life. The *puruṣārthas* clearly demonstrate the evolution within the retroprogressive context, therefore, it is important to explain them in any study of Vedanta.

The Vedas classify the human goals into four main ones:

- *Dharma*: ethics, righteousness.
- *Artha*: security, wealth.
- *Kāma*: pleasure, enjoyment, happiness, desire.
- *Mokṣa*: liberation.

They are mentioned in the *Gaṇapaty-atharva-śīrṣa Upanishad* in this way:

sarvatrādhīyāno 'pavighno bhavati
dharmārtha-kāma-mokṣaṁ ca vindati

> Studying this Upanishad in all situations will remove obstacles and the devotee will obtain *dharma*, *artha*, *kāma*, and *mokṣa*.
>
> (*Gaṇapaty-atharva-śīrṣa Upanishad*, 11)

The four *puruṣārthas* are further classified into two groups:

1. Those shared by human beings and animals: *artha* (the search for security) and *kāma* (the search for pleasure).
2. Those that belong only to human beings: *dharma* (ethical behavior) and *mokṣa* (the search for liberation).

Artha or "wealth, security"

Artha literally means "objective," but in the context of *puruṣārthas*, it means "livelihood," that is, the search for wealth and occupations that earn an income to make a living. However, behind the search for wealth hides the desire to achieve security.

In one way or another, almost every living being seeks security and protection. Instinct leads mice to accumulate cheese; ants, leaves; dogs, bones; and bees, pollen. Animals can only behave according to a natural program of survival that already includes the search for security. On the other hand, as human beings evolve, they overcome instinct and their search for security becomes more refined.

Behind any search for wealth, beauty, fame, or power lies the fear of feeling insecure. This fear is expressed in our efforts to achieve things that would help us feel protected.

However, none of the achievements we reach with so much effort manage to calm our fear of physical and emotional insecurity. Regardless of how much money, fame, health, beauty, or power we have, we continue to feel insecure. Through money, we can attain some comfort but not security; through beauty, we can attract admiration but not eliminate the fear of insecurity. Otherwise, the rich, the famous, the powerful, and the beautiful would be the happiest and most secure people in the world.

We aspire to an experience of absolute security, but our results are limited. On the dual platform, every gain involves a loss: obtaining means giving something up, winning means losing. For example, if I want a new car, I must invest time and energy in finding the vehicle I want and then take care of all the paperwork. Buying the car involves spending the money I have saved with much sacrifice. Any acquisition implies a detachment and, therefore, any initial relief is offset by a sense of loss. Although Vedanta is not opposed to the search for security in this world, it warns that *artha* is unable to relieve our fundamental pain.

The real problem is not that we lack protection but that we perceive ourselves to be vulnerable and unprotected. Since this feeling of insecurity is not in harmony with our original nature, we seek solutions to escape from it. In fact, we are not trying to obtain something but to get rid of our deep dread of insecurity. Unfortunately, nothing we might possess can alter the idea that we have about ourselves. As long as we consider ourselves unprotected, nothing and no one can eradicate our sense of insecurity. The experience of insecurity does not occur in the objective dimension but on the subjective plane. Since it is the result of what we believe ourselves to be, it is clear that we will not find a solution in the phenomenal world.

Since our original identity is unlimited, nothing limited can satisfy us. Our insatiable needs cannot be pacified in the finite world. We long for an experience of absolute and unlimited protection and security. As long as we exist as something or someone separate, we will experience fear of insecurity.

In the revelation of our authenticity, we will not find security but the absence of fear of insecurity. To fear insecurity is to escape and live afraid of life itself. Security is death; insecurity is life. Awakened beings embrace insecurity with deep love.

Kāma or "pleasure"

Kāma means "desire, craving, yearning, or appetite." Within the context of the *puruṣārthas*, the term refers to the yearning for the complete spectrum of pleasure, enjoyment, and happiness.

Three factors are required to attain *kāma*: an object, a sense organ, and the right mood. First, access to the object of enjoyment is essential. Second, the corresponding sensory organ must perceive the object;

in addition, it has to be healthy to experience pleasure. For example, a deaf person cannot enjoy beautiful music. We will not enjoy ice cream if we have a strong toothache. The third factor is the appropriate mental framework. Although the object and the organ may be available, we will not enjoy if we are not in the right mood. If we are sad, we will not enjoy objects that would cause us pleasure in a different mood.

Undoubtedly, modern society is very dynamic, but it has not yet realized the implications of its frantic pace. Today, we live at such a speed that it is almost impossible to find the time and place to sit quietly with ourselves without being disturbed by entertainment. Moments of peace and tranquility are scarce, when we can reflect without our attention being diverted to a cellphone, computer, or television. This inclination of the masses is fully exploited by the entertainment industry. In fact, enjoyment acts as a temporary painkiller that prevents us from solving the real problem. Every pleasure does nothing but delay facing our fundamental issue.

Both animals and human beings feel attracted to pleasure. Every mosquito in this world moves in search of happiness. At the instinctive level, the search is simple and gross, but in humans it becomes more sophisticated. Human beings enjoy art, poetry, music, dance, and philosophy. Animals satisfy their needs but lack the ability to cultivate enjoyment and refine the sources of pleasure. Animals enjoy their food, but only human beings have developed a complete gastronomic culture with restaurants, chefs, dishes, and manners. Beasts can enjoy sex, but human beings have developed the pornography industry. Humans are not content with merely satisfying their biological need but go beyond in search for pleasure provided by the satisfaction of these needs.

The desires of animals come from instinct while humans' faculty of free will allows them to express their desires with personal preferences. People find pleasure in very different objects. Pleasure can be sensory, physical, mental, artistic, intellectual, emotional, biological, contemplative, and so on. At different stages of life, our sources of pleasure may vary. During childhood, we enjoy toys; in adolescence, music, sports, and dancing; as adults, our family, spouse, and children; and in old age, our grandchildren. Although everyone has sought happiness in the history of humanity, very few have managed to free themselves from suffering, from that feeling of dissatisfaction that lies in the depths of every heart.

Our self-perception through imperfect means leads to the erroneous conclusion that we are limited, unhappy, unfortunate, and incomplete. We see ourselves as embodied creatures that live at the mercy of diseases, old age, and death. However, we do not accept this and wish to see ourselves happy and satisfied. Therefore, just as any search for security is an escape from insecurity, any search for pleasure is an escape from the feeling of unhappiness. We live with the incorrect impression that by acquiring a new car, a new home, or a beautiful husband or wife, we will become happy and complete. Although these achievements might momentarily calm our suffering, they do not provide a radical solution.

The world is full of unhappy millionaires, unsatisfied couples, and frustrated beautiful people.

The egoic phenomenon consists of perceiving ourselves as separate beings. To be disconnected from paradise is undoubtedly a situation that arouses panic. To be banished from our eternal home is extremely frightening. The ego is afraid of the future, rejection, other people, change, insecurity, suffering, and so on. Fear motivates every selfish pursuit: the dread of the part mistakenly feeling uprooted from the Whole.

There is a radical qualitative difference between the pursuit of happiness and the escape from suffering. Like people who say they love but actually escape from loneliness, our intimate aspiration is not bliss but fleeing from affliction, bitterness, and sorrow.

What the egoic phenomenon considers happiness is a mere reduction of suffering. Within egoic territory, bliss cannot be found. Therefore, the ego can only try to minimize its misery.

The real problem lies not in the pursuit of pleasure but in the exaggerated expectations that we have of people, objects, and situations. We erroneously hope that they will not only grant pleasure but totally eradicate our deep dissatisfaction.

Only self-satisfaction or the realization of our true nature, which is complete in itself, will naturally and spontaneously stop any pursuit of pleasure. Therefore, the Bhagavad Gita refers to the wise as those who do not seek happiness in the objective world because they have found it in the Self.

āpūryamāṇam acala-pratiṣṭhaṁ
samudram āpaḥ praviśanti yadvat
tadvat kāmā yaṁ praviśanti sarve
sa śāntim āpnoti na kāma-kāmī

Just like the ocean that rests quietly as rivers fill it, one who stands still despite the incessant flow of desires attains peace, not those who crave their desires.

(Bhagavad Gita, 2.70)

vihāya kāmān yaḥ sarvān
pumāṁś carati niḥspṛhaḥ
nirmamo nirahaṅkāraḥ
sa śāntim adhigacchati

Having abandoned all desires, moving without longing, a sense of "mine," and selfishness, that person attains peace.

(Bhagavad Gita, 2.71)

eṣā brāhmī sthitiḥ pārtha
naināṁ prāpya vimuhyati
sthitvāsyām anta-kāle 'pi
brahma-nirvāṇam ṛcchati

This is the Brahmic state (eternal state), O son of Pṛthā! Having achieved this, nothing is illusory. Being within in it, even at the end of life, one reaches unity with Brahman.

(Bhagavad Gita, 2.72)

The bliss of the enlightened sage does not depend on any pleasure offered by the phenomenal world. Although enlightened beings have desires, their desires are not binding, so they do not enslave, chain, or tie them. When a binding desire is not satisfied, it causes discomfort. Ordinary people enjoy it if they manage to satisfy a desire and get frustrated if they do not. The desire of the ordinary person is born from a lack or deficiency; not so the desire of the sage, which emerges from plenitude. Enlightened beings constantly rest in their true nature of bliss, whether they achieve sensory enjoyment or not. If pleasure manifests, they enjoy it; but if not, the absence of pleasure does not tarnish their transcendental bliss. Recognizing themselves as consciousness itself, enlightened sages do not seek to be completed by anything or anybody.

Dharma or "ethics or righteousness"

Like many other Sanskrit terms, *dharma* has a variety of meanings. Although there is no exact English equivalent, it has been translated as religion, law, duty, conduct, and so on. When reading a Sanskrit text, we must consider the context in which it is used. In regard to the *puruṣārthas*, the closest meaning is "cosmic duty." That is to say, *dharma* refers to actions that are in accordance with universal order and balance.

Śaṅkarācārya defines the word *dharma* in this way:

> *prāṇināṁ sākṣāt abhyudaya niḥśreyasa-hetuḥ yaḥ*
> *sa dharmaḥ.*

> *Dharma* is that which directly promotes the prosperity and emancipation of living beings.
> (Śaṅkarācārya, introduction to *Bhagavad Gītā Bhāṣya*)

In a civilized society of individuals seeking to satisfy their desires, it is essential to establish an ethical system that safeguards the well-being and safety of the community. In contrast to the animal kingdom, which is governed by the laws of nature, human society requires a system of social rules and regulations that places cosmic law above personal goals. Unlike animals, human beings have the ability to understand, accept, and follow *dharma*.

Vedanta recognizes the existence of desires and allows individuals to fulfill them without disturbing harmony in society. It does not condemn pleasure achieved by legitimate and peaceful means. Any damage caused to others constitutes a violation of the cosmic order and universal harmony, but pleasure that is free of violence is not condemnable because it does not hurt others or ourselves. Both our objectives and the means to achieve them should be devoid of violence. *Dharma* offers an elaborate system of ethical and moral values that can be applied to both personal choices and the means to achieve them. This system confirms the norms of common sense while adding wise principles.

Dharma includes the concepts of *puṇya* (merit) and *pāpa* (demerit or sin).

> *yathā-kārī yathā-cārī tathā bhavati—sadhu-kārī sādhur bhavati, papa-kārī pāpo bhavati; puṇyaḥ puṇyena karmaṇā bhavati, pāpaḥ pāpena.*
>
> Just as someone does and acts, so becomes; by doing good the person becomes good and by doing evil, becomes evil.
>
> (*Bṛhad-ārāṇyaka Upanishad*, 4.4.5)

Puṇya and *pāpa* are Sanskrit terms that refer to the results of right and wrong actions, respectively. Every action has immediate and tangible results as well as invisible and unknown ones. The latter subtly accumulate in our karmic account and in due course they become either pleasant or unpleasant tangible experiences, in this life or successive lives. The subtle result of *puṇya* unfolds as pleasure (*sukha*); the subtle result of *pāpa* unfolds as pain (*duḥkha*). *Puṇya* and *pāpa karmas* have three stages: *bīja* (seed), *vṛddhi* (development), and *anubhava* (experience). *Bīja* can be eliminated through knowledge; *vṛddhi*, or the development of wrong actions, can be controlled by meritorious acts. However, one will inevitably experience (*anubhava*) of both karmas to some extent.

We are born within a family. Relationships with our family members entail a series of duties and rights: as sons and daughters, we must respect and obey our progenitors; as parents, we have the duty to protect and educate our children, and so on. We also have obligations to the large family of human society: neighbors, community, city, nation, and so on. If we fulfil our purpose in life as well as the duties that we have been assigned, we act in harmony with *dharma* and therefore, with the universe. If we act in harmony with universal law, we are in tune with the entire cosmic manifestation.

Dharma is not a series of rules and regulations originating from a human tradition or culture. Universal law palpitates spontaneously in every human being because it was revealed along with creation. Otherwise, the law of nature would be defective. It is like instruction manuals that usually come with electronics. We are all able to discern between right and wrong because we have directly experienced what causes us suffering or pain. Since we expect others to behave toward us in a certain way, we can infer what behavior others expect from us. However, although we are all aware of universal dharmic principles, not everyone lives according to them. Since we have free will, we can choose to follow universal law or walk away from it. Desires and attachments often deter us from living according to cosmic law. Selfish ambitions do not always harmonize with *dharma* and most people feel inclined to transgress *dharma* in order to satisfy their own ambitions. In the present Age of Kali, humans are unable to resist the pressure of their desires and constantly violate the law of *dharma*, even though they know their actions are wrong.

Although *dharma* deserves to be respected, we should not expect that it will lead us to liberation. Neither *dharma*, *artha*, nor *kāma* offer a radical solution to the essential problem. The fulfillment of *dharma* gives us a very subtle and elevated pleasure: that of fulfilled duty. But no matter how elevated this goal might be, it is still limited. *Dharma* purifies but it is not the final solution. Following universal law bestows the great joy of doing what should be done, but it does not eradicate our deep dissatisfaction and our feeling of being incomplete.

There are two types of *dharma*: *pravṛtti* and *nivṛtti*.

1. *Pravṛtti-dharma*: People seek satisfaction through *kāma* and *artha* but in a regulated manner. Only when they realize the futility of seeking satisfaction in the limited objective world do they adopt *nivṛtti-dharma* and start seeking liberation, or *mokṣa*.
2. *Nivṛtti-dharma*: This is the renunciation of worldly desires and acceptance of spiritual practices intended for purification. People rise above the animal level through the acceptance of *pravṛtti-dharma* and rise from the human level to the divine through *nivṛtti-dharma*.

sa bhagavān sṛṣṭvedaṁ jagat, tasya ca sthitiṁ cikirṣuḥ, marīcyādīn agre sṛśṭvā prajāpatīn, pravṛitti-lakṣaṇaṁ dharmaṁ grāhayāmāsa vedoktam. tataḥ anyān ca sanaka-sanandanādīn utpādya, nivṛtti-lakṣaṇaṁ dharmaṁ jñāna-vairāgya-lakṣaṇaṁ grāhayāmāsa. dvi-vidho hi vedokto dharmaḥ – pravṛtti-lakṣaṇaḥ, nivṛtti-lakṣaṇaś ca, jagataḥ sthiti-kāraṇam.

Having created the cosmos and seeking to ensure its existence, the Lord brought forth in the beginning the progenitors (Prajāpatīs)

> Marīci and the rest. Then he imparted to them the Vedic *dharma* of works (*pravṛtti-lakṣaṇa-dharma*). Later, bringing forth others like Sanaka and Sanandana, he imparted to them the *dharma* of cessation of work (*nivṛtti-lakṣaṇa-dharma*) marked by the knowledge of detachment. Indeed, the *dharma* declared by the vedas, for the world's stability is two-fold: embracing work and embracing cessation.
> (Śaṅkarācārya, introduction to *Bhagavad Gītā Bhāṣya*)

Although living in harmony according to universal law is extremely beneficial for our evolution, it cannot eliminate our essential problem. Our desires and inclinations vary over the years. Preferences and values fluctuate at different times of life. Human beings aspire to all kinds of collective and personal changes. In their eagerness to change, they reveal a deep longing to change themselves. Dissatisfaction motivates them to seek experiences to eradicate this discomfort. Their desires to make objective changes only reveal discontentment with what they believe they are. However, these experiences and changes do not eliminate the essential problem: their incorrect perception of themselves.

Mokṣa or "liberation"

The word *mokṣa* comes from the root *muc* (to become liberated) and means "liberation." It is the highest *puruṣārtha* and the main goal of human life. There is no higher aim than liberation. It is discussed last because it is sought after only by people who have realized the limitations of all other goals in life. *Mokṣa* is reserved for those who have understood the futility of trying to complete themselves through *dharma*, *artha*, and *kāma*. When we mature, we are able to assess our experiences and discover that behind our dharmic search for safety, pleasure, and love, there is a basic desire to free ourselves from insufficiency. Only then do we realize that this desire cannot be satisfied by any amount of *dharma*, *artha*, or *kāma*.

With maturity comes the understanding that the pleasure produced by the satisfaction of our desires does not last. The world only offers objective pleasure and enjoyment, which is limited by time and space, while our desire is eternal and absolute bliss.

Animals and humans share the pursuit of *artha* and *kāma*; *dharma* belongs to humans alone; *mokṣa* is not for the masses but is reserved for a minority of highly developed human beings. Liberation is a yearning that manifests after one becomes aware that true happiness is not achieved through the enjoyment in the relative world.

The egoic phenomenon is an experience of absence or lack. The idea of "I" resembles a very deep well that is impossible to fill up. Throughout our lives, we strive to throw heavy stones into the well, in the form of money, jewels, objects, people, and so on, but it remains empty. On the contrary, the more objects we throw into this great egoic hole, the more it seems to grow and enlarge. Unhappiness, sadness, and pain depend on the idea of "I." The egoic phenomenon is the basis and foundation of all dissatisfaction. Therefore, we can say that the unqualified original desire is the desire to be complete and get rid of the feeling of limitation. This is the desire from which every other desire originates.

The deep sense of limitation that we all suffer from leads us to focus our quest on objects. We aspire to get rid of that feeling of limitation to experience fullness and wholeness. The feeling of insecurity motivates our search for security. Suffering impels us to pursue happiness. Our need for love stems from our loneliness.

We experience a variety of desires for things such as fame, prestige, recognition, respect, and so on, and all of them originate in our feeling of deficiency. The experience of lacking something motivates our efforts to complete ourselves by satisfying mental demands in the limited objective world. That is to say, desire is a response to the feeling of lacking something. Our original nature of unlimited bliss drives us to find happiness or to avoid suffering.

Nothing and no one in the objective world has the ability to liberate us from the pursuit of pleasure. Begging is inherent in our slavery.

What we seek is our true original nature, our own authenticity. When we strive to stop feeling limited and dissatisfied, we are actually looking for Brahman, or the Absolute.

Although we do not learn from anyone to yearn for happiness, we look for it beginning in childhood. To aspire for plenitude is not taught to us, but we strive for it from when we are very young. Mistakenly, we try to find it in the relative world. We are looking for an objective solution for a subjective problem. Due to ignorance, we are looking for the unlimited in places, objects, circumstances, times, and our own bodies.

Many feel inclined to change places, houses, cities, or countries in the course of their life. They think that their anxiety and discomfort comes from the place where they are. However, after some time, when the new place is no longer a novelty, they return to the same uneasiness.

There are those who constantly wait for better times and recall the past, which was supposedly better than the present. They cultivate an irrational idealization of "the good old days."

Many people strive to make money to upgrade their refrigerator, stereo, car, house, and so on. They blame their possessions for their discomfort and think that replacing them or owning better ones will increase their happiness and peace.

Bachelors want to get married, husbands want children, and fathers want a divorce. Human beings change jobs, convinced that their dissatisfaction lies in the special circumstances they are facing.

People start and end relationships. They think their parents are the cause of their unhappiness and the guru will be the cause of their bliss. They constantly put the responsibility for their happiness in others' hands. They believe that they will reach the peak of happiness when they find the right person. In the same way, they give others the responsibility for their own misfortune.

Many people think that happiness is obtained through the senses, so they seek sensual pleasure throughout their lives: they eat as much as possible, smoke, have a lot of sex, watch TV, take drugs, drink coffee, tea, and alcohol, and so on. For many people, the satisfaction of the senses and physical well-being are synonymous with happiness and they focus on things in the phenomenal world.

Instead of condemning efforts to satisfy the senses, Vedanta recommends exploring the nature of desire in depth. It does not suggest a blind and ignorant repression of desires but to become liberated from the constant search for enjoyment.

Clearly, any search for the unlimited in the limited, for the eternal in the temporal, for the Absolute in the relative, will end in frustration. Our original nature of infinite bliss urges us to free ourselves from feelings of sadness, grief, limitation, discontent, and frustration. If deficiency was part of our original nature, we would not be disturbed by it. If our real nature was limited, limitation would not bother us: we would be pleased experiencing limitation at all levels. If sadness and suffering were natural to us, we would be content being sad or we would feel good feeling bad. Liberation means transcending the profound sense of limitation, uncertainty, dissatisfaction, disconnection, separation, unhappiness, and discontent. To satisfy our mental demands and whims is only to take pain-killers that do not really solve the problem. Authentic bliss is to become free from dissatisfaction itself.

After experiencing many disillusionments and disappointments, we eventually realize that nothing and nobody can give us what we really yearn for: unlimited and absolute bliss. We believe we are limited and relative. What we really are is infinite and absolute.

Chapter 13

The five afflictions or *kleśas*

Jñāna-yoga is a path toward *vimukti*, or "the final liberation." In order to inquire about emancipation, it is necessary to have a clear definition of captivity. In fact, few people can grasp the essence of liberation or even understand the nature of captivity. The Bhagavad Gita (18.30) indicates that only those who have a sattvic *buddhi*, or "intellect," can identify captivity. A rajasic or tamasic intellect is unable to discriminate between bondage to *saṁsāra* and freedom from it.

The intellect, due to its proximity to the Self, is the highest mental faculty in sentient creatures. Its main functions are to observe, analyze, classify, discern, decide, discriminate, reason, and desire. Only a sattvic *buddhi* has enough clarity to perceive that which is subtle and recognize his or her own conditioning. For this reason, one of the main purposes of yogic *sādhana* is to create *sattva*.

Patañjali Maharṣi helps us identify the five components of slavery:

avidyāsmitā-rāga-dveṣābhiniveśāḥ kleśāḥ

> The five afflictions that hinder the balance of consciousness are ignorance, egoism, attachment, aversion, and the desire to cling to life.
>
> (*Yoga Sūtra*, 2.3)

These afflictions, or *kleśas,* can be classified as intellectual (ignorance and egoism), emotional (attachment and aversion), and instinctive (clinging to life). These five obstacles may be latent or manifest, attenuated or aggravated, repressed or active; but even when a lion is asleep or relaxed, its mere presence implies danger.

We cannot become liberated without overcoming the *kleśas*. However, repressing them does not lead to salvation. To escape from prison, we must first know it well enough. To live beyond the cell bars, we must first be aware of them. For this reason, masters such as Patañjali were dedicated to analyzing afflictions. Now we will delve into each of them.

Ignorance or *avidyā*

Ignorance is the first on the list of afflictions since Patañjali considers it the source of all the others. In fact, *avidyā* is the absence or lack of knowledge of our Brahmanic essence. Just like darkness and light, ignorance and knowledge cannot coexist: the presence of one means the absence of the other. When ignorance is removed, our true nature reveals itself.

The term *vidyā* means "knowledge" and the prefix *a* implies negation; therefore, *avidyā* literally means "not knowledge." More than an absence of knowledge, *avidyā* comes from a mistaken interpretation of reality. It is not only being ignorant about our essence and the true nature of the world, but also having incorrect information about it. Worse than not knowing something is believing that we know it, like believing the rope is a snake.

Ignorance is not in the mind, rather, it *is* the mind: to transcend it is to go beyond the mental plane. *Avidyā* is the basis of the conditioning that restricts the freedom of human beings. In his commentary on the *Vedānta Sūtra* (3.4.52), Śaṅkara confirms that liberation is the complete eradication of ignorance. Patañjali himself describes the symptoms of *avidyā*:

anityāśuci-duḥkhān ātmasu nitya-śuci-
sukhātma-khyātir avidyā

> Ignorance is confusing temporal with eternal, impure with pure, pleasure with pain, and what is not the Self with the Self.
>
> (*Yoga Sūtra*, 2.5)

Ignorance is confusing what is temporal with what is eternal. Therefore, we relate to our possessions, family, and even our bodies as if they were perennial. We do not accept that all possessions are relative, forgetting that eventually we will have to separate from all that we consider ours.

Ignorance leads us to believing the impure is pure. We think that our ideas are pure, as well as our opinions, intentions, motives, feelings, and actions. However, they are mostly produced by our own inclinations, weaknesses, addictions, needs, and selfish interests.

Ignorance means confusing pain with pleasure. Certain attitudes and actions seem pleasant as long as we deny the pain that they cause us. For example, the apparent pleasure that comes from attachment to people, places, or objects brings suffering when we lose them.

> *evam aviruddhaḥ pratyag ātmany apy anatmādhyāsaḥ. tam etam evam lakṣaṇam adhyāsaṁ paṇḍitā avidyeti manyante. tad vivekena ca vastu svarūpāvadhāraṇaṁ vidyām āhuḥ.*
>
> Thus, the superimposition of the non-Self on the inner Self is possible. Learned men regard this superimposition as *avidyā* (nescience). Ascertaining the true nature of a thing through discrimination, they say, is called *vidyā* (knowledge).
>
> (Śaṅkarācārya, introduction to *Brahma Sūtra Bhāṣya*)

Ignorance is mixing up the Self and the non-Self. When we believe we have a specific name and a personal story, we confuse the Self with the non-Self. We identify ourselves with our body, country, profession, ideas, and conclusions; we believe we are someone or something and we identify with the idea "I." Our reality becomes covered by what we believe ourselves to be, which is a complete misconception about ourselves. Instead of saying: "I think," we should say: "My ego thinks." As a result, our lives inevitably become filled with errors and, thus, the rest of the afflictions arise.

ātmano vikriyā nāsti
buddher bodho na jātviti
jīvaḥ sarva-malaṁ jñātvā
jñātā draṣṭeti muhyati

> Ātman never does anything, and intellect of its own accord has no capacity to experience "I know." But the individuality in us delusorily thinks to be the seer and the knower.
>
> (*Ātma-bodha*, 26)

Let us say that ignorance is the clouds and knowledge is the sun. When it is cloudy, we cannot see the sun. However, we notice that the day is cloudy because the sun is up. Just as the sun hides behind the clouds, consciousness is the background of the ego. Due to ignorance, we cannot see reality as it is. Instead it is consciousness that allows for all perception.

Even if it is temporarily hidden, consciousness is always present. Similarly, the sun never disappears, even when clouds prevent us from seeing it. Consciousness never withdraws, but it is hidden by the ego. The ego arises when the observer identifies with the body–mind complex; it crystallizes by seeing names and forms as separate realities. When the ego is removed, consciousness shines again in its entire splendor.

In the darkness of night, the sun disappears from our sight. In our ignorance, we believe that we must do something to make it appear again. However, it never ceased to shine, and at dawn, it will be revealed again.

If ignorance is the root cause of slavery, then knowledge is clearly the path to liberation, as affirmed by the *Aṣṭāvakra-gītā*:

ātma 'jñānāj jagad-bhāti
ātma-jñānān na bhāsate
rajjvajñānād ahir bhāti
taj jñānād bhāsate na hi

> The universe appears with ignorance of the Self and disappears with the knowledge of the Self, just as the snake appears from not understanding the rope and disappears when this is grasped.
>
> (*Aṣṭāvakra-gītā*, 2.7)

In the *Advaita-bodha-dīpikā* of Śrī Karapatra Swami (2,1–2) we read:

> Disciple: "Master, it is said that ignorance has no beginning and therefore has no end. How can ignorance that has no beginning disappear? Ocean of mercy, please explain this to me." Master: "Yes, my son. You are intelligent and

> capable of understanding subtle concepts. You spoke well. Indeed, ignorance has no beginning but it does have an end. It is said that the emergence of knowledge is the end of ignorance. Just as the dawn dissipates the darkness of night, the light of knowledge dispels the darkness of ignorance."

If we turn intellectual knowledge into an end in itself, we only increase our ignorance. Theology and philosophy are only means. In our attempt to free ourselves from *māyā*, we should be very careful not to end up being enslaved by a book, however holy it may be. Books are important, but only as maps to help us reaching the promised land. Knowledge purifies, but we need to abandon it upon reaching our goal. A boat is useful for crossing a river; however, it only hinders our progress if we continue to carry it on our shoulders after reaching the other side. Similarly, the thorn of ignorance stuck in a hand may be removed with the thorn of knowledge. But after removing it, we should toss both away.

Knowledge helps us purify ourselves: acting as an acid, it dissolves us as an egoic entity. It is part of a destructive spiritual process.

The world is created out of ignorance of the Absolute. As was explained before, this ignorance has two different *śaktis*: *āvaraṇa-śakti*, or "concealing power," and *vikṣepa-śakti*, or "projecting power." While *āvaraṇa-śakti* covers the reality of Brahman, *vikṣepa-śakti* projects the world on the screen of the veiled reality. These two powers are clearly described in the *Vedānta-sāra* (The Essence of Vedanta) written by Sadānanda:

> *asyājñānasyāvaraṇa-vikṣepa-nāmakam asti śakti-dvayam.*
>
> This ignorance has two powers. They are called the power of concealment (*vikṣepa*) and the power of projection (*āvaraṇa*).
>
> (*Vedānta-sāra,* 51)

> *āvaraṇa-śaktis tāvad alpo 'pi megho 'neka-yojanāyatam āditya maṇḍalam avalokayitṛ nayana patha-pidhāyakatayā yathācchādayatīva tathājñānaṁ paricchinnam apy ātmānam aparicchinnam asaṁsāriṇam avalokayitṛ buddhi pidhāyakatayācchādayatīva tādṛśaṁ sāmarthyam. tad uktaṁ ghanac channa-dṛṣṭir ghanac channa-markaṁ yathā manyate niṣprabhaṁ cātimūḍhaḥ. tathā baddhavad bhāti yo mūḍha-dṛṣṭeḥ sa nityopalabdhi-svarūpo 'ham ātmā iti(hastāmalakam 10).*
>
> Just as the sun is covered from an observer's eyes by a small cloud, despite the size of the sun being millions of kilometers, so ignorance, despite being limited, obstructs the intellect of the observer and seems to hide the Self that is unlimited and not subject to transmigration. Such is the force of this power of concealment. It is thus said

(by Śaṅkarācārya in the *Hastāmalaka*, 12): "Just as the sun appears to be covered by a cloud and hidden from the ignorant whose vision is obstructed by the cloud, what to the unenlightened seems to be enslaved is my real nature, the Self, the eternal knowledge."

(*Vedānta-sāra*, 52)

nayā āvṛtasyātmanaḥ kartṛtva-bhoktṛtva-sukhitva-duḥkhitvādi-saṁsāra sambhāvanāpi bhavati yathā svājñānenāvṛtāyāṁ rajjvāṁ sarpatva-sambhāvanā.

The Self covered by this (the concealing power of ignorance) may become subject to *saṁsāra* (relative existence), which is characterized by one believing oneself to be the agent and the experiencing subject, who may be happy, miserable, and so on, just as a rope may become a snake due to the concealing power of one's own ignorance.

(*Vedānta-sāra,* 53)

vikṣepa-śaktis tu yathā rajjvajñānaṁ svāvṛta rajjau svaśaktyā sarpādikam udbhāvayaty evam ajñānam api svāvṛtātmani svaśaktyā 'kāśādi prapañcam udbhāvayati tādṛśaṁ sāmarthyam. tad uktam—vikṣepa-śaktir liṅgādi brahmāṇḍāntaṁ jagat sṛjet iti. (vākyasudhā 13)

Just as ignorance regarding the rope, by its inherent power, gives rise to the illusion

> that the rope is a snake, so also ignorance, by its own power, creates in the Self such phenomena as *ākāśa* (space or ether). This power is called the power of projection. It is thus said in the *Vākya Śudha* (13): "The power of projection creates everything, from subtle bodies to the cosmos."
>
> (*Vedānta-sāra*, 54)

> *śakti-dvayavad ajñānopahitaṁ caitanyaṁ sva-pradhānatayā nimittaṁ svopādhi pradhāna tayopādānaṁ ca bhavati.*

> Consciousness associated with ignorance and its two powers (concealing and projecting), when considered from its own standpoint, is the efficient cause (*pradhāna*), and when considered from the standpoint of its limitation (*upādhi*) is the material cause (*upādāna*) [of the universe].
>
> (*Vedānta-sāra*, 55)

Let us compare the states of dreaming and being awake. The dream world is a product of forgetfulness of the waking state. The world we experience while awake is a product of forgetting Brahman.

Let us call the dream state "the first world of dreams" and the waking state, "the second world of dreams." The first world of dreams disappears when we wake up and become aware of the waking world. However, the world we see while awake is but another world of dreams. Like the Russian dolls called *matryoshkas*, the first world of dreams is a smaller doll inside a larger doll, which is the waking world or the second world of dreams. Only when we get rid of the larger doll—or when grace grants us enlightenment—do we access to our Brahminic nature.

> *tad anena antaḥkāraṇādy avacchinnaḥ pratyagātmā idam-anidaṁ-rūpaś cetanaḥ kartā bhoktā kārya-kāraṇāvidyā-dvayādhāraḥ…*
>
> …the inner self defined by the internal organ, and so on, the intelligent being made of the 'this' and the 'not this,' is the *jīva*, the agent, the enjoyer, the support of the two kinds of ignorance—the result and the cause…
>
> (Vācaspati, *Bhāmātī Catus-sūtrī* on Śaṅkara's *Brahma Sūtra Bhāṣya*, chapter 1, "*Adhyāsa*")

Ignorance is the origin of the universe that we perceive through the senses. The ignorance of Brahman in the waking state is called primary ignorance (*mūlāvidyā*) or causal ignorance (*kāraṇāvidyā*). In this state, we also have secondary or relative ignorance (*tulāvidyā*) or effective ignorance (*kāryāvidyā*), which is the ignorance of other people's thoughts or of subjects such as physics, mathematics, chemistry, and so on.

When we fall asleep, we lose awareness of the world we experience while awake. While dreaming, we experience a completely different world, which is produced by our own mind. It is necessary to forget the waking reality in order to create the world of dreams. This ignorance of the waking world while dreaming is called the original or causal ignorance (*mūlāvidyā* or *kāraṇāvidya*). While we sleep, we are aware of people, animals, and objects, but we are not aware of many details such as the thoughts of others, objects that we cannot see, and so on. We call this ignorance of details the second or effective ignorance (*tulāvidyā* or *kāryāvidyā*). After enough rest, we wake from our dream. But what wakes us up from the waking state is enough knowledge. When the knowledge of Brahman is awakened in us, this second world of dreams is annihilated. What remains is Brahman, the only reality.

Since ignorance is non-existent and is only perceived through its symptoms, inquiring about its origin makes no sense. What we call *ignorance* is no more than a lack of knowledge about ourselves. As waves form and then dissolve back into the ocean, *avidyā* arises and vanishes in *vidyā*. There is no difference between the waves and the ocean: any difference between ignorance and knowledge is only verbal. Even reflecting upon *vidyā* is considered ignorance. Reality is only perceived when both notions are renounced. When reality is revealed, all differences evaporates and what remains is only what is, as it is.

The ego hides its ignorance behind knowledge of information, but information corrupts ignorance and tarnishes its purity. Ignorance becomes innocence when we accept it and illuminate it with the light of consciousness. Ignorance becomes conscious innocence in a *bodhi-dharma* who does not know who he is, or in

Socrates, who only knows that he does not know.

Ignorance disconnects us from our authentic reality. It keeps us in the dark, so enlightenment is the absence of ignorance. With the cultivation of wisdom, the perceived duality of the soul and Brahman evaporates, allowing the realization that they are one and the same. The awakening to our real nature evaporates ignorance forever.

Egoism or *asmitā*

dṛg-darśana-śaktyor-ekātmata-iva-asmitā

> Egoism is the identification of the seer with
> the instrument of seeing.
>
> (*Yoga Sūtra*, 2.6)

Egoism is born from *avidyā*. Egoism is the identification of the Self with the mind, or the instrument of perception; it is consciousness objectifying itself and perceiving itself as an object of observation.

Although the mind–body complex is different from the Self, *avidyā* causes them to appear as one and the same, just as an iron ball placed inside a hot oven seems like a ball of fire. Even though the qualities of fire and of iron are completely different, the light and heat of the fire mixed with the hardness and shape of iron seem to be a ball of fire. Despite the difference between *ātmā* (the seer) and the mind (the seen), in the act of seeing, what is seen appears to be the seer: this phenomenon is *asmitā*, or "egoism."

What we call "personality" is, in fact, the personalization of the mind. Egoism is when the Self identifies with mental fluctuations and thereby suffers or enjoys. I think that "I" enjoy or suffer, but enjoyment and suffering are nothing but temporary experiences. They are mere waves of thoughts that arise in the mind. We should not allow thought waves to limit the infinite ocean of consciousness. When mental activity ceases, personality evaporates.

A clay pot seems to contain the space inside, but when it breaks, what was its interior space is revealed to be infinite space. Similarly, when the mind evaporates so does a separate personality; only infinite consciousness remains. When the subject–object experience is transcended, the veil covering reality drops.

Reality is as omnipresent as the space inside a pot; it is emptier than space yet is a vacuum filled with consciousness. If we eliminate all conceptualization, we will see that all beings are nothing more than empty expressions of emptiness.

Attraction and repulsion, or *rāga* and *dveṣa*

Rāga is "attraction or attachment" and *dveṣa* is "repulsion, aversion, dislike, or disgust." If we feel pleasure, this means that we have followed *rāga*; if we experience discomfort or suffering, we did not manage to avoid *dveṣa*. This is mentioned in the Bhagavad Gita:

rāga-dveṣa-vimuktais tu
viṣayān indriyaiś caran

ātma-vaśyair vidheyātmā
prasādam adhigacchati

> But one who has a disciplined (lower) self, which have been mastered by the higher Self, and is free from attraction and aversion even while using sense objects, attains peace.
> (Bhagavad Gita, 2.64)

The three main thoughts (*vṛttis*) are *rāga* (attraction), *dveṣa* (aversion), and *taṭastha* (indifference). We are drawn to certain aromas and repelled by others; we like certain foods and not others. There are people we get along with and others we cannot stand. We enjoy adulation, respect, and honor but are hurt by criticism, disrespect, disrepute, and disgrace. The same is true of melodies, colors, clothing, places, languages, and so on. In summary, we like comfort and enjoyment; we dislike discomfort and suffering. We live our lives escaping what we detest and chasing after all that we like. Thus, our lives are restricted to obsessive escape and pursuit.

Actually, all our attractions and aversions exist only in the mind. Attachments and rejections are part of our yesterdays because they are related to past experiences, whether pleasant or unpleasant. Our attachments and repulsions are memory; therefore, any pursuit of happiness aimed at escaping pain will take place within the limits of the mind. On the contrary, the search for the Truth or reality is beyond the limits of thought, so it cannot have anything to do with escaping from suffering.

Attraction and aversion are the two powers that dominate our lives. We live linearly: drawn by what we like and escaping from what we dislike. We are under the absolute control of these forces. Moreover, we suffer not only from what we dislike, but also from that which attracts us: the things we like create attachment and addiction and the threat of losing them makes us suffer.

Because our senses are directed outward, we are drawn to seek pleasure in the limited phenomenal world. Actions that seek pleasure, enjoyment, or happiness on the relative plane are called *kāmya-karma*. When our actions are selfish, our attention is directed toward the outcome. We dissociate from the reality of the present and direct our attention to the future. We disconnect from the moment to focus on what comes next. There are only two reactions to a *kāmya-karma* action: if we like the result, the response is favorable and there will be *rāga*, or "attraction." If the result is unpleasant, our response will be unfavorable and there will be *dveṣa*, or "repulsion." This is how we relate to every situation in life, in dualistic terms of attraction or repulsion: we like it or dislike it. Far from being associated with happiness, *kāmya-karma* is the cultivation and development of *rāga* and *dveṣa*. Attachments and repulsions are what Vedanta calls *impurities*. They fuel new desires to achieve what we like and escape from what we dislike. By triggering new desires, *rāga* and *dveṣa* enslave us in the perpetual karmic chain of action and reaction. As the source of all activity, attractions and repulsions keep us trapped within the *saṁsāra* of repeated births and deaths.

Although *kāmya-karma* actions promise happiness,

their results do not help eliminate our deep inner dissatisfaction. Through discrimination, or *viveka*, serious aspirants understand the limitations of any *kāmya-karma* activity. A logical analysis leads them to the conclusion that any outcome of their actions is limited and unable to give them the absolute bliss they seek.

To expect bliss or security from the world is a mistake that originates in ignorance. We cannot find bliss in a prison cell, bound by the chains of *rāga* and *dveṣa*. Only by going beyond both can we realize bliss. When we experience of Brahman, our attractions and repulsions immediately evaporate.

Abhiniveśa or "clinging to life"

Abhiniveśa, or "the attachment to life," is the fear of dying:

> *sva-rasa-vāhī viduṣo 'pi tathārūḍho 'bhiniveśaḥ*

> The attachment to life is firmly established,
> even in the sages.
>
> (*Yoga Sūtra*, 2.9)

Our fear of death is proportional to our attachment to life. When we accumulate things, it is not our possessions that contaminate our soul, but our craving to possess. In reality, our fear of death is only due to attachment.

Behind the fear of physical death lies the fear of the disappearance of the mind and the destruction of the ego. The egoic phenomenon is not only frightened of losing the body but of anything that threatens to diminish it in any way. For this reason, we feel threatened when faced with any attempt to offend or minimize us and we react aggressively to anything that may break the integrity of our ego.

Afraid to evaporate as idea-beings, we seek an illusory security that offers us certain solidity. We seek economic security through savings accounts, emotional security through marriage, and so on. Out of the need to experience continuity, we become attached to objects, places, situations, and people. It is the panic of disappearing as "someone" that keeps us from risking what is trivial and heading toward bliss. In the end, we finally accept being condemned to a life of conformity and secure mediocrity.

The path of liberation means abandoning everything that is false in us so that our true natural qualities shine: consciousness, knowledge, and bliss. The problem is that we do not want to let go of everything that binds us: our habits, ideas, opinions, fears, and desires. We have built the bars of our cell out of them. Freeing ourselves from our prison requires us to abandon the treasure that we have been accumulating for years. If we abandon the treasure chest, the bars and walls will fall away and we will be free!

Let us enjoy life, let us live with joy, without trying to possess or accumulate, but only with the awareness that all we receive—from the body to our home and its comforts—are all things that existence has loaned us temporarily. Let us use them with respect and profound appreciation, without possessing or accumulating.

Death only frightens those who live their lives half way, who feel they are missing out on life, who are not really present in each moment, who do not live in the here and now. Death threatens only those who have left many things pending, who have postponed too much because they lack the courage to live with intensity. Death only frightens those who worry about life but forget to live. Death does not threaten those who live deeply, intensely, and completely.

The longing that we feel in our heart to caress the Divine is the basis of all of our fears, because it is the aspiration of the soul that threatens the mind. The passion of the spirit frightens the ego and the union of the soul with its source represents the greatest danger to our dreams.

We may be great scholars and know the sacred scriptures by heart, but the only remedy for this fear is exactly what we fear: death itself. This fear will only disappear with the end of what we believe ourselves to be. In other words, this deeply rooted terror will only cease with enlightenment.

The Vedantic view

The essential problem is the ignorance about our true identity. However, there is absolutely nothing we can do about this. This may seem strange because we have been programmed to solve problems. But in this case, we do not lack what we are looking for; we just do not know it exists. We do not lack our original nature but have not recognized it yet. The opposite of ignorance is knowledge, not action. In regards to ignorance, action can only purify or prepare us for revelation. Action helps create the proper conditions to absorb the Truth. Yoga minimizes the inhibiting factors of our reality, principally attraction and repulsions. The yogic system makes it possible to follow a lifestyle committed to the Vedantic vision. Although the path of knowledge and the path of action reinforce each other, the solution will depend much more on knowing than acting.

Without purifying ourselves, we lack the openness required for revelation. In this respect, the practical contribution that yoga makes through action is essential. Selfishness makes us stupid; desires and attachments blur our vision. Our selfish interests decrease our clarity and prevent understanding reality. Without prior preparation, we declaim recycled knowledge and even teach it without really having digested what we are expressing.

However, we should not forget that the essential problem is ignorance and, therefore, the only remedy is knowledge. This is ignorance of ourselves. We know too much about the universe of names and forms and too little about our subjective reality. We are not aware of our reality, our essential nature, who we really are. When Vedanta mentions knowledge, it refers to knowing ourselves, to the recognition of the foundation of our existence.

Life as it is perceived on the dual plane consists of two aspects: the objective and the subjective. Within the relative dimension of existence, there are only two levels: the objective world and the experiencer or the subject, the observed and the observer, everything that can be perceived and the perceiver. *Object* refers to what is observed, be it people, animals, or things. S*ubject* refers to the "I" or the observer. Everything that can be perceived as an object is material; only the observer or subjectivity is spiritual. The existence of happiness cannot be denied because everyone has experienced it, even if only for a fraction of a second. Yet happiness is certainly subjective and not objective.

If the nature of salt is salty, its taste will be the same at any time and under any circumstances. Even if you taste it one, ten, or a hundred times, its taste will not change. Sweetness is an integral part of honey, which will be equally sweet at all times and in any situation. Similarly, if the nature of the objects of the world were happiness, they would always make us happy. For example, ice cream seems to make many people happy. However, if we wake up someone in the middle of the night to offer them an ice cream, there is no reason to believe this would be a welcome offer. The first bite of ice cream may be tasty, the second will be fine, the third will no longer cause us pleasure, and the fourth could be torture. We can similarly analyze any object, substance, or person in the universe. If happiness is not the nature of any object, then according to the rule of elimination called *pariśeṣa-nyāya*, it must be the nature of the subject. Therefore, you, the observer, are the source of bliss. You are what you are looking for. This is the Vedantic revelation. Bliss is the nature of consciousness.

We often try to avoid afflictions (*kleśas*) with objects that bring us joy such as paintings, chocolate, beer, or cigarettes. However, if we open them and look inside, we will not find happiness. If we test them in a laboratory, we will find chemicals and other elements, but not joy or pleasure. The happiness that we experience when we consume these objects lies within us. In the depths of our hearts rests the infinite source of bliss that is the Self, consciousness, that is, what we really are. You are unlimited but you have not recognized this yet. The big problem of human beings is that they do not know what their problem is or where it lies.

Human beings are desperately seeking an objective solution to a subjective problem or a material solution to a spiritual problem. Their difficulty lies in perceiving themselves incorrectly. They are not aware of their real nature and this ignorance does not allow them to perceive themselves as they are. Far from preaching a belief or faith, Vedanta proposes doubting our own conclusions about what we are. The legacy of the old sages is a profound uncertainty about our limited condition. It is a vision that welcomes investigation, exploration, and questioning.

To achieve a perspective that would allow us to overcome afflictions, a more objective and clear vision of reality is essential. For this purpose, we need to cultivate *vairāgya*, or "detachment," which allows us to observe the world without adding subjective values. Generally, we do not see the world as it is but as it seems to us. When we observe life, we superpose our memory upon it. A discerning view of the world is impossible without *vairāgya*.

We read in the *Viveka-cūḍāmaṇi*:

vairāgya-bodhau puruṣasya pakṣivat
pakṣau vijānīhi vicakṣaṇa tvam
vimukti-saudhāgra-talādhirohaṇaṁ
tābhyāṁ vinā nānyatareṇa sidhyati

> O wise one! Know that *vairāgya* (renunciation) and *bodha* (true understanding) are two means, like the two wings of a bird. The ascent to the upper floor of the palace of *vimukti* (liberation) is not ensured by either of the means alone.
>
> (*Viveka-cūḍāmaṇi*, 374)

The expectation of eradicating our inner afflictions motivates us to seek changes and experiences. But what we really seek is to eliminate what we think we are. Thus, we only postpone dealing with the real difficulty. We strive to be considered valuable, successful, and worthy of appreciation based on our achievements. Like a dog chasing its tail, our efforts will not bring us bliss. Every effort based on what is limited will lead to limited results. It is like the idiom, "you cannot make a silk purse from a sow's ear." If we expect something to change, it is impossible to realize the joy we aspire to.

According to Vedanta, there are two kinds of achievements: to achieve what we lack and to achieve what we have. The former refers to the ordinary achievement that we are familiar with. If I am missing something, I need to invest time and energy to get it. I strive to acquire something that time and space keep away from me. Enlightenment is the second type: the distance between the seeker and what is sought is ignorance, like when we look for our glasses and find them on our own head. Vedanta does not seek for what we lack, but for what we have but have not recognized yet.

In the search for our true nature, ignorance creates an illusory distance. Our real problem is the belief in what is not and the ignorance of what really is. Only by perceiving ourselves properly can we stop feeling limited. What we long for resides in us; it just needs to be recognized.

Chapter 14

The fourfold spiritual discipline or *sādhana-catuṣṭaya*

Upanishadic literature repeatedly mentions the moral values that aspirants should cultivate to realize Brahman. The following verse says that an authentic disciple must have a calm mind (*praśānta-citta*) and self-control (*śamānvita*).

tasmai sa vidvān-upasannāya samyak
praśānta-cittāya śamānvitāya
yenākṣaram puruṣaṁ veda-satyaṁ
provāca tāṁ tattvato brahma-vidyām

To the disciple who has thus approached the master in the proper manner, whose mind is at rest, and whose senses are subdued, let the wise master truly teach *Brahma-vidyā*, through which the true immortal Puruṣa is known.

(*Muṇḍaka Upanishad*, 1.2.13)

Jñāna-yoga is considered to be the most demanding among all the yogic paths since it requires preliminary study and practicing other branches of classical yoga. Before embarking upon the path of the knowledge of the Self, it is essential that the aspirant grow and develop in:

- *Karma-yoga*: the yoga of service.
- *Haṭha-yoga*: the yoga of psychophysiological development.
- *Bhakti-yoga*: the yoga of devotion.
- *Rāja-yoga*: the yoga of meditation.

These yogic paths are true spiritual pillars that strengthen our different aspects. Someone who dares to walk this path without proper preparation takes the risk of getting stuck at Vedanta of lips: an informational speech devoid of any practical value.

Another important requirement is a tremendous curiosity about who we are, our existence, ourselves as reality, about who really dwells behind our heart. I am not referring to a childish curiosity but a burning spirit of inquisition that keeps us awake at night, to a true passion for discovery. This path is not a creed or a faith, nor does it conform to dogmas or legends; rather, it is a search for what is most authentic within.

The *Kaṭha Upanishad* affirms that the truth of the Self is only revealed to those who have a focused and a subtle intellect:

eṣa sarveṣu būteṣu
gūḍho ''tmā na prakāśate

dṛśyate tvagryayā buddhyā
sūkṣmayā sūkṣma-darśibhiḥ

The Self that is hidden within all beings is not evident; it is only perceived through the subtle and acute intellect of the seers.
(*Kaṭha Upanishad*, 1.3.12)

The keenness necessary for studying *jñāna-yoga* is developed through *sādhana-catuṣṭaya*, or "the fourfold spiritual discipline," which involves cultivating the four requirements or instruments of Vedanta. All serious students of *jñāna-yoga* should be equipped with these four essential virtues.

Śrī Śaṅkarācārya mentions the preparations that Truth seekers should undertake before they will be able to understand Brahman:

ucyate-nityānitya-vastu-vivekaḥ ihāmutrārtha-bhoga-virāgaḥ, śama-damādi-sādhana-saṁpat, mumukṣutvaṁ ca. teśu hi satsu, prāg api dharma-jijñāsāyā ūrdhve ca śakyate brahma-jijñāsituṁ jñātuṁ ca; na viparyaye.

It should be noted that there are a few prerequisites to proceed and reflect on the Absolute. The requirements are discerning between what is eternal and non-eternal (*nityānitya-vastu-viveka*), detachment from the enjoyment of the fruits of current and future work (*ihāmutrārtha-bhoga-virāgaḥ*), perfection

> in practices such as control of the mind (*śama-damādi-sādhana-saṁpat*), senses, and genitals, and a strong desire for liberation. Provided these prerequisites are fulfilled, it is possible to reflect on the Absolute whether before or after the desire to perform our duty (*dharma*), but not otherwise.
>
> (Śaṅkarācārya, *Brahma Sūtra Bhāṣya,* 1.1.1)

Later on, Śrī Śaṅkarācārya himself explained the steps to follow on the non-dual path in books such as *Dṛg-dṛśya-viveka*, *Aparokṣānubhūti*, *Upadeśa-sāhasrī,* and *Viveka-cūḍāmaṇi.*

ādau nityānitya-vastu-
vivekaḥ pariganyate
ihāmutra-phala-bhoga-
virāgas tad-anantaram
śamādi ṣaṭka-sampattir
mumukṣutvam iti sphuṭam

> First there is discrimination (*viveka*) between the permanent and the impermanent, then a stilling of the craving for the enjoyment of the fruits of our actions (*vairāgya*) in this life and the next, followed by the six-fold treasure (*ṣaṭ-sampat*), which begins with control of the mind (*śamādi*). Finally, the desire for liberation (*mumukṣutva*) is clearly established.
>
> (*Viveka-cūḍāmani,* 19)

The *Vedānta-sāra* of Sadānanda also mentions *sādhana-catuṣṭaya* as a set of virtues every disciple should cultivate.

> *sādhanāni— nityānitya-vastu-vivekehāmutrārtha-phala-bhoga-virāga-śamādi-śaṭka-sampatti mumukṣutvāni.*
>
> The means to realizing wisdom are discriminating between permanent and transient things (*nityānitya-vastu-viveka*), renouncing enjoyment of the fruits of actions in this world and hereafter (*ihāmutrārtha-phala-bhoga-virāga*), fulfilling the six observances such as control of the mind (*śamādi-śaṭka-sampatti*), and desiring spiritual freedom.
>
> (*Vedānta-sāra*, 15)

The Vedic scriptures emphatically and explicitly state that without cultivating these qualifications, it is impossible to advance even a single step on the involutive process. Without these qualifications, all that we study and read will only be a waste of time and a bother to those around us.

Serious seekers on a religious path should be certain they are equipped with these four virtues, because only those who have become firmly rooted in these practices will be able to advance on the path of wisdom. We will now examine each of these four requirements.

1. *Viveka* or "discernment"

brahma satyaṁ jagan mithyety evaṁ-rūpo viniścayaḥ
so 'yaṁ nityānitya-vastū-vivekaḥ samudāhṛtaḥ

> *Viveka* is discernment between what is real and what is unreal (*nityānitya-vastū-viveka*) on the basis of a strong conviction that only Brahman is reality and the phenomenal world is unreal.
>
> (*Viveka-cūḍāmaṇi*, 20)

nityānitya-vastu-vivekas tāvad brahmaiva nityaṁ vastu tato 'nyad akhilam anityam iti vivecanam.

> Discernment between permanent and transient things is the discernment that Brahman alone is the permanent substance (*brahmaiva nitya vastu*) and that all other things are transitory.
>
> (*Vedānta-sāra*, 16)

Viveka is the power to discern between the apparent and the real, the temporal and the eternal, the relative and the Absolute. It is this power that helps us become aware of what is really important in life. Only those who have cultivated and developed *viveka* will be able to transcend desire without falling into mere repression. Instead of fighting earthly desires, they will simply become aware of their futility.

A person who is very discerning will comprehend that stealing is dangerous simply by hearing this from a trustworthy authority. Someone less evolved will need to study the matter thoroughly by reading the crime section in the news before reaching the conclusion that stealing has drawbacks. Others will only understand this when they see a thief arrested by the police, since "seeing is believing." Still others will only be able to give up delinquency after spending some time in prison. And there are even those whose power of discernment is so weak that even after hearing warnings, seeing what has happened to others, and suffering the consequences themselves, they repeat the same mistakes without being able to differentiate between what is pleasant and what is beneficial.

Discernment allows us to separate elements that have been mixed together and to identify their respective qualities. For example, when a metal ball is in contact with fire, the characteristics of metal and fire mix. The resulting fireball has the shape of the metal and the luminosity and heat of the fire. The human condition is similar, as it is a mixture of the Self, or Ātman, and the body–mind complex. As a result, consciousness seems to be confined to a particular form, and the human body appears to be conscious. A person thinks: "I am a human being," thus connecting "I am" (which refers to the Self) with "a human being" (which refers to the body–mind complex). By saying "I am happy," one blends "I am" (which refers to consciousness) with "happy" (which refers to the emotional aspect). When one declares: "I am beautiful," one joins the same "I am" with "beautiful," which refers to one's physical appearance.

Having a certain level of discriminative power, we can easily tell the difference between light and darkness, day and night, and so on. However, it is more difficult to distinguish more subtle realities such as physical, astral, and causal bodies.

Great keenness is also required to grasp the essential difference between a student and a disciple, which is the difference between studying and learning. The accumulation of information through studying is different from the existential phenomenon of learning. Greater sensitivity is needed to differentiate between attachment and love and between the internal happiness of the Self (*śreyas*) and that which comes from sensory satisfaction (*preyas*). That is to say, the development of *viveka* is part of cultivating discipleship. When we develop the spiritual capacity to discern, we rise above the worldly plane. Only with subtle discrimination can we separate the temporal from the eternal, the real from the apparent, and what we are from what we think we are.

Most humans suffer from *aviveka,* or a lack of discernment. Attachments, addictions, and egoistic desires interfere with our ability to reason and distinguish between right and wrong. When we meet new people or visit new places, we often form incorrect ideas about them. Worse still, since we are the first thing we perceive in this life, we develop incorrect ideas about what we are. Since we live as a mixture of consciousness and the body–mind complex, we confuse the Self, which is our true nature, with the non-Self. We are infinite and eternal consciousness but we feel limited because we perceive ourselves as being mixed with the non-Self. This painful experience of limitation is the main reason for human suffering.

Behind any human effort to feel happy hides the desire to break free from this sense of limitation. In order to escape our restrictions we pursue wealth, beauty, youth, fame, knowledge, and so on. We wish to expand our limits and so we strive to buy bigger houses and cars and accumulate more wealth. Yet the search for happiness within the world is merely a consequence of our limited perception of ourselves and what we are.

In fact, the moral rules of different religions are attempts to compensate for our lack of *viveka*. If we could distinguish between what is important and what is not, we would not need rules and regulations such as *yama* and *niyama* or the Ten Commandments.

Cultivating discernment allows us to put different situations in life into proper perspective. As *viveka* is directly related to one's degree of purity, it reaches its height in enlightened beings. The faculty of discernment, however, does not flourish from imposed guidelines. If we obey a list of laws, our conduct will necessarily not be the fruit of *viveka*. Rather than becoming free, we will turn into well-programmed robots. On the contrary, *viveka* can only be cultivated through attentive watchfulness because discernment is nothing more than the active aspect of observation.

vapus tuṣādibhiḥ kośaiḥ
yuktaṁ yuktyāvaghātataḥ
ātmānam antaraṁ śuddhaṁ
vivicyāt taṇḍulaṁ yathā

> Through discriminative self-analysis and reasoning, one should separate the pure Self within from its sheaths as one separates the rice from the husk, bran, and so on, that covers it.
>
> (*Ātma-bodha*, 16)

Our indifference and insensitivity cause us to ignore what really matters. If we manage to discern that everything except for Brahman is transient and temporal, we will certainly change our priorities in life. For this reason, *viveka* is not just the most important but the *only* requirement for experiencing that only the Self *is*.

Vedanta begins and culminates in the development of discernment, which is essential to experience that *brahma satyaṁ jagan mithyā*, or "Brahman is the reality; the (dual and relative) world is false." *Viveka* leads to the realization that the world is magic and reality is the magician.

Only God really is. Besides the Self, there is nothing here.

2. *Vairāgya* or "dispassion, detachment"

Vairāgya means renouncing all enjoyment that this or the next world may offer. It is an abandonment of the search for pleasure, be it material or spiritual.

tad vairāgyaṁ jihāsā yā
darśana-śravaṇādibhiḥ
dehādi-brahma-paryante
hy anitye bhoga-vastuni

> *Vairāgya* is the desire to renounce all impermanent sensory pleasures, from those of the body [via seeing, hearing, and so on] to those of [the abode of] Brahmā.
>
> (*Viveka-cūḍāmaṇi*, 21)

> *aihikānāṁ srak-candana-vanitādi-viṣaya bhogānāṁ karma-janyatayānityatvavad āmuṣmikāṇām apy amṛtādi-viṣaya bhogānām anityatayā tebhyo nitarāṁ viratiḥ ihāmutrārtha-phala-bhoga-virāgaḥ.*

> Since the objects of enjoyment in this world—such as a garland of flowers, sandalwood paste, and sexual pleasure—are transitory, being the results of actions, and since the objects of enjoyment in the hereafter, such as the nectar of immortality (*amṛta*), are transitory as well, an utter disregard for all of these is the renunciation of the enjoyment of the fruits of actions in this world and beyond (*ihāmutrārtha-phala-bhoga-virāgaḥ*).
>
> (*Vedānta-sāra*, 17)

If we do not want our studies on religion in general, and on *jñāna-yoga* in particular, to remain solely theoretical, we must develop detachment and renunciation. As our discernment sharpens, attachments and addictions decline on their own, naturally and spontaneously. The relative reality of names and forms is constantly changing, and therefore, any attachment to a source of pleasure will sooner or later become the cause of pain and suffering. However, beyond this changing world is the transcendental Self, unborn, unalterable, eternal, while the world is nothing but the Self's manifestation.

As we discover new truths, they force us to detach from our previous concepts, ideas, attitudes, beliefs, and ideologies, which were comfortable and useful in the early stages of our development but have now become inappropriate. Surprisingly, it can be much easier to detach from objects, money, and material possessions than from comforting sentimental attitudes and intellectual beliefs.

In *Viveka-cūḍāmaṇi*, Śaṅkarācārya warns about the danger that resides in the senses and their demands:

doṣeṇa tīvro viṣayaḥ
kṛṣṇa-sarpa-viṣād api
viṣaṁ nihanti bhoktāraṁ
draṣṭāraṁ cakṣuṣāpy ayam

> The sense-objects are more dangerous than the poison of a cobra, which is only fatal for one who is bitten, whereas the objects of the senses can be fatal even for one who only looks at them through the eyes.
>
> (*Viveka-cūḍāmaṇi*, 77)

Discernment (*viveka*) is essential for cultivating detachment and indispensable for realizing the Self.

Vairāgya is not the result of a life of repression, instead it flourishes from *viveka*. Repression without discernment only leads us to neurotic obsession. Proper discernment reveals the futility of worldly desires and of the pursuit of fleeting earthly pleasures.

3. *Ṣaṭ-sampat* or "the treasure of the six virtues"

Ṣaṭ-sampat, or "the treasure of the six virtues," consists of six attributes required to develop the mastery over the mind necessary for concentration and meditation. These are not six typical steps or stages, but qualities that should be developed simultaneously, as each one is a natural consequence of all the others.

> *śamo damas-titikṣoparatiḥ śraddhā tataḥ param*
> *samādhānam iti proktaṁ ṣaḍ evaite śamādayaḥ.*

> These six are said to be serenity of the mind (*śama*), control over the senses (*dama*), tolerance (*titikṣā*), renunciation of worldly desires (*uparati*), faith (*śraddhā*), and attention to the Self (*samādhāna*).
>
> (Śaṅkarācārya, *Sarva-vedānta-siddhānta-sāra-saṅgraha*, 95)

> *śamāday astu śama-damoparati-titikṣā-samādhāna-śraddhākhyāḥ.*

> These six virtues are limiting extroverted mental tendencies (*śama*), restraining external sense-organs (*dama*), internalizing into oneself (*uparati*), tolerance (*titikṣā*), deep contemplation (*samādhāna*), and faith (*śraddhā*).
>
> (*Vedānta-sāra*, 18)

3.1. *Śama* or "serenity"

virajya viṣaya-vrātād
doṣa-dṛṣṭyā muhur muhuḥ
sva-lakṣye niyatāvasthā
manasaḥ śama ucyate

> *Śama* is the state in which the mind continuously rests in contemplation of its goal, having become detached over and over again from the host of sensory objects through seeing their faults.
>
> (*Viveka-cūḍāmaṇi*, 22)

śamas tāvat śravaṇādi-vyatirikta-viṣayebhyo manaso nigrahaḥ.

> *Śama* is the restraining of the mind from all objects except listening to the scriptures, contemplating on their meaning, and meditating upon them.
>
> (*Vedānta-sāra*, 19)

The mind constantly seeks to externalize itself through the senses. *Śama* is usually translated as the control or mastery over the mind, but in reality it is the internalization of the mind; it is the serenity and tranquility that come from dispassion and detachment.

Due to the constant effort to obtain pleasure through the senses, the mind gets exhausted. *Śama* refers to the rest or relaxation of the mind that comes from the complete renunciation of sensory enjoyment. This virtue only manifests itself when we realize that sensory pleasure cannot grant us true peace, which only comes from Brahman, our authentic nature.

Śama is the liberation from pain that comes from detaching from sensory gratification. It is a state of serenity produced by mastery over the mind.

The craving for enjoyment creates emotional and energy states that become real obstacles to religious life. Peace, serenity, and tranquility are essential for creating favorable conditions for meditation.

3.2. *Dama* or "control over the senses"

viṣayebhyaḥ parāvartya
sthāpanaṁ sva-sva-golake
ubhayeṣām-indriyāṇām
sa damaḥ parikīrtitaḥ

> Withdrawing the two groups of sense organs from the sense objects and placing them in their respective centers is called *dama*.
>
> (*Viveka-cūḍāmaṇi*, 23a–b)

damḥ—bāhyendriyāṇāṁ tad-vyatirikta-viṣayebhyo nivartanam.

> *Dama* means keeping external organs away from all objects except those related to that (listening to the scriptures, thinking about their meaning, and meditating upon them).
>
> (*Vedānta-sāra*, 20)

Dama refers to control over the *indriyas*, or "the ten external senses," which include the five *jñānendriyas* (senses of knowledge) and the five *karmendriyas* (senses of action).

While *dama* (control over the senses) is mentioned as a different virtue from *śama* (mastery over the mind), in fact they are closely related since the mind and the senses are two aspects of the same phenomenon. The senses are extensions or continuations of the mind. The consequence of mental mastery is the equilibrium of the senses.

The mind activates the senses and is in turn influenced by them. This relationship is explained in the Bhagavad Gita:

yatato hy api kaunteya
puruṣasya vipaścitaḥ
indriyāṇi pramāthīni
haranti prasabhaṁ manaḥ

> The senses are very troublesome, O son of Kuntī, and forcibly steal the mind even of a wise person who is making an effort [to control them].
>
> (Bhagavad Gita, 2.60)

If we look carefully, we will notice the exaggerated importance that modern society gives to the senses and their demands. But rather than suppressing the senses or fighting against them, *dama* means putting them in their place in our life and giving them their true value.

Dama is not the result of blind repression but the natural consequence of wisdom. It is important to understand this because a blind struggle against the senses can constitute a serious obstacle to meditation. If the senses are unhealthily repressed, they unbalance our emotions. Repression in the absence of understanding tends to exaggerate the importance of what is repressed and create neurotic obsessions. On the other hand, one who enjoys the senses without any restrictions whatsoever clearly closes the door to all opportunities for enlightenment. Authentic tranquility can only blossom when the senses remain both healthy and awake in a balanced way.

3.3. *Uparati* or "renunciation of worldly desires"

bāhyān-ālambanaṁ vṛtter
eṣoparatir uttamā

> *Uparati* is inner absorption, or retreat into oneself. The highest *uparati* is when thoughts (*vṛttis*) do not take hold of anything external.
>
> (*Viveka-cūḍāmaṇi*, 23c)

nivartitānām eteṣāṁ tad-vyatirikta-viṣayebhya uparamaṇam uparatir athavā vihitānāṁ karmaṇāṁ vidhinā parityāgaḥ.

> *Uparati* is the cessation of the activity of these external organs; it means restraining them from pursuing external objects. It may also mean abandoning activities mandated by scripture.
>
> (*Vedānta-sāra*, 21)

The word *uparati* stems from *uparam*, or "to cease action, to be calm," and it means withdrawing and turning away from temptation. It is a conscious effort to resist external stimuli. It means abstaining from activities that are inessential for maintaining our physical or spiritual life. For this reason, it also means renouncing the belief in the ego as the actor or doer.

With *uparati*, one overcomes the dualities that affect most people such as pleasure and pain, honor and shame, happiness and sorrow, diversion and boredom. Only those who detach themselves from the pairs of opposites, such as attraction and repulsion, enjoy steadiness, which is indispensable for the aspirant.

Uparati means no longer thinking about objects that have been enjoyed in the past and resist bad habits; it is a struggle against our acquired vices and habits but not against our true nature. It is not escape from society, but no longer seeing reality with worldly eyes and opening the eyes of the soul.

3.4. *Titikṣā* or "tolerance"

sahanaṁ sarva-duḥkhānām
apratīkārā-pūrvakam
cintā-vilāpa-rahitaṁ
sā titikṣā nigadyate

> The capacity to withstand affliction with resignation and without rebelling is *titikṣā*, or "tolerance."
>
> (*Viveka-cūḍāmaṇi*, 24)

titikṣā— śītoṣṇādi-dvandva-sahiṣṇutā.

Titikṣā is the endurance of heat and cold and the other pairs of opposites.

(*Vedānta-sāra*, 22)

It is easy to keep a calm and relaxed mind in a peaceful environment. However, only those who have developed *titikṣā* can remain even-tempered even in the face of life's inconveniences. Such people do not bear grudges against their enemies and forgive harm done to them; if slapped, they turn the other cheek.

The great Bengali saint Caitanya, in his famous *Śikṣāṣṭaka* (3), advises us to be more tolerant than the trees (*taror api sahiṣṇunā*). When one has cultivated the virtues of tolerance and acceptance, it is possible to face difficulties and offenses without being bothered. The power to contain our reactions is not a product of mere repression but arises from observation.

Every reaction comes from the past. Only those who act in the now can develop authentic *titikṣā*. Solely from the position of the witness can one be really tolerant. Yogis who have developed this virtue can patiently contemplate the pairs of opposites like heat and cold, happiness and sadness, pleasure and pain.

Kṛṣṇa refers to tolerance in the Bhagavad Gita:

mātrā-sparśās tu kaunteya
śītoṣṇa-sukha-duḥkha-dāḥ
āgamāpāyino nityās
tāṁs titikṣasva bhārata

> O son of Kuntī! Due to the contact of the senses with objects, there appears to be cold and heat, happiness and distress, states which are transitory and have a beginning and an end. O descendent of Bharata, you must learn to tolerate them (without being bothered).
>
> (Bhagavad Gita, 2.14)

In a world that is temporary, relative, and illusory, and that ultimately is just a projection of the mind, what really matters is one's attitude. Life is a wheel; sometimes we are at the summit and other times at the very bottom. In a dual world, nothing can exist without its opposite. Whoever desires pleasure will know pain, and whoever runs after happiness will taste grief and sorrow. Those who pursue pleasure in this reality of dualities will never be able to know peace and serenity. Only those who remain calm before the pairs of opposites can aspire to the peace that lies beyond all logic.

The development of tolerance leads to acceptance, which allows us to renounce the habit of judging and condemning ourselves, as well as others. To live wisely is to live with acceptance. Only this way do we experience life as it really is, not as we wish it to be. Without going beyond the pairs of opposites, there is no possibility of observation, since we usually hope to see things as we want them to be. Acceptance is essential for meditation to occur.

The sequence begins with tolerance, continues with acceptance, and culminates in *śraddhā*, or "faith." Only beings of unconditional acceptance who trust existence are capable of surrendering to God.

3.5. *Śraddhā* or "trust, faith"

śāstrasya guru-vākyasya
satya-buddhy-avadhāraṇam
sā śraddhā kathitā sadbhir
yayā vastūpalabhyate

> The sages define *śraddhā*, or 'faith,' as the acceptance of the truth of the scriptures and the words of the guru. This faith makes the realization of reality possible.
>
> (*Viveka-cūḍāmaṇi*, 25)

gurūpadiṣṭa-vedānta-vākyeṣu viśvāsaḥ— śraddhā.

> *Śraddhā* is the faith in the assertions of Vedanta as taught by the guru.
>
> (*Vedānta-sāra*, 24)

Śraddhā means trust in the spiritual master, in the sacred scriptures, in God, in oneself, in life. The mind is our defensive, protective, and resistant attitude; therefore, it is our main obstacle to surrendering.

Śraddhā is not a mental state but a way of being. The realization of the Self calls for absolute surrender, a complete letting go, total relaxation in the very essence of existence. *Śraddhā* is the trust that swimmers have in water: when they jump from the diving board, they know that they will rise up and float in the water, even if they first go under water. It is this trust that helps them relax. Have you ever seen what happens to those who cannot swim? Lacking confidence in water, their bodies stiffen, and this rigidity becomes the main obstacle to keeping afloat.

Our defenses, fears, and concerns prevent us from surrendering to the Whole. Trust and faith begin where egoism and pride end.

Kṛṣṇa says in the Bhagavad Gita:

śraddhāvāl labhate jñānaṁ
tat-paraḥ saṁyatendriyaḥ
jñānaṁ labdhvā parāṁ śāntim
acireṇādhigacchati

> Those who have faith, mastery over the senses, and dedication achieve true wisdom. Having achieved wisdom, they soon realize supreme peace.
>
> (Bhagavad Gita, 4.39)

ajñaś cā śraddadhānaś ca
saṁśayātmā vinaśyati
nāyaṁ loko 'sti na paro
na sukhaṁ saṁśayātmanaḥ

> But the ignorant one who doubts and lacks wisdom and faith is lost, because for those who doubt, there can be no happiness, either in this world or in the next.
>
> (Bhagavad Gita, 4.40)

We are an integral part of life. We are existence. We are what we are and where we are because life desires it so for some reason. Our existence has meaning. We are something more than a sack of flesh and bones and our life is much more than a path from the cradle to the grave.

The religious process is similar to a drop of water allowing itself to slide into the ocean. This leap of faith is impossible if the drop lacks sufficient trust to give up its existence as a drop and be reborn as the ocean. Having religion means no longer existing as a part in space and time in order to exist in eternity.

3.6. *Samādhāna* or "attention to the Self"

sarvadā sthāpanaṁ buddheḥ
śuddhe brahmaṇi sarvadā
tat-samādhānam ity uktaṁ
na tu cittasya lālanam

Samādhāna is said to be constant, undivided (complete) attention on pure Brahman and not on merely indulging the mind.

(*Viveka-cūḍāmaṇi*, 26)

nigṛhītasya manasaḥ śravaṇādau tad-anuguṇa-viṣaye ca samādhiḥ— samādhānam.

Samādhāna is the constant concentration of the mind, restrained in this way, in listening, contemplating and meditating on

> the passages of the scriptures and anything else dealing with the same subject matter.
>
> (*Vedānta-sāra*, 23)

The mind, like a butterfly, constantly flits from one object to another in search of happiness. Its attention wanders without stopping and it becomes scattered. *Samādhāna* means stopping the mind's incessant wandering and focusing attention on attention itself, on the Self, on Brahman. As the mind concentrates, fixed and absorbed in the Self, it frees itself from anxiety and suffering and becomes integrated and unified.

Samādhāna manifests itself as a natural consequence of the development of *śama*, *dama*, *uparati*, *titikṣā*, and *śraddhā*. Once our attention moves to attention itself, we transcend attractions and repulsions, which leads to a state of satisfaction with ourselves. Experiencing *samādhāna*, we feel comfortable with life and self-satisfied.

Students of *jñāna-yoga* who lack *samādhāna* will continue looking for something in the world of names and forms. Only those who delight in their own being will truly devote themselves to knowing instead of obtaining.

4. *Mumukṣutvā* or "the aspiration for liberation"

ahaṅkārādi-dehāntān
bandhān ajñāna-kalpitān
sva-svarūpāvabodhena
moktum icchā mumukṣutā

> *Mumukṣutvā*, or "spiritual aspiration," is the yearning to break free from all bondage

> fabricated by ignorance, beginning with the feeling of "I" (ego) and ending with the fetters of the body through the realization of our authentic nature.
>
> (*Viveka-cūḍāmaṇi*, 27)

mumukṣutvaṁ mokṣecchā.

> *Mumukṣutva* is the yearning for liberation.
>
> (*Vedānta-sāra*, 25)

Desire enslaves whereas aspiration liberates. Aspiration is the sublimation of desire. Although the destruction of desire is impossible, it can be sublimated into a sincere aspiration for freedom.

This yearning of the soul is so necessary on the spiritual path that I would say it is essential. Experiencing this yearning is undoubtedly grace manifested and channeled through the spiritual master:

manda-madhyama-rūpāpi
vairāgyeṇa śamādinā
prasādena guroḥ seyaṁ
pravṛddhā sūyate phalam

> This longing for liberation, however torpid or mediocre, can bear fruit through the grace of the guru, [being developed] through renunciation (*vairāgya*), peace (*śama*), and so on.
>
> (*Viveka-cūḍāmaṇi*, 28)

Any desire for worldly pleasure is diminished by the aspiration for the Self, which is an essential requirement for enlightenment. It is this spiritual longing that leads us to give ourselves in body, mind, and soul to religion and the search for God. It involves changing our addictive attitude toward misery: a change that clearly implies much more than just an intellectual decision. *Mumukṣutvā* means completely renouncing our chains. It is the aspiration to free ourselves not only from sorrow and pain, but also from the misery brought about by what we mistakenly call *happiness*. May every moment of our lives become filled with spiritual aspiration.

The "I" cannot be free because the ego is slavery itself. Slavery cannot be freedom. In the same way that the appearance of the light means the disappearance of darkness, the appearance of freedom means the disappearance of slavery.

The search for enlightenment is synonymous with the aspiration for liberation from everyone and everything, including ourselves. We are of freedom: from freedom we have come and to freedom we go. Freedom resides as much in our origin as our destination. It is not something one achieves, but something one becomes.

As long as we remain confined by the mind, we continue to be slaves. Liberation is the absence of "I": it is the absence of you. Even though the mind cannot conceive of enlightenment, it can become aware of its slavery. Ultimately, freedom involves liberating oneself even from the need for freedom.

The path of wisdom does not offer loopholes, evasions, or escapes from the ego. It does not advise us to ignore the ego but suggests that we investigate it, analyze it, understand it, confront it, and look it straight in the eye, which will eventually dissolve it completely, like acid.

Jñāna-yoga does not promise liberation but the direct realization that in fact nothing has ever existed and there is nothing and no one to be liberated from. There have never been any locks or chains. Misery does not enslave us; we are the ones who cling to it and do not let it go.

Religion is the most wonderful phenomenon that can occur in a human heart, if there is a genuine passion for freedom. We should bear in mind that if we use religion only to calm our fears and insecurities, it will destroy us, damage our dignity, obstruct our intelligence, and obscure our soul.

There is only one true religion and I am not referring a single "ism" among many. True religion is what arises from the passionate pursuit of Truth and the thirst to know who or what we are, that is, the hunger to know ourselves.

It is very important that students of Vedanta develop the four virtues mentioned above. Otherwise, their *jñāna-yoga* will be no more than an intellectual game of words that will only inflate the ego. They will only listen to lectures or read about Advaita Vedanta without it having any real effect on their life. Religion is not merely theory or information; above all, it is transformation.

With the cultivation of discernment (*viveka*), detachment (*vairāgya*), tranquility (*śama*) stemming from our mastery over the mind, self-control (*dama*), the renunciation of worldly desire (*uparati*), tolerance (*titikṣā*), placing attention on the Self (*samādhāna*), faith (*śraddhā*), and a sincere longing for liberation (*mumukṣutvā*), our study of Vedanta will transcend the limits of mere theory.

These qualities are the true pillars to base our path on, authentic treasures that we need to be equipped with in our journey toward ourselves.

As a consequence of *sādhana-catuṣṭaya*, we turn our attention away from what is ephemeral and focus it on the Self.

Chapter 15

The disciplines on the path of self-discovery

According to *jñāna-yoga*, there are three fundamental disciplines on the path of self-discovery that lead to *ātma-sākṣātkāra*, or "the direct experience of the Self." As the *Viveka-cūḍāmaṇi* explains:

tataḥ śrutis tan mananaṁ satattva-
dhyānaṁ ciraṁ nitya-nirantaraṁ muneḥ
tato 'vikalpaṁ parametya vidvān
ihaiva nirvāṇa-sukhaṁ samṛcchati

Next there is listening (*śravaṇa*), reflecting (*manana*), and a long, continuous, and uninterrupted meditation on the Truth (*nididhyāsana*). Next, the wise seeker (*muni*) reaches the supreme state of enlightenment (*nirvikalpa*) and realizes the bliss of final liberation (*nirvāṇa*) even in this life.

(*Viveka-cūḍāmaṇi*, 70)

These disciplines leading to the realization of the Self are also mentioned in the *Bṛhad-āraṇyaka Upanishad*:

> *ātmā vā are draṣṭavyaḥ śrotavyo mantavyo nididhyāsitavyaḥ.*
>
> The Ātman is worthy of being seen. One should listen to, think about, and meditate upon the Ātman.
>
> (*Bṛhad-āraṇyaka Upanishad*, 2.4.5)

Śaṅkarācārya, in his *Bhāṣya* on this *Upanishad* elaborates:

> *tasmāl loka-prasiddham etad— ātmaiva priyo nānyat. "tad etat preyaḥ putrāt" (Bṛ. U. 1.4.8) ity upanyastam. ...tasmād ātma-prīti-sādhanatvāt gauṇī anyatra prītir ātmany eva mukhyā. tasmād ātmā vai are draṣṭavyo darśanārho, darśana-viṣayam-āpādayitavyaḥ; śrotavyaḥ pūrvam ācāryata āgamataś ca ; paścān-mantavyaḥ tarkataḥ; tato nididhyāsitavyo niścayena dhyātavyaḥ. evaṁ hy asau dṛṣṭo bhavati śravaṇa-manana-nididhyāsana-sādhanair nirvartitaiḥ. yadaikatvam etāny upagatāni, tadā samyag darśanaṁ brahmaikatva-viṣayaṁ prasīdati, na anyathā śravaṇa-mātreṇa.*
>
> Hence, it is widely acknowledged that the Self alone is dear and nothing else. It has already affirmed: "This [Self] is dearer than a son," etc. (*Bṛ. U.* 1.4.8). ...Therefore,

> our affection for other objects is secondary since they contribute to the pleasure of the Self, and our love for the Self is primary. Hence: "The Self, my dear Maitreyi, should be realized, is worthy of realization, or should be made the object of realization. It should first be heard of from a teacher and from the scriptures, then reflected upon, through reasoning, and finally steadfastly meditated upon." It is realized only through engagement with these means: hearing (*śravaṇa*), reflection (*manana*), and meditation (*nididhyāsana*). Only when these three are combined, actual realization of the unity of Brahman is achieved, and not through hearing alone.
>
> (*Bṛhad-āraṇyaka Upanishad Bhāṣya*, 2.4.5)

Next we will give a brief explanation of each of these disciplines.

1. *Śravaṇa* or "listening"

> *śravaṇaṁ nāma ṣaḍ-vidha-liṅgair aśeṣa-vedāntānām advitīya-vastuni tātparyāvadhāraṇam.*

> Listening (*śravaṇa*) is the proof, through the six characteristic signs established by the Vedanta philosophy (beginning and conclusion, repetition, originality, result,

eulogy, and demonstration), that Brahman is the One without a second.

(*Vedānta-sāra*, 182)

Śaṅkarācārya, in his *Bhāṣya* on *Bṛhad-āraṇyaka Upanishad*, emphasizes:

kathaṁ dṛṣṭa ātmani? iti ucyate pūrvam ācāryāgamābhyāṁ śrute...

How is the Self perceived? This is being explained: First, by hearing from the spiritual master and the scriptures.

(*Bṛhad-āraṇyaka Upanishad Bhāṣya*, 4.5.6)

Śravaṇa refers to systematically studying with a bona fide guru over a long period of time. The Vedic scriptures advise us to learn directly from a qualified spiritual master. The *Kaṭha Upanishad* affirms:

uttiṣṭhata jāgrata
prāpya varān nibodhata
kṣurasya dhārā niśitā duratyayā
durgaṁ pathas tat kavayo vadanti

Arise, awake! Having found the great enlightened masters, you will attain understanding. The seers say that the path is sharp as a razor.

(*Kaṭha Upanishad*, 1.3.14)

It is impossible to realize the Self only through books, courses, or teachers. They may prepare us for the encounter with our eternal guru, but wisdom only flourishes in close association with spiritual masters. Authentic disciples need to be situated in *śravaṇa*. With a calm and free mind of preconceived ideas and concepts, they become pure silence and receptivity.

2. *Manana* or "reflection"

> *mananaṁ tu śrutasyādvitīya-vastuno vedāntānu-guṇa-yuktibhir anavaratam anucintanam.*
>
> Reflection (*manana*) is the uninterrupted contemplation of the one real essence that has no second (Brahman), of which one has heard from the guru through reasoning that is in accordance with Vedanta.
>
> (*Vedānta-sāra*, 191)

A serious and deep contemplation of the truths springing forth from the lips of the *sad-guru* turns what is hidden into obvious. The spiritual master's teachings must be assimilated until they remove all doubts. Skepticism is a defense mechanism of the mind. While our skepticism persists, we will maintain our defenses and continue to resist the Truth.

The Sanskrit word *manana* means "negation of the mind"; it is not another speculative process that strengthens the mind. Although it is impossible to understand the Truth through the mind, the mind helps us become aware of this. *Manana* is actually a mental process, but a self-destructive one.

Listening will be ineffective if we do not spend time digesting what we have heard. It is essential that spiritual aspirants contemplate, in seclusion, on the implications of what they have heard may have on their lives. In religion, knowledge is ours only when we can live according to it. Thus, if our behavior is incoherent with what we hear, we are nothing but highly informed ignoramuses. From the daily reflection on the master's teachings, self-inquiry flourishes.

3. *Nididhyāsana* or "Vedantic meditation"

> *vijātīya-dehādi-pratyaya-rahitādvitīya-vastu-sajātīya-pratyaya-pravāho nididhyāsanam.*
>
> Meditation (*nididhyāsana*) is a stream of ideas about the One real essence which has no second (Brahman), leaving aside other ideas such as those related to the body and so on.
>
> (*Vedānta-sāra*, 192)

Nididhyāsana is meditative reflection upon the knowledge until merely intellectual concepts become reality. In this way, one assimilates the truths and theoretical philosophy is transformed into experience.

Nididhyāsana is a meditative search for the very roots of consciousness, for it is in consciousness that we existentially experience the truths learned from spiritual masters and holy scriptures. During this process, knowledge is transformed into wisdom and theory becomes a subjective experience.

Śravaṇa is listening to the scriptures from our guru, *manana* is internalizing them, and *nididhyāsana* is experiencing them as the Truth and living accordingly.

Ātma-sākṣātkāra or "the direct perception of the Self"

Ātma-sākṣātkāra, or "the direct perception of the Self," refers to self-realization, which is the natural consequence of the three disciplines described above.

It is impossible to understand *ātma-sākṣātkāra* intellectually. We learn about the perception of the Self from books and sermons, but as egos, we create our own concept of it. Therefore, in our search for the Truth we run the risk of striving for a goal that is merely a mental interpretation.

In our ordinary state of consciousness, we do not live based on an authentic perception of ourselves, but a belief about what we are. The egoic phenomenon is a self-objectivization: we perceive ourselves as something separate and disconnected from the Whole. *Ātma-sākṣātkāra* is our disappearance as "someone" and our evaporation as an "I-idea" or "I-concept."

We cannot become enlightened because when the light of Truth appears, it only reveals our absence; therefore, there is nobody there to be enlightened. To think that you or I can be enlightened is simply absurd, because that "I" is just an obstacle. In essence, we all are enlightened. But as egos, we have no relation to enlightenment since it completely transcends what we believe ourselves to be. Society has trained us to increase our purchasing power: the more successful we become, the more it increases. However, on the spiritual path we develop our capacity to renounce, which leads us to stop acquiring: not because it is forbidden, but because we transcend our feeling of lacking something, and therefore, our need to possess and accumulate.

Enlightenment is not about adding but subtracting; it is not gaining anything that is missing but divesting ourselves of excess. It is not acquiring something that we lack but renouncing ideas, beliefs, concepts, and conclusions that we have accepted as our identity.

Religion is a path that leads from darkness to light, but it is a path for losers, because the more you advance, the less you possess. Our great problem is not the lack of something, but the lack of awareness of what we are. In *ātma-sākṣātkāra*, there is nothing left to possess, since we have renounced everything. We exist but we are nowhere... We are no one.

aprākṛtena nityena
nirmalenāvikāriṇā
vyāpakenātisūkṣmeṇa
pareṇa jñāna-cakṣuṣā

viśuddhaṁ śāśvataṁ nityaṁ
aprameyaṁ anaupamam
nirvikalpaṁ acinyaṁ ca
hetu-dṛṣṭānta varjitaṁ

sutṛptaṁ nirguṇaṁ śāntaṁ
tattvātītaṁ nirañjanam
avibhāvyaṁ asandehyaṁ
paśyantīśānam ātmani

With the eye of consciousness which is not created by the evolutes of *prakṛti*, and is eternal, pure, immutable, pervasive, extremely subtle and supreme, he sees within his own self the Absolute One, which is always pure, imperishable, incomparable, unaffected by modifications and changes, beyond the reach of thought, eternally free from the three impurities, inexplicable through logical reasoning and illustration, content, free from the attributes, expressive of serene calmness, beyond the range of *tattvas*, undefiled by limiting factors, inconceivable and which defies all sorts of doubt.

(*Sarva-jñānottara Āgama*, 2.7.17–19)

Chapter 16

Vedantic epistemology

Both animals and humans share four propensities: eating, sleeping, procreating, and defending themselves. As long as the basis of our life is just these four activities, it cannot be called *human life*. The main difference between human beings and beasts is epistemological, because is related to the quest for knowledge. Only humans have the level of consciousness necessary to inquire about the absolute Truth. The *Vedānta Sūtra* suggests that we inquire about Brahman:

athāto brahma-jijñāsā

Now the inquiry about Brahman.
(*Vedānta Sūtra*, 1.1)

According to Vedic epistemology, the means to acquire knowledge can be grouped into three categories: *pratyakṣa*, *anumāna*, and *śabda* or *śruti*.

- ***Pratyakṣa***, or "that which is evident," refers to empirical knowledge. First we acquire information through the senses and then we use our mind to analyze it and reach conclusions.
- ***Anumāna***, or "inference," uses logic to reach conclusions from premises that are considered valid.
- ***Śabda***, or "revealed knowledge that comes from the Vedas," descends orally through *paramparā*, directly from the Absolute.

Only by understanding the limitations of our own means of knowledge will we feel the need for an external source that can reveal to us what is inaccessible through our mind and senses. By studying Vedantic epistemology, we identify the limitations of our intellect and appreciate Vedanta as a means for revealing reality.

According to Vedic scriptures, there are two methods of attaining knowledge. The first is *āroha-panthā*, or "the ascending method." It refers to knowledge grasped through the senses and includes both deductive and inductive reasoning. The second is *avaroha-panthā*, or "the descending method." It refers to the acceptance of knowledge from an authority on the subject.

Āroha-panthā or "the ascending method"

The ascending method is a process of investigation and exploration through *pratyakṣa* and *anumāna*. It is an effort to discover the Truth through personal investigation. This method begins with perception through our gross and subtle senses (eyes, ears, nose, tongue, skin, mind, and intelligence) and the subsequent mental processing that leads us to certain conclusions. Because of our sensory limitations, *pratyakṣa* leads to relative knowledge, although scientists sometimes try to present it as absolute. *Anumāna* means "to follow the mind." Although it is more subtle than *pratyakṣa*, it is still on to the relative plane and does not give us access to perfect knowledge. Knowledge gained through the senses is faulty. Inference based on imperfect information will definitely lead to erroneous conclusions. How can we accept as truth a premise that comes with a lot of phrases such as "perhaps," "in my opinion," "I think," "could be," and so on?

It is impossible to access the transcendental through this method for the simple reason that human beings are finite and limited. Their limitations can be categorized as four essential defects:

- ***Karaṇāpāṭava***, or "sensorial imperfection." It is an indisputable fact that our senses are limited. For example, we cannot hear sounds above or below certain frequencies. We see the sun and it seems to us to be the size of a coin, but it is bigger than the very planet that we live on. There are many people who are unaware of their own sensory limitations and say that they will accept God only if they can see him.
- ***Bhrama,*** or "error." All human beings make mistakes because of their sensory limitations. It is even said that to err is human. In other words,

no matter how important, intelligent, skillful, learned, beautiful, strong, or rich human beings may be, they will surely make mistakes.

- ***Pramāda,*** or "the illusion in which we live due to complete ignorance of our own identity." Ignorant of our true spiritual nature, we identify with a physical body and believe that we have a particular nationality and belong to a specific race, group, and so on. However, these are all identifications based on the erroneous bodily concept of life.
- ***Vipralipsā,*** or "cheating propensity." Instead of seeing what is as it is, we defend our own conclusions. We do not only deceive others, but ourselves as well. We interpret situations to make a version of reality that does not contradict our self-image. We arrange the facts to make a story that enables us to live in peace with our own conscience.

tatra puruṣasya bhramādi-doṣa-catuṣṭaya-duṣṭatvāt sutarām alaukikācintya-svabhāva-vastu-sparśāyogyatvāc ca tat-pratyakṣādīny api sa-doṣāṇi.

To start with, an ordinary person's means of knowing—sensory perception and so on—are imperfect: they are tainted by four defects beginning with incorrect judgment, and moreover, they are simply inadequate for establishing contact with a reality whose nature is otherworldly and inconceivable.

(Jīva Gosvāmī, *Tattva-sandarbha*, 9)

yady api pratyakṣānumāna śabdārthopamāṇārthā-patty-abhāva-sambhavaitihya-ceṣṭhākhyāni daśa pramāṇāni viditāni, tathāpi bhrama-pramāda-vipralipsā-karaṇāpāṭava-doṣa-rahita-vacanātmakaḥ śabda eva mūlam-pramāṇam.

If one carefully examines the ten kinds of evidence, namely *pratyakṣa*, *śabda*, *anumāna*, *arya*, *upamāna*, *arthāpatti*, *abhāva*, *sambhava*, *aitihya*, and *ceṣṭha*, one will find that all of them are contaminated by the four defects of material life: cheating, imperfect senses, illusion, and mistakes. Therefore, of all of these, revelation (*śruti*) is considered to be superior for it is above the four defects. *Śruti* is, therefore, the root of all evidence.

(Jīva Gosvāmī, *Sarva-saṁvādinī* on *Tattva-sandarbha*, 9)

Due to these four basic flaws, we cannot receive or impart perfect knowledge. In other words, as limited beings we are not reliable. Our opinions are influenced by our attachments. Without transcending our addictions, we will not be reliable sources of knowledge. In fact, as long as we do not overcome the slavery to our mental and emotional demands, we cannot even trust ourselves.

Avaroha-panthā or "the descending method"

The word *avaroha* is related to the word *avatāra,* which means "that which descends." Due to its transcendental nature, Vedic wisdom is not the result of experiments. For the followers of *Sanātana-dharma,* Vedic knowledge is axiomatic. We receive Vedic truths by listening, not by experimenting; they are clear and self-evident. Moreover, the origin of the Vedas is transcendental, not human. *Avaroha* is the process for obtaining perfect knowledge through *śabda.* Transcendental wisdom descends from the perfect supreme Lord through the authorities of the line of disciplic succession. Unlike human knowledge, this wisdom is reliable.

Although the superiority of *śabda* is accepted, *pratyakṣa,* and *anumāna* are not rejected. However, if ever there is a conflict between them, we turn to *śabda* as the reliable source of authoritative knowledge.

Pramāṇas or "the means of acquiring knowledge"

Advaita Vedanta accepts the three Vedic *pramāṇas* and adds three more. This is how it describes the six means to acquire valid knowledge:

> *tāni ca pramāṇāni ṣaṭ-pratyakṣānumanopamānāga-mārthāpatty-upalabdhi-bhedāt.*
>
> These means of knowledge are six in number and they are perception, inference, comparison, verbal testimony, presumption,

and non-apprehension.

(*Vedānta-paribhāṣā* of Dharma-rāja Adhvarīndra, chapter 1)

1. *Pratyakṣa*, or "direct perception": This refers to knowledge obtained through our physical senses: sight, hearing, smell, taste, and touch, plus an internal one called *manas*, or "mind."

There are two kinds of *pratyakṣa*: *nirvikalpaka* and *savikalpaka*. *Nirvikalpaka-pratyakṣa* is an undetermined perception in which we perceive an object but we do not know what it is: we see something but we cannot identify it. *Savikalpaka-pratyakṣa*, on the other hand, is a perception that allows us to identify the object with the help of our memory. Our ability to define something is due to a previous perception of a similar concept. In *nirvikalpaka-pratyakṣa*, only the senses are involved, but in *savikalpaka-pratyakṣa* we use our judgment and capacity for interpretation. In light of our previous experience, we are able to recognize an observed object.

2. *Anumāna*, or "inference": According to traditional or Aristotelian logic, inference is a form of deductive reasoning. What is inferred is not perceived directly; it is deduced based on the invariable relationship that it has with the perceived indications. The classic example of *anumāna* is seeing smoke in the distance. There is an invariable and universal relationship between smoke and fire. Seeing smoke, we infer there is fire. Smoke is the external indication that allows us to infer the existence of fire even though we cannot see the fire directly.

3. *Upamāna*, or "comparison": This is knowledge obtained through analogies. We acquire knowledge by comparing an unknown object with a known one. For example, in the past I visited the Atacama Desert in northern Chile. When I travel to the United States and see the Chihuahua desert, I recognize that the terrain is very similar. Therefore, I am able to acquire knowledge about the Chihuahua desert based on my experiences of the Atacama. Such knowledge is acquired through comparison.

4. *Arthāpatti*, or "assumption": This refers to the knowledge acquired through a postulate. *Arthāpatti-pramāṇa* is the assumption of an imperceptible fact that explains what we perceive when we lack other explanations.

5. *Anupalabdhi*, or "non-perception": This refers to inexistence that is grasped through its lack of apprehension. Vedanta argues that when the senses do not perceive an object, perception does in fact take place: that of non-existence. For example, if we do not see a pencil in its place, we know it is not there. This *pramāṇa* is used when one asserts "the lawyer is not in his office" or "the flower has no perfume." Both perception and non-perception are useful in this type of knowledge acquisition.

6. *Āgama* or *śabda*, or "reliable testimony": These are the affirmations of the sacred scriptures or the knowledge obtained through the *śāstras*. This is the transcendental testimony of the enlightened sages, who are considered reliable. Much of the knowledge we acquire at a school or university cannot be perceived

by the naked eye. We simply accept the testimony of books, historians, and scientists of proven reliability. Likewise, the sacred scriptures contain the wisdom of the revelation received by the wise seers of antiquity. These *ṛṣis* possess the degree of purity necessary to be recipients of the absolute knowledge of the divine revelation. *Śabda* is the only *pramāṇa* that can provide us with knowledge about Brahman, or the Absolute.

Chapter 17
Consciousness

In searching for the Truth, many have accepted the existence of a superior being called God. Trying to understand the message and teachings of great enlightened beings, they have concluded that there is an almighty creator who dwells in heaven. They postulate a separation between the individual and God, whom they consider part of objective reality. This belief sees God as someone or something separate and suggests worshipping him as a different reality. However, according to the Advaitic view, God and consciousness are two terms for the same thing.

yac ca sthāvaraṁ sarvaṁ tat prajñā-netraṁ.
prajñāne pratiṣṭhitaṁ prajñā-netro lokaḥ prajñā
pratiṣṭhā prajñānaṁ brahma.

All these have consciousness as the giver of their reality; all these are impelled by consciousness; the universe has

> consciousness as its eye and consciousness as its end. Consciousness is Brahman.
>
> (*Aitareya Upanishad*, 3.1.3)

Sensory perception is possible due to consciousness. Everything that happens in our inner world depends on consciousness such as thinking, remembering, feeling, and imagining. Whatever can be touched, heard, smelled, tasted, thought about, imagined, and felt is only a temporary projection of imperceptible consciousness.

Although consciousness cannot be imagined, it is real because it would be impossible to imagine anything without it. It cannot be defined, but without it we could not define anything. It cannot be conceptualized, but without it we could not conceptualize anything. It cannot be seen, but without it we could not see anything. Thus reality is not a temporary and impermanent projection; it is what makes such projections possible.

Any mental or emotional activity means there is a presence that perceives it. In other words, every thought, idea, and experience depends on a presence that witnesses it. Consciousness is what knows and knows that it knows. In other words, it is the presence that not only knows, but also knows itself knowing. The first two *sūtras* of the *Śiva Sūtra* say:

caitanyam ātmā
jñānaṁ bandhaḥ

> Consciousness is the Self. Limited knowledge, which is equal to ignorance, is captivity.
>
> (*Śiva Sūtra*, 1–2)

Consciousness is indivisible. If it could be divided, we would have a finite part and an infinite minus that part. Hence, there can be no pieces of consciousness and consciousness is not a whole composed of parts. The part is not real: whatever we think might be a part is actually consciousness in its totality. If consciousness is reality, then anything perceived as a part is necessarily an illusion.

We refer to consciousness as ours and we believe we possess it to a greater or lesser degree. However, it is consciousness that possesses us and not the other way around. It does not reside within us; we reside within it. It is not a quality of our mind because it precedes the mind. Since it exists prior to thought, consciousness cannot be limited by mental concepts such as time or space. This is very clear in the Hebrew language: the word *olam* is synonymous with both space (*olam* is "world") and time (*le'olam* is "forever"). Moreover, *olam* is related to *he'almut*, or "disappearance." Thus, the world (*olam*), as we perceive it, is nothing but the disappearance (*he'almut*) of consciousness behind time and space. The word *olam* is in the Jewish prayer *Aleinu*, which according to tradition was composed by Joshua. This prayer glorifies God for allowing us to serve Him and says *letakken olam bemalchut shadai*, which means "to repair the world under divine sovereignty"; in other words, the world (*olam*) will become perfect when God is recognized and all idolatry disappears (*he'almut*).

Consciousness lies at the base and root of all experience and makes it possible to perceive objective reality. Hence without consciousness there is no experience, since both are one and the same.

In Sanskrit, experience is *anubhāva*. Our lives can be defined as *anubhāva-dhārā*, or a "flow of experiences": a long succession of various situations. Perceptions in this world of names and forms are experiences. We interact with a book, a tree, or a friend as if they were external objects, when in fact, they are merely our experiences. Even ourselves, as somebody called "I," is nothing more than another experience.

The ego is just the forgetfulness of our own nature, which is consciousness. Although consciousness is always here and now, our conditioning and habits lead us to ignore it. The Vedantic teachings guide us toward the recognition of it.

Consciousness is absolute stability, which perceives our own existence here and now. It is the stillness that remains unaffected by our constantly fluctuating moods, thoughts, and emotions. It remains indifferent to the succession of experiences that appear and disappear in space and time. It is the absolute presence that knows that we exist in the present.

Many spiritual seekers make the mistake of confusing enlightenment with a mystical experience. A divine or spiritual experience can be beautiful; however, just as any worldly experience, it is temporary. Any experience, whether divine or worldly, has a beginning and an end. Enlightenment is the experience of the permanent, of eternity. It is the infinite where all experiences take place.

When we perceive the objective world, we think that the senses are part of the subject that observes. However, if we see the mind as the subject, the senses become part of the objective world. Finally, if we observe the mind from the point of view of consciousness, we will discover that it is part of the object.

Your reality is the ultimate unmanifested subjectivity or pure consciousness, which is the authentic substantiality of both the thought and the thinker. Even if the observer and the observed switch roles, consciousness remains as the stable reality. Consciousness can assume different perspectives. For example, in the dream state, consciousness is both the dreamer and the objects in the dream. That is, consciousness creates a reality where it assumes the function of the subject and the object.

On the path toward recognizing itself, consciousness goes through different states of observation. The doctrine that deals with states of consciousness is called *catuṣpād*, or "the doctrine of four feet or parts." Earlier Upanishads mention three states: wakefulness (*jāgrat*), sleep with dreams (*svapna*), and deep sleep without dreams (*suṣupta*). At the time of the *Māṇḍūkya Upanishad*, a fourth state called *turīya*, or "the undifferentiated state," was added.

Consciousness experiences the world created in dreams as if it were real. In the waking state, it considers the world stored in memories to be true. In deep sleep, it experiences the state of the absence of dreams. However, consciousness is capable of observing reality itself, in which the observer is not different from what is observed. Meditation is directed at the existential experience of the most solid and stable aspect of reality.

During sleep, consciousness cannot be recognized because consciousness itself creates the dreamed reality and accepts it as true. Neither can it be recognized in wakefulness, since this state is a succession of recollections based on memory. However, the present is a cognitive state that is neither created nor evoked.

During the states of both dreaming and ordinary wakefulness, we recognize people and objects but not consciousness. Consciousness remains hidden behind apparent diversity. Our perception of the world depends on whether it is a mental creation, an evocation, or an event captured without mental intervention. The dream state is a mental creation and the waking state is a projection of memories; however, the present is a reality of facts. The now is the most conducive situation for self-realization or self-recognition. The present is the ideal cognitive state for the self-recognition of consciousness. By continuously establishing ourselves in the now, we perceive events while allowing the recognition of consciousness to happen.

Consciousness is not just a theory or a mere idea but a substantial reality that can be recognized and experienced.

When attention—the dynamic aspect of consciousness—settles on attention itself, what happens is "the consciencization of consciousness." Cognition no longer differentiates between the subject and object, even though both preserve their existence as the knower and the known.

Along with self-realization, we recognize that consciousness is no different from the object of perception. When consciousness recognizes itself and knows itself, we realize that it is the foundation of everything; moreover, only consciousness is. With this recognition, consciousness simultaneously perceives itself as both the subject and the object. This consciencization completely transforms our perspective of the world and life: reality adopts an undifferentiated character of simultaneity.

In order to experience this, one needs to meditate and turn the cognitive process toward cognition itself: place attention on attention, or to direct observation toward observation itself. These teachings are an invitation to recognize the ultimate subjectivity: our authentic nature.

Since attention is the dynamic aspect of consciousness, it is essential to cultivate meditative attention in order to recognize consciousness and become familiar with it. Meditation is relaxed wakefulness without the interference of the mind. To cultivate it, it is necessary—under the expert guidance of a realized spiritual master—to do exercises that can facilitate the revelation that everything is pure consciousness.

Consciousness always remains here and now regardless of what we feel or think, since it is at the foundation of every thought and emotion. It is the screen that our experiences are projected onto. It is the space where our emotions, thoughts, and ideas take place. Consciousness is the stable background against which experiences come and go, as they are born and die like waves in the ocean.

Every one of us can find that infinite stable space deep within and discover the permanent stability that is at the foundation of every experience. The only obstacle to recognizing consciousness is our conditioning.

Vedanta suggests we commit to constantly recognizing consciousness at the root of every experience through meditation, which reveals the stable presence of what always remains.

Chapter 18

Liberation or *mukti*

Mukti or *mokṣa* are Sanskrit terms that mean "emancipation or ultimate liberation." The word *mukti* comes from the root *muc*, which means "liberate, release, or emancipate." When the suffix *ktin* is added, it forms *mukti*, or "liberation." The prefix *vi* comes from the term *viśeṣa-rūpeṇa*, which means "with distinction, merit, excellence, or superiority"; thus, the terms *vimukti* and *vimokṣa* mean "final or ultimate liberation."

Eschatologically, *mukti* and *vimukti* refer to liberation from the cycle of repeated births and deaths, or *saṁsāra*. Epistemologically and psychologically, they mean freedom, self-realization, or self-knowledge.

mukti-śrī-nagarasya durjayataraṁ dvāraṁ yad astyād imaṁ
tasya dve arare dhanaṁ ca yuvatī tābhyāṁ pinaddhaṁ dṛḍham
kāmākhyārgala dāruṇā balavatā dvāraṁ tad-etat-trayam
dhīro yas tu bhinatti sorhati sukhaṁ bhoktuṁ vimukti-śriyaḥ

> However, there is another city: the sacred city of absolute freedom. There is a strong gate at the entrance to that city. Women and wealth are the two sides of the gate, while lust is like a powerful bar that locks it from the inside. But heroes make their way through this gate. Only they are ready to enjoy the bliss of final liberation.
>
> (*Sarva-vedānta-siddhānta-sāra-saṅgraha*, 90)

Defined negatively, liberation is the burning of all our karma. Defined positively, it is union with Brahman. According to Advaita Vedanta, the path that leads us to realize the unity of Brahman and *ātman* is called *jñāna-yoga*.

Since incarnate beings are unaware of their authenticity, they are motivated by egoism and are thus dragged into the slavery of *saṁsāra*. Liberation from this slavery is reached through the direct knowledge of reality, or Brahman. We access this revelation through study and understanding of the sacred scriptures under the proper guidance of an enlightened spiritual master. When we are blessed with liberation, we recognize that we are in fact consciousness.

While it is true that the term *liberation* hints at a supernatural achievement, in fact it is our original state of complete harmony with the Absolute. *Mukti* or *vimukti* is union with immeasurable eternity, the very essence of what we are. In enlightenment, what is temporal, relative, and limited discovers its origin in the eternal, absolute, and unlimited. It is the revelation of our reality, which transcends *nāma* and *rūpa*, or "name and form."

Just as we cannot lift ourselves up by pulling our belt, no active effort of a human being as an egoic phenomenon can lead to liberation. Clearly, no ego can go beyond itself.

Liberation is the immediate consequence of the realization of reality and not the effect of our actions, as *mīmāṁsakas* believe. *Sādhana* is meant to create the appropriate conditions, but enlightenment is not the result or byproduct of practice.

The path to liberation does not entail getting, reaching, acquiring, gaining, seizing, appropriating, or grabbing something we lack but going after a revelation. The spiritual process is not a series of systematic practices to satisfy needs. No spiritual effort should be carried out from a feeling of lack. Instead of acquiring what we do not have, we should try to discover what has always been. *Mukti* cannot be obtained because it is our authentic original nature, what we originally are. *Mukti* is simply being, without the intervention of the mind and its interpretations. The spiritual process is not about acquiring something but about getting rid of everything: our conclusions, concepts, ideas, prejudices, and in general, of our acquired conditioning. Enlightenment is not something we obtain but what remains after our ignorance vanishes.

The word "liberation" refers to the direct experience of our reality. But in fact, it does not involve freedom from anything tangible but from our acquired conditioning. It means ceasing to relate to life through a mental prism and stopping to project what is known upon reality.

Mukti is recognizing consciousness where every experience happens. It is an awakening to our reality as the origin of all that is. Consciousness is believed to be a personal and individual quality of the human being, separated from the universe. In this way, we create an illusory inner fracture called *ego*. Liberation is the recognition of consciousness as what we really are. When revelation happens, you realize yourself as the very essence of the phenomenal universe, as the unique nature that lies behind everything and everyone.

Fundamental conditioning consists in believing ourselves to be someone or something separate from the rest. Since we are integral parts of the Whole, this separation is illusory. Liberation is understanding that we are not disconnected from the universe. As long as I believe that I exist in time and space, I am limited by that idea and I lose my existence to become a simple mental creation. Freedom is transcending the idea that I am a person and accepting that I have no limits. Limits only exist as long as I consider myself someone, but nothing can limit nothingness.

Jīvan-mukta or "the one liberated in life"

jīvan-muktas tu tad vidvān
pūrvopādhi-guṇās tyajet
sac-cid-ānanda-rūpatvāt
bhaved bhramara-kīṭa-vat

Liberated ones, endowed with self-knowledge, give up the traits of their previously explained conditioning (*upādhis*) and because of their nature of *sac-cid-ānanda*, they truly become Brahman, like the worm that grows to be a bee.

(*Ātma-bodha*, 49)

nanu jīvan-muktaḥ kaḥ? yathā deho 'haṁ puruṣo 'haṁ brāhmaṇo 'haṁ śūdro 'ham asmīti dṛḍha-niścayas tathā nāhaṁ brāhmaṇaḥ na śūdraḥ na puruṣaḥ kintu asaṅgaḥ sac-cid-ānanda-svarūpaḥ prakāśa-rūpaḥ sarvāntaryāmī-cid-ākāśa-rūpo 'smīti dṛḍha-niścaya rūpo 'parokṣa-jñānavān jīvan-muktaḥ.

So who is a *jīvan-mukta*? Many have the conviction that 'I am a body, I am a man, I am a *brāhmaṇa*, or I am a *śūdra*.' But a *jīvan-mukta* has the firm belief and the direct experience that "I am not a *brāhmaṇa*, I am not a *śūdra*, I am not a man, I am detached, I am absolute existence–knowledge–bliss, I am effulgent, I am the inner dweller of everything, I am the formless awareness."

(*Tattva-bodha*, 11)

The *jīvan-mukta*, or "the being liberated while still in a physical body," lives in union with the Absolute. It is important to keep in mind that any description of the Absolute happens on the dual platform. Therefore, the means of description are from the relative plane, which obviously distorts a faithful description of direct experience. While words can point to the Truth, we must always remember that they cannot describe reality itself.

An enlightened person is rarely appreciated by those on the relative platform. Those who live every moment in the present are unpredictable. Therefore, it is impossible to generalize about the behavior of enlightened beings because they do not act condicioned by the past or what is known.

It would be difficult to recognize enlightened beings from the outside because they only differ from others on the inside. *Jīvan-muktas* remain in physical form even after their realization, simply out of compassion. They retain their physical form in order to guide human beings mired in ignorance and illusion. Śrī Śaṅkarācārya refers to these great *ācāryas* in his famous commentary on the *Chāndogya Upanishad*. He describes such great personalities in the following way:

> *parama-kāruṇikaṁ kañcit sad-brahmātma-vidaṁ*
> *vimukta-bandhana brahmiṣṭaṁ.*
>
> An extremely merciful person who is a knower of Sat-brahman or the Self, who is free from all bonds (*vimukta-bandhana*) and is devoted to Brahman.
>
> (Śaṅkarācārya, *Chāndogya Upanishad Bhāṣya* 6.14.2)

Kṛṣṇa also refers to sages who have seen the Truth and are able to impart knowledge:

tad viddhi praṇipātena
paripraśnena sevayā
upadekṣyanti te jñānaṁ
jñāninas tattva-darśinaḥ

Know that by approaching those who know through humble exploration and service, those who have seen Truth will teach you wisdom.

(Bhagavad Gita, 4.34)

There are three types of karma but only two of them are eradicated through knowledge. The first type is *sañcita-karma*, which is the accumulated karma that has not yet produced results or reactions. The second type is *āgāmi-karma*, which is the karma obtained in the present life with results that will manifest in the future. This karma cannot affect those who are liberated since they lack an ego; therefore, there is no personal agent that is trapped by such reactions. The third type of karma is called *prārabdha-karma* and it refers to karma that manifests the results of past actions in the present. This karma is also the source of the current body and therefore, it cannot be eliminated with knowledge and the results must manifest until the present body is abandoned.

Jīvan-muktas remain in physical forms and before abandoning their present body, they must inevitably experience the reactions of *prārabdha-karma*. But even within a physical body, *jīvan-muktas* are aware of their true identity as Brahman. Likewise, they know that their true nature cannot be really embodied, because the body is not real, since it is only a form and a name. The body and the world, like reflections in a mirror, lack substantiality. What drags us into the transmigratory process of repeated births and deaths is not the body but ignorance. The cause of slavery lies in not knowing our true nature and believing that we are a body. Enlightenment is the disappearance of ignorance, not the physical form. Thus, the recognition of our true nature as identical to Brahman does not conflict with embodied existence.

Enlightenment conflicts with the phenomenal experience but not with the presence of the phenomenal world. It is possible to awake to the recognition of consciousness without leaving the physical world. The proof is in the large number of master *ācāryas* of the past who achieved enlightenment during their lives. This state is especially accepted within the context of Advaita. Dualism, in general, refers to liberation as the enjoyment of an association with a personal God in a paradise after the abandonment of the physical body. For non-dual Vedanta, however, liberation in life is like salt dissolving in water. When dissolved in the Absolute, the human being ceases to have a separate existence from Brahman: both are one and the same. In *nirvikalpa-samādhi*, consciousness expands to become one with infinity. It is not a loss of our identity, but the realization of our true original identity.

Mumukṣu or "the ideal aspirant"

> *mumukṣutvaṁ kim? mokṣo me bhūyād iti dṛḍecchā.*
>
> What is *mumukṣutva*? It is the intense desire to achieve liberation.
>
> (*Tattva-bodha*, 1.4)

Mumukṣus are ideal aspirants who are completely sure that *mokṣa* is what they want in life. *Mumukṣutva* is the burning aspiration for Truth. It is an aspiration to realize the reality that far exceeds all other urges, ambitions, or desires. People have a large number of wishes. Those who have grasped the limitations of *artha*, *kāma*, and *dharma* do not strive for security, pleasure, and religiosity nor do they expect that these things will solve the essential problem. Only these people are in a position to undertake the search for liberation.

Mumukṣus have only one aspiration that eclipses all others. Such aspiration is the result of maturity and understanding that originate from inquiry, or *vicāra*. Of all the types of inquiry, the inquiry into our own authenticity is the highest one. *Vicāra* consists in questioning the true nature of what is observed. The desired answer is the silence that remains in the experience of fusion with absolute consciousness. It is an evolutionary process that goes from the identification with an objective world to a fusion with its source and origin. For this purpose, it is essential to intuit the possibility of objectless consciousness not as a quality of the person but as the basis and foundation of reality. Beliefs and dogmas are conditioning. What really matters is exploration, investigation, analysis, and questioning.

Śrī Śaṅkarācārya writes:

vairāgyaṁ ca mumuṣutvaṁ
tīvraṁ yasya tu vidyate
tasminn evārthavantaḥ syuḥ
phalavantaḥ śamādayaḥ

> Only if one's resignation and yearning for freedom are intense will tranquility and other practices really bear fruit.
>
> (*Viveka-cūḍāmaṇi*, 29)

If one is equipped with *viveka* (discernment), *vairāgya* (detachment), and *ṣaṭ-sampat* (the six virtues), the intense desire for liberation from repeated births and deaths will manifest. In fact, the desire for liberation is not about wanting to gain something. Rather, it is the aspiration to get rid of all selfish worldly longings. The true seeker of Truth is one who is aware of the fundamental problem. Those who lack intense aspiration will be unable to withstand temptations. This clarity reflects a very advanced level on the spiritual path. When starting on the path, most of us face difficulties, doubts, distractions, and obstacles. At times the path is clear, but at other times it becomes confusing and we stumble. It is only possible to advance with *mumukṣutva* and determination, patience, courage, detachment, faith, willpower, and joy. *Mumukṣus* evolve through yogic life relatively quickly because their direction is clear: the commitment to transcend ignorance and to achieve self-knowledge.

Truth is not a means

A spiritual search that is only about escaping pain and pursuing pleasure cannot lead us to real liberation. By running away from hell we will not reach God, because such an attitude will ruin every attempt.

If we see meditation as a means to escape the suffering of illusion and experience Truth, our focus will be on these achievements. Any action performed with a solution-oriented attitude lacks value: it becomes only a means focused on a reward or result.

What is the value of serving others if we do it only for the sake of enlightenment? What is the meaning of love that only seeks to obtain the position of a saint? Why meditate if we focus on the future outcome?

The yoga of action, or karma yoga, teaches us that God should not be sought through action, but in action itself. Truth is not revealed *through* service and meditation but *in* service and meditation. If one is meditatively attentive and situated in the present, Truth is revealed in every action and movement.

The motivation of the seeker

Motivation, or its absence, plays a key role in the effectiveness of our search. The term *motivation* comes from the Latin *motivus*, which means "the cause or reason for a movement," and is closely tied to willingness and interest. It is the stimulus that moves us to perform certain actions and stay until they are finished. Motivation is composed of mental factors that activate, direct, and maintain the behavior by directing it toward certain goals.

Every effort we make in life in pursuit of a goal requires a certain incentive external to the goal. However, the search for God should be free from any motivation. Reality simply is and it lacks any cause or support. Motivation implies an external goal, but nothing can be left out of totality. Reality is unmotivated since it does not have any external support. Most of humanity has a utilitarian attitude, but those who try to experience reality with this approach are on the wrong path. The search for Truth is more like a game than a business. Motivation is desire; consciousness is free from desires and is transcendental to these: the way to achieve consciousness is by emptying ourselves of desires.

A petty demand for Truth only gives rise to new doctrines. The result of a weak urge for reality is another philosophical theory. On the contrary, a sincere and honest thirst for Truth leads to a revealing vision that transcends thought and goes beyond it, to caress authenticity. Only a vital search can illuminate what is, as it is.

Epilogue

The acceptance of solitude

Besides informing and teaching us, *jñāna-yoga* is here to remind us of our eternal solitude. Although we try to escape it, we find it in all times and places. Even if we manage to hide from loneliness in the company of friends, a partner, children, and grandchildren or to cover it up with a career, position, fame, and money, in the end, we will discover that it is impossible to completely destroy, annihilate, or make it disappear.

There are those who have danced a lot without being fond of dancing and those who have sung for hours without any real interest in music. Many people have written books without liking literature, have painted without an inclination for art, or have studied intensively without a passion for knowledge. So many people have converted the most beautiful things of this world into cold currency used to buy a handful of attention. Moreover, so many have hugged without sincere feelings, ready to prostitute themselves for a moment of warmth.

We need sincerity to recognize if we are really interested in clothes, cars, jewelry, money, trees, flowers, romance, family, stars, or strolls along the seashore. It is brave to admit that life has never really interested us and we have not lived but have only used life as a means to buy the energy of others and escape from the anguish produced by that immense emptiness called *loneliness*. But we should not forget that to use life as a means to obtain something else is the worst business deal of all. We should never be tempted to use our life to buy something else. Whatever we are offered in return is an illusion since, apart from life, nothing exists.

To look for a partner, get married, create a family, have children, and dream of grandchildren is beautiful if what we look for is love. Yet it would be really awful to discover that we have converted other human beings into the ground where we have buried our loneliness. Authentic friendship can only bloom when we do not need it. True appreciation and love can manifest only if we do not need to utilize someone as a means to solve our own problems. To escape from solitude is to try to flee from that infinite void; it is to attempt to rip away the feeling of insecurity, of not belonging to anyone or any place in particular.

However, *jñāna-yoga* reminds us that solitude is what we are, our authenticity.

We come into and depart from this world surrounded by people but completely alone. We live on this planet with many people, our blood relatives, kith and kin, and our close friends, yet none of them is close enough to reach us where we really are and put an end to our loneliness. *Jñāna-yoga* proposes acceptance: accept yourself and you will be revealed in all your glory. Accept the solitude within and your true nature will be unveiled in its full splendor.

To accept solitude is to climb the last four rungs of the ladder to our reality: enlightenment, evolution, elevation, and emancipation.

The first step is enlightenment, or awakening to our authenticity.

manuṣyāṇāṁ sahasreṣu
kaścid yatati siddhaye
yatatām api siddhānāṁ
kaścin māṁ vetti tattvataḥ

> Out of thousands of humans, only one strives for perfection and out of those who strive for and have attained perfection, only one knows me in essence.
>
> (Bhagavad Gita, 7.3)

Only by becoming aware of our solitude will we attain the realization of the One without a second, *sac-cid-ānanda*, which is the Self.

Oṁ prajñānaṁ brahma

> *Oṁ*. Consciousness is Brahman.
>
> (*Aitereya Upanishad* of the *Ṛg Veda*, 3.3)

The second step is evolution, or the jump from what we think we are to what we really are.

Oṁ ahaṁ brahmāsmi

Oṁ. I am Brahman.
(*Bṛhad-āraṇyaka Upanishad* of the *Yajur Veda*, 1.4.10)

The third step is elevation, or the perception of our soul beyond our ideas, concepts, and conclusions.

Oṁ tat tvam asi

Oṁ. You are that.
(*Chāndogya Upanishad* of the *Sama Veda*, 6.8.7)

And the fourth step is emancipation or liberation, when God ceases to be *that* in order to be realized as *this*, what is closer to you than yourself.

Oṁ ayam ātmā brahma

Oṁ. The Self (Ātman) is Brahman.
(*Māṇḍūkya Upanishad* of the *Atharva Veda*, 1.2)

Only reality is

It is difficult to distinguish and appreciate the details when distance surpasses the limits of our visual capacity. Too much distance blurs our perception, but without any distance it is impossible to see. *Jñāna-yoga* teaches us that the obstacle to seeing God is of the latter type. With distance we can build airplanes, boats, or spaceships, but with extreme proximity, the situation becomes insolvable.

Neither God nor the Truth are distant. The problem is us and our difficulty in perceiving what is close and intimate.

There is no distance between the Truth and ourselves, because it is closer to us than even ourselves. The effort of the *jñānī* to realize the Self does not consist in overcoming distance but closeness, which, with its hypnotic capacity, transforms what is miraculous into obvious and what is mysterious into evident, wrapping it with the gray mist of vulgarity. This happens with situations, places, and persons. But the same happens with God, the Truth, existence, and finally, with ourselves.

Lost in the proximity of our horizon, what is ordinary tends to disappear. By ignoring what is obvious, we decrease its value and interest. Faced with the dilemma of closeness, nothing remains but the existential alternative of being.

Jñāna-yoga reminds us not to forget that there is no distance, that we are in fact what we are trying to find. Since we have forgotten this, we search far away, in the future, somewhere else: anywhere but where we really are. And we abandon the here, the now, and thus, reality. We expect something to happen, forgetting that God and life are undeniably happening now, and that nothing more extraordinary could ever occur.

In your illusion, you believe that something has concealed reality from you and you dream of finding it in the future. Never forget that what you discover that day will not have arisen in that moment; rather, it is already here and now. Observe yourself, because by observing you will discover that while though you are life and reality, you have been striving in vain to obtain it: you have been trying to reach existence while already being it.

The encounter with ourselves is only possible in the now. To renounce the ego is to renounce the past and to give up acting and reacting to yesterday. By asking "who am I?" we situate ourselves in the present moment.

Your authenticity is not found in some distant place. The Self is not a memory, a wish, or a hope. It is not a purpose or a goal to achieve. To be situated in the Self is to be settled in the here and now.

The past was the present only when we experienced it, and the future will be the present only when we will experience it. The experience of reality only takes place in the now. Yesterday and tomorrow are nothing but an illusion, a dream, a fantasy.

We live absent. Thus, the path of wisdom invites us to live in the present, which means living every moment with the profound realization that we can only remain in the now, that there is no alternative but to be in the present. Apart from this moment, there is nowhere else to go. To be present is to see that life is not our remembered past or our desired future: existence is just this precious moment, and apart from this moment, everything else is illusion.

This present cannot be categorized as time, because to be in the now is to leap out of the scale of time into timelessness. If we are present every moment of our life, we do not have to wait for physical death to reach eternity.

Appendix

The life and work of Śrī Śaṅkarācārya

Ādi Śaṅkara (788–820 CE) is considered to be one of the greatest luminaries of Hinduism. At the age of twelve, he was granted the title of respect *ācārya* and from that point on he was called Śaṅkarācārya.

Without a doubt, he is the greatest exponent of Advaita. Faced with the challenges that Buddhism presented to Hinduism in his time, Śaṅkara reorganized and adapted the Vedic tradition. He reaffirmed the foundations of Upanishadic monism and included deity worship as a means to access the realization of ultimate formless reality.

There are fourteen biographies of Śaṅkarācārya. Of these, the oldest is Citsukha's *Bṛhat-śaṅkara-vijaya*, but only parts of it have been preserved. The oldest and most reliable complete biography is Mādhava's *Mādhavīya Śaṅkara-vijaya* or *Śaṅkara-dig-vijaya*. Its authority is largely based on the fame of its author, Vidyāraṇya Svāmī from Śṛṅgerī. The *Mādhavīya* has two commentaries: the

Advaita-rājya-lakṣmī (1824 CE) by Achyutarāya Moḍaka and the *Ḍiṇḍimā* (1978 CE) by Dhanapati Sūri.

Ānandagiri's *Śaṅkara-vijaya* is not trustworthy or credible. Although the author's name is Ānandagiri, it does not seem to be the same Ānandagiri who lived in the thirteenth century CE and wrote famous commentaries (*ṭīkās*) on Śaṅkarācārya's writings. Most of the manuscripts are incomplete and some appear to have been tampered with. In addition, there are numerous inconsistencies and disagreements.

There are two other important biographies, the *Cidvilāsīya Śaṅkara-vijaya* by Cidvilāsa (fifteenth to seventeenth centuries CE) and the *Keralīya Śaṅkara-vijaya* (seventeenth century CE). The rest of the biographies were written centuries after Śaṅkara's disappearance. They include legends and stories about him that sometimes contradict each other. The *Śaṅkara-dig-vijaya* by Mādhavācārya or Vidyāraṇya Svāmī, as well as other biographies, refers to Śaṅkara as an incarnation of Śiva who descended to Earth to neutralize Buddhism, counter dualism, and restore the original Vedic tradition.

Parents and birth

The *Śaṅkara-dig-vijaya* describes the birth of Śaṅkara as follows:

ajñānāntar-gahana-patitān ātma-vidyopadeśais
trātuṁ lokān bhava-dava-śikhā-tāpa-pāpacyamānān
muktvā maunaṁ vaṭa-viṭapino mūlato niṣpatantī
śambhor mūrtiś carati bhuvane śaṅkarācārya-rūpā

> Lord Dakṣiṇāmurti (Śiva), who was sitting under a Banyan tree, who is the master of the supreme Truth through silence, abandoned his place of meditation. He now moves in the form of Śaṅkarācārya, imparting his precious and knowledgeable advice to the people of the world, who have been trapped in the dense and endless forests of ignorance and are seriously threatened by the approaching forest fire of family bonds.
>
> (*Śaṅkara-dig-vijaya*, 4.60)

He was born into a family of *brāhmaṇas* in a town called Kālaḍi on the banks of the Pūrṇa River, six miles east of Alwaye in southern India. Today the river is known as the Periyār River in Kerala.

Śaṅkara's grandfather Vidyādhirāja worshipped Lord Śiva in a temple in Kālaḍi. His son, named Śivaguru, married Āryāmbā, who, like her family, belonged to the Nambūdiri *Brāhmaṇa* caste. Both worshipped Lord Śiva daily and asked for children. The couple went on a pilgrimage to Thrissur where they performed a *pūjā* to Lord Vadakkunathan (Śiva) for forty-eight days. Satisfied with their devotion, he promised to manifest as their son. Āryāmbā became pregnant, but before she gave birth, the Lord appeared to them again and asked if they preferred several ordinary children with long lives or only one brilliant and extraordinary son with a short life. The couple chose the latter, preferring quality over quantity. One afternoon in the spring, at the auspicious moment of *abhijit-muhūrta* under the constellation of Ārdra, Ādi Śaṅkara was born.

When Śaṅkara was seven, his father died and the full responsibility of raising the child fell on the young mother. In the same year, the *upanāyana* ceremony was performed, and the little Śaṅkara received his sacred thread. The pious Āryāmbā took care of her son's education, ensuring that he would be instructed in the sacred scriptures. From his earliest childhood, Śaṅkara showed a supernatural intelligence, completing his studies in just a few years.

His faith and devotion were evident from the very beginning of his intense life, which was full of supernatural events. When he was a young *brahmacārī*, he went to the house of a woman who lived in poverty to ask for alms. When she opened the door and saw the saint, her heart was filled with devotion. However, she had no food to offer and gave him the only dry *āmalaka* fruit left in the house. Śaṅkara was so moved by the woman's devotion that he composed a hymn on the spot to the goddess Lakṣmī called *Kanaka-dhārā Stotra* (the stream of gold hymn), pleading for relief in the home.

dadyād dayānupavano draviṇāmbu-dhārām
asmin na kiñcana-vihaṅga-śiśau viṣaṇṇe
duṣkarma gharmam apanīya cirāya dūraṁ
nārāyaṇa-praṇayinī nayanāmbu-vāhaḥ

May goddess Lakṣmī bestow (upon us) a stream of wealth through the wind of

> her mercy, for I, utterly destitute and discouraged by poverty, am as helpless as a bird's newborn chick. May the goddess Lakṣmī remove the suffering caused by past sins, O, beloved of Nārāyaṇa, may your eyes rain upon me (the shower of your mercy).
>
> (*Kanaka-dhārā Stotra*, 9)

Lakṣmī heard Śaṅkara's hymn and immediately poured a shower of gold *āmalakas* (gooseberries) on the poor woman's house.

The renounced order of life or *sannyāsī*

Śaṅkara's aspirations were in conflict with his mother's wishes. Āryāmbā wanted to see her beloved son become a family man. But even as a child, he wished to completely devote himself to a spiritual life. Śaṅkara's aspiration was not to marry but to live as a monk. His mother was worried that there would be no one to perform the funeral rites on the day of her death. Śaṅkara solemnly promised her that he himself would take care of her funeral when her time came. Nevertheless, Āryāmbā refused to grant her consent. Once, when they were standing on the bank of a river, a fierce crocodile grabbed Śaṅkara by the leg and tried to drag him into the river. "Dear mother," the boy shouted, "a crocodile is dragging me into the river. At least let me die as a *sannyāsī*: grant me your permission to accept the renounced order of life!" The scared mother granted his last wish and gave her consent. As soon as he received her permission, a miracle happened: the crocodile released him without causing any harm. Thus, Śaṅkara mentally assumed the *sannyāsī* order.

The mother was so happy to see her child safe and sound that she completely forgot she had given her permission. Śaṅkara, however, reminded her that from now on his family was all of humanity, and his home was no longer Kālaḍi but the entire universe. Śaṅkara made all the necessary arrangements to leave his mother in the care of his family and left them the small property he had. He again promised his mother that when the time came, he would take care of her funeral. Having said goodbye to his mother and relatives, he left the comfort of his home in search for a spiritual master.

tasmāt sva-mātur api bhakti-vaśād anujñām
ādāya saṁsṛti-māhābdhi-viraktimān saḥ
gantuṁ mano vyadhita sannyasanāya dūraṁ
kiṁ nau-sthitaḥ patitum icchati vāri-rāsau

Śrī Śaṅkara, out of devotion, took leave from his mother and Lord Kṛṣṇa. Being very detached from the world and anxious to renounce everything, he wanted to go far away and be ritually initiated as an ascetic. When there is a boat available for transport, no one falls into the sea. Similarly, people who have firm a belief in renunciation do not fall into the sea of worldly life.

(*Śaṅkara-dig-vijaya*, 5.80)

In search of his spiritual master

Śaṅkara knew that the great master Govindapāda, a disciple of Gauḍapāda, resided to the north, on the banks of the Narmadā River. After two months of traveling through jungles, villages, and forests, he finally arrived at a cave where Govindapāda was meditating. The aspiring disciple entered the cave and began to sing hymns in glory of the guru. Hearing the singing, the saint stopped meditating and asked the boy who he was. In response, Śaṅkara recited the ten verses known as *Daśa-ślokī*, in which the true nature of the ultimate reality is explained:

atha daśa-ślokī

Here comes *daśa-ślokī*, a hymn of ten verses about liberation.

na bhūmir na toyaṁ na tejo na vāyuḥ
na khaṁ nendriyaṁ vā na teṣāṁ samūhaḥ
anekāntikatvāt suṣupty eka-siddaḥ
tad eko 'vaśiṣṭaḥ śivaḥ kevalo 'ham

I am neither earth nor water, nor fire nor air nor space. I am none of the faculties nor I am a combination of them. However, I can be proven solely in the experience of deep sleep. I am the One that remains, auspicious and pure.

na varṇā na varṇāśramācāra-dharmā
na me dhāraṇādhyānayogādayopi
anātmāśrayāhaṁ-mamādhyāsa-hānāt
tad eko 'vaśiṣṭaḥ śivaḥ kevalo 'ham

There are no castes (*vārṇas*) in me, nor observances nor duties for the stages of life (*varṇāśrama*). There is no concentration, meditation, or yoga in me. The mistaken meanings of "I" and "mine" lay in the non-Self should be abandoned. I am the One that remains, auspicious and pure.

na mātā pitā vā na devā na lokā
na vedā na yajñā na tīrthaṁ bruvanti
suṣuptau nirastātiśūnyātmakatvāt
tad eko 'vaśiṣṭaḥ śivaḥ kevalo 'ham

The sages say there is no mother nor father, nor gods nor areas of experience, nor the Vedas nor sacrificial sites, nor any sacred places. Because in the state of deep sleep, all these are negated by the experience of complete void. I am the One that remains, auspicious and pure.

na sāṅkhyaṁ na śaivaṁ na tat pāñca-rātraṁ
na jainaṁ na mīmāṁsakāder mataṁ vā
viśiṣṭānubhūtyā viśuddhātmakatvāt
tad eko 'vaśiṣṭaḥ śivaḥ kevalo 'ham

I do not follow *Sāṅkhya* or *Śaiva* philosophy. I do not follow *Pāñca-rātra* or *Jaina* or *Mīmāmsa* philosophy. I am that distinct knowledge that is absolutely pure. I am the One that remains, auspicious and pure.

na cordhvaṁ na cādho na cāntarna bāhyaṁ
na madhyaṁ na tiryaṅ na pūrvā 'parā dik
viyad vyāpakatvād akhaṇḍaika-rūpaḥ
tad eko 'vaśiṣṭaḥ śivaḥ kevalo 'ham

There is nothing above or below me. There is nothing inside or outside of me. There is nothing in me or through me. There is no east or any other direction in me. All-pervasive, I have an undivided form. I am the One that remains, auspicious and pure.

na śuklaṁ na kṛṣṇaṁ na raktaṁ na pītaṁ
na kubjaṁ na pīnaṁ na hrasvaṁ na dīrgham
arūpaṁ tathā jyotir ākārakatvāt
tad eko 'vaśiṣṭaḥ śivaḥ kevalo 'ham

I am not ruled by anyone. There is no scripture for me. I do not have any disciples. I do not have any instructions. There are no distinctions between 'you' and 'I', and there is no world for me. The knowledge of one's true Self does not admit of different perceptions. I am the One that remains, auspicious and pure.

na śāstā na śāstraṁ na śiṣyo na śikśā
na ca tvaṁ na cāhaṁ na cāyaṁ prapañcaḥ
svarūpāvabodho vikalpāsahiṣṇuḥ
tad eko 'vaśiṣṭaḥ śivaḥ kevalo 'ham

I am not ruled by anyone. There is no scripture for me. I do not have any disciples. I do not have any instructions. There are no distinctions between 'you' and 'I', and this world is my true self. I am the One without a second, I am knowledge itself. I am the One that remains, auspicious and pure.

na jāgran na me svapnako vā suṣuptiḥ
na viśvo na vā taijasaḥ prājñako vā
avidyātmakatvāt trayāṇaṁ turīyaḥ
tad eko 'vaśiṣṭaḥ śivaḥ kevalo 'ham

There is no state of wakefulness, nor dreaming nor deep sleep. I am not the Lord of waking (*Viśva*) nor dreams (*Taijasaḥ*) nor deep sleep (*Prājña*). These states appear in me out of ignorance but I am *Turīya*, who is beyond these three states and their lords. I am the One that remains, auspicious and pure.

api vyāpakatvāt hitatva-prayogāt
svataḥ siddha-bhāvād ananyāśrayatvāt
jagat tuccham etat samastaṁ tad anyat
tad eko 'vaśiṣṭaḥ śivaḥ kevalo 'ham

> Benevolent, the desired goal, self-evident, dependent on nothing external, this world and everything else is worthless in comparison to it [to the Self].. I am the One that remains, auspicious and pure.

na caikaṁ tad anyad dvitīyaṁ kutaḥ syāt
na kevalatvaṁ na cākevalatvam
na śūnyaṁ na cāśūnyam advaitakatvāt
kathaṁ sarva-vedānta-siddhaṁ bravīmi

> How can one be when there is no second? There is neither oneness nor lack of oneness. It is neither a void nor a non-void. Since there is not a second entity, how can I even speak about that, which is the essence of the entire Vedanta?

iti śrimac chaṅkarācārya-viracitaṁ daśa-ślokī samāptaṁ

> Thus concludes the splendid *Daśa-ślokī* composed by Śaṅkarācārya.

Govindapāda was very pleased with the excellent expression of Vedanta coming from the lips of such a young aspirant and Śaṅkara was accepted as a disciple. He stayed with his guru for three years, was instructed in the sacred scriptures, and practiced the prescribed *sādhana*. As an exemplary disciple, he was formally initiated and instructed in the deep meanings of the *mahā-vākyas*.

One day, the Narmadā River overflowed, threatening to flood the surrounding villages and sweep away the houses and their inhabitants. When Śaṅkara saw that the cave where his guru was meditating was about to be flooded, he recited the *jalākaraṣaṇa* mantra and put his water vessel at the entrance of the cave. As soon as the torrent reached the vessel, it stopped and began to recede. In a few minutes, the river returned to its normal course, saving the population from imminent disaster.

Kashi

Govindapāda sent Śaṅkarācārya to Kashi, today called Benares, to expound the meaning of the *Vedānta Sūtra*, the Bhagavad Gita, and the Upanishads for the benefit of the general public. He also ordered him to write a commentary on the *Viṣṇu-sahasra-nāma*. Then Govindāpada went into a deep meditation, left his body, and entered *mahā-samādhi*.

Faithfully fulfilling his guru's instructions, Śaṅkara set out on his journey and in time arrived at the city of Kāśi, an important center for such studies. There he settled near the temple of Viśvanātha, dedicating himself to meditation and teaching Vedanta. Some of the people who attended his lessons asked for initiation and stayed to live with him. The first to become his disciple was Viṣṇuśarma, a boy from Chola-desa in southern India who received the spiritual name Sānanda. As time went by, some of the disciples began to complain that Śaṅkara had an unjustified preference for Sānanda. They could not understand why Śaṅkara treated him differently, so the master decided to reveal his disciple's holiness. One day, Śaṅkara was bathing in the sacred Ganga with some disciples. He saw Sānanda on the other shore and called him. To everyone's amazement, Sānanda stepped on the water without any hesitation and walked across the river. With every step he took, a lotus flower appeared to keep him above the water. This is how he came to be called Pādmapāda (lotus feet).

One day, as Śaṅkara was returning from his daily ritual bath in the Ganges, he encountered a *caṇḍāla* (untouchable) and had four dogs that were blocking his path. The master politely asked the *caṇḍāla* to get out of the way and allow him to pass. To his surprise, the man asked what should get out of the way and of what. The *caṇḍāla* said: "O venerated saint! You teach that the Absolute resides in every place since it is omnipresent; however, you treat me as if I were something different from you. Do you want to separate the consciousness that is in this body from that which lies in that one? Is there any difference between the sun reflected in the Ganges and the sun reflected in a puddle in the *caṇḍāla* neighborhood?"

The great *ācārya* immediately recognized his mistake, for the omnipresent Absolute resides in everything and everyone and the lowest in society is also Brahman. Inspired by this encounter, Śaṅkara composed the *Manīṣā-pañcaka* and bowed down at the untouchable's feet.

jāgrat svapna suṣuptiṣu sphuṭatarā yā saṁvid ujjṛimbhate
yā brahmādi pipīlikānta-tanuṣu protā jagat-sākṣiṇī
saivāhaṁ na ca dṛśya-vastviti dṛḍha-prajñā 'pi yasyāsti cet
cāṇḍālo 'stu sa tu dvijo 'tu gurur ity eṣā manīṣā mama

> If someone has attained the firm knowledge that he or she is not an object of perception, but pure consciousness that shines clearly in the states of waking, dream, and deep sleep, and that, as the witness of the whole universe, dwells in all bodies from the body of the creator Brahmā to the body of the ant, then he is my guru, irrespective of whether he is an outcast or a *brāhmaṇa*. This is my conviction.
>
> (*Manīṣā-pañcaka,* 1)

Then the *caṇḍāla* vanished, transforming himself into Lord Śiva. The Lord blessed him and ordered him to eliminate superstition and reestablish religion by writing commentaries on the sacred scriptures and sharing the message with all mankind.

Another day, while walking down the street, Śaṅkara heard the voice of an old scholar teaching Sanskrit grammar. Full of compassion, he approached the old man and lovingly told him that instead of wasting his valuable time and energy with Sanskrit grammar, at his age he should worship God. This encounter inspired him to compose a twelve-verse hymn called the *Bhaja-govinda,* also known as *Dvā-daśa-mañjarīka-stotra,* or "a hymn of twelve verses." It can be also interpreted that these verses glorify his master Govindapāda. Each of the fourteen disciples that were with Śaṅkara on that occasion added one verse each. These fourteen additional verses are collectively called *Catur-daśa-mañjarīka-stotra,* or "a hymn of fourteen verses" and are highly respected in Advaita literature.

(1)

bhaja govindaṁ bhaja govindaṁ
govindaṁ bhaja mūḍha-mate
samprāpte sannihite kāle
na hi na hi rakṣati ḍukṛṅ karaṇe

Revere Govinda, worship Govinda, adore Govinda. O fool! The rules of grammar will not save you at the time of your death.

(2)

mūḍha jahīhi dhanāgama-tṛṣṇāṁ
kuru sad-buddhiṁ manasi vitṛṣṇām
yal labhase nija-karmopāttaṁ
vittaṁ tena vinodaya cittam

O fool! Give up your thirst for wealth and devote your mind to thoughts about what is real. Be content with what comes from past actions.

(3)

nārī-stana-bhara-nābhī-deśaṁ
dṛṣṭvā mā gā mohāveśam
etan māṁsa-vasādi-vikāraṁ
manasi vicintaya vāraṁ vāram

Do not drown in illusion, wildly chasing the passions and lust aroused by seeing a woman's navel and breasts. These are nothing but a modification of flesh, fat, and blood. Be sure to think of this again and again in your mind.

(4)

nalinī-dala-gata-jalam ati-taralaṁ
tad vaj jīvitam atiśaya-capalam
viddhi vyādhy abhimāna-grastaṁ
lokaṁ śoka-hataṁ ca samastam

The life of persona is as uncertain as a raindrop trembling on a lotus leaf. Know that the whole world remains prey to disease, ego, and grief.

(5)

yāvad vittopārjana-saktas
tāvan nija-parivāro raktaḥ
paścāj jīvati jarjara dehe
vārtāṁ ko 'pi na pṛcchati gehe

As long as a man is healthy and able to support his family, everyone around him is affectionate. But once his body trembles from old age, not even those in his own house bother talking to him.

(6)
yāvat pavano nivasati dehe
tāvat pṛcchati kuśalaṁ gehe
gatavati vāyau dehāpāye
bhāryā bibhyati tasmin kāye

When he is alive, his family members kindly inquire about his well-being. But when his soul departs his body, even his wife flees out of fear of the corpse.

(7)
bālas tāvat krīḍā-saktaḥ
taruṇas tāvat taruṇī-saktaḥ
vṛddhas tāvac cintā-saktaḥ
parame brahmaṇi ko 'pi na saktaḥ

Childhood is lost because of attachment to playfulness. Youth is lost because of attachment to women. Old age leaves us lost in thoughts of the past. Hardly anyone wants to get lost in Para-brahman.

(8)
kā te kāntā kas te putraḥ
saṁsāro 'yam atīva vicitraḥ
kasya tvaṁ kaḥ kuta āyātas
tattvaṁ cintaya tad iha bhrātaḥ

Who is your wife? Who is your son? Strange is this *saṁsāra* (world). Do you belong to someone? Where do you come from? Brother, reflect on these truths.

(9)

sat-saṅgatve nissaṅgatvaṁ
nissaṅgatve nirmohatvam
nirmohatve niścala-tattvaṁ
niścala-tattve jīvan-muktiḥ

From *sat-saṅga* (association with the Truth) comes detachment; from detachment comes freedom from deception, which leads to inner stability. From inner stability comes liberation while living (*jīvan-mukti*).

(10)

vayasi gate kaḥ kāma-vikāraḥ
śuṣke nīre kaḥ kāsāraḥ
kṣīṇe vitte kaḥ parivāraḥ
jñāte tattve kaḥ saṁsāraḥ

What is lust when youth is over? What is a lake with no water? Where is the family when wealth is gone? Where is *saṁsāra* (the continuation of birth and death) when the Truth is known?

(11)

mā kuru dhana-jana-yauvana-garvaṁ
harati nimeṣāt kālaḥ sarvam

māyā-mayam idam akhilaṁ hitvā var budhvā
brahma-padaṁ tvaṁ praviśa viditvā

Do not show off wealth, friends, or youth. They can all be destroyed in a minute. Having known that all this is illusionary, free yourself from the world of *māyā* and attain the timeless Truth.

(12)
dina-yāminyau sāyaṁ prātaḥ
śiśira-vasantau antau punar āyātaḥ
kālaḥ krīḍati gacchaty āyus
tad api na muñcaty āśā-vāyuḥ

Daylight and darkness, dusk and dawn, winter and spring come and go. Time dances and life wanes. But the storm of desire never goes away.

(13)
kā te kāntā dhana-gata-cintā
vātula kiṁ tava nāsti niynatā
tri-jagati saj-jana-saṅgatir ekā
bhavati bhavārṇava-taraṇe naukā

O mad man! Why this engrossment in thoughts of wealth? Is there no one to guide you? The association with wise people (*sat-jana-saṅga*) is the only thing in the three worlds that can serve you as a boat to quickly cross the sea of birth and death (*saṁsāra*).

(13a)

dvādaśa-mañjarikābhir aśeṣaḥ
kathito vaiyākaraṇasyaiṣaḥ
upadeśo 'bhūd vidyā-nipuṇaiḥ
śrīmac-chaṅkara-bhagavac-charaṇaiḥ

This bouquet of twelve verses (2–13) was imparted to a grammarian by Śaṅkara who knows everything, adored as Bhagavatpāda.

The following verse is attributed to Padmapāda:

(14)

jaṭilo muṇḍī luñchita-keśaḥ
kāṣāyāmbara-bahu-kṛta-veṣaḥ
paśyann api ca na paśyati mūḍho
hy udara-nimittaṁ bahu-kṛta-veṣaḥ

Many have matted hair and others have clean and shaven heads. Many have had their haired pulled out. Some wear saffron clothes and and adorn themselves with various other things. All that just to make a living. Even when the Truth is revealed right in front of them, fools cannot see it.

The following verse is attributed to Toṭācārya:

(15)
aṅgaṁ galitaṁ palitaṁ muṇḍaṁ
daśana-vihīnaṁ jātaṁ tuṇḍam
vṛddho yāti gṛhītvā daṇḍaṁ
tad api na muñcaty āśā-piṇḍam

Strength has left the old man's body. His head has gone bald, his gums are toothless and he walks with the help of a stick. Even in this state, he still is not free of his mountain of desires.

The following verse is attributed to Hastāmalaka:

(16)
agre vahniḥ pṛṣṭhe bhānuḥ
rātrau cubuka-samarpita-jānuḥ
kara-tala-bhikṣas taru-tala-vāsas
tad api na muñcaty āśā-pāśaḥ

Behold, here we have a man who warms his front with a fire and his back with the sun. At night, he curls up to stay warm. He receives alms in his hand and sleeps under a tree. Even living like this, he is still not free of the bonds of desire.

The following verse is attributed to Subodha:

(17)
kurute gaṅgā-sāgara-gamanaṁ
vrata-paripālanam athavā dānam
jñāna-vihīnaḥ sarva-matena
muktiṁ na bhajati janma-śatena

One can go on a pilgrimage to Gangā-sāgara (the holy place where the Ganges joins the sea), fast, or donate riches for charity! But if you lack wisdom (*jñāna)*, you will not experience *mukti*, even after a hundred births.

The following verse is attributed to Vārttikakāra (Sureśvara):

(18)
sura-mandira-taru-mūla-nivāsaḥ
śayyā-bhūtalam ajinaṁ-vāsaḥ
sarva-parigraha-bhoga-tyāgaḥ
kasya sukhaṁ na karoti virāgaḥ

Live in temples or under a tree, sleep on the ground, and dress yourself with a deer skin. Renounce all attachments and enjoyment. Who wouldn't be happy with such detachment?

The following verse is attributed to Nitānanda:

(19)
yoga-rato vā bhoga-rato vā
saṅga-rato vā saṅga-vihīnaḥ
yasya brahmaṇi ramate cittaṁ
nandati nandati nandaty eva

Let one delight in yoga or in sensory pleasure. One can be attached or detached. But only one whose mind delights in Brahman is happy, certainly happy.

The following verse is attributed to Ānandagiri:

(20)
bhagavad-gītā kiñcid adhītā
gaṅgā-jala-lava-kaṇikā pītā
sakṛd api yena murāri samarcā
kriyate tasya yamena na carcā

Reading a little of the Bhagavad Gita, drinking only a drop of water from the Ganges, worshipping Murāri (Kṛṣṇa) only once. One who does this will have no discussion with Yama (the lord of death).

The following verse is attributed to Dṛḍhabhakti:

(21)
punar api jananaṁ punar api maraṇaṁ
punar api jananī jaṭhare śayanam

iha saṁsāre bahu-dustāre
kṛpayā 'pāre pāhi murāre

Being born again, dying again, and returning to a mother's womb. This *saṁsāra* is very difficult to cross. O Murāri! Save me through your mercy.

The following verse is attributed to Nityanātha:

(22)
rathyā car paṭa-viracita-kanthaḥ
puṇyāpuṇya-vivarjita-panthaḥ
yogī yoga-niyojita citto
ramate bālonmattavad eva

There is no shortage of clothes for a monk as long as there are discarded rags in the street. Freed from vice and virtue, the monk wanders. This yogi, who lives in communion with God, enjoys pure and uncontaminated happiness, like a child or an intoxicated person.

The following verse is attributed to Yogānanda:

(23)
kas tvaṁ ko 'haṁ kuta āyātaḥ
kā me jananī ko me tātaḥ
iti paribhāvaya sarvam asāram
viśvaṁ tyaktvā svapna-vicāram

Who you are? Who am I? Whence do I come? Who is my mother? Who is my father? Meditating thus, see that everything lacks essence and leave this world as if it were a vain dream.

The following verse is attributed to Surendra:

(24)
tvayi mayi cānyatraiko viṣṇuḥ
vyarthaṁ kupyasi mayyasahiṣṇuḥ
bhava sama-cittaḥ sarvatra tvaṁ
vāñchasy acirād yadi viṣṇutvam

Viṣṇu is the only one who dwells in me, in you, and everywhere. Your anger and impatience make no sense. If you are in equanimity (*samabhāva*) in all situations, you will soon attain the quality of Viṣṇu.

The following verse is attributed to Medhātithira:

(25)
śatrau mitre putre bandhau
mā kuru yatnaṁ vigraha-sandhau
sarvasminn api paśyātmānaṁ
sarvatrotsṛja bhedājñānam

Do not waste your efforts on winning someone's love or arguing against enemies, friends, children, or relatives. See yourself in everyone and give up completely all feelings of differences.

The following verse is attributed to Bhārativaṁśa:

(26)
kāmaṁ krodhaṁ lobhaṁ mohaṁ
tyaktvā 'tmānaṁ bhāvaya ko 'ham
ātma-jñāna-vihīnā mūḍhāḥ
te pacyante naraka-nigūḍhāḥ

Renounce lust, anger, greed, and delusion and reflect on your true nature. Fools are devoid of self-knowledge (*ātma-jñāna*). They are being burned in a hidden hell.

The following verse is attributed to Sumati:

(27)
geyaṁ gītā nāma-sahasraṁ
dhyeyaṁ śrī-pati rūpam ajasram
neyaṁ saj-jana saṅge cittaṁ
deyaṁ dīna-janāya ca vittam

Recite the Bhagavad Gita and the *Viṣṇu-sahasra-nāma* regularly, meditate on Viṣṇu in your heart, and sing his thousand glories. Rejoice in being with noble and holy people and distribute your wealth in charity among the poor and the needy.

The following verse is attributed to Sumati:

(28)
sukhataḥ kriyate rāmā-bhogaḥ
paścād dhanta śarīre rogaḥ
yady api loke maraṇaṁ śaraṇaṁ
tad api na muñcati pāpācaraṇam

One who gives in to lust for pleasure leaves the body in the grip of disease. Even though death puts an end to everything in the world, human beings do not abandon the sinful path.

(29)
artham anarthaṁ bhāvaya nityaṁ
nāsti tataḥ sukha-leśaḥ satyam
putrād api dhana bhājāṁ bhītiḥ
sarvatraiṣā vihitā rītiḥ

Wealth offers no advantage. This should be reflected upon always. There is no joy in it, this is the reality. Rich people fear even their own children. This is the path of wealth everywhere.

(30)
prāṇāyāmaṁ praty āhāraṁ
nityānitya viveka-vicāram
jāpya sameta samādhi-vidhānaṁ
kurvavadhānaṁ mahad-avadhānam

Regulate the vital airs (*prāṇāyāma*) and withdraw the senses (*pratyāhāra*), discern between real and unreal (*nityānitya viveka*), silence the turbulent mind by singing the holy names of God. Perform all these with great care.

(31)

guru-caraṇāmbuja-nirbhara-bhakataḥ
saṁsārād acirād bhava muktaḥ
sendriya-mānasa niyamād evaṁ
drakṣyasi nija hṛdaya-sthaṁ devam

Being completely devoted to the lotus feet of the guru, you may soon be free from *saṁsāra*. Through disciplined senses and a controlled mind, you will see the Lord that resides in your heart!

(32)

mūḍhaḥ kaścana vaiyākaraṇo
ḍuḥkṛṅ-karaṇādhyayana-dhurīṇaḥ
śrīmacchaṅkara-bhagavac-chiṣyair
bodhita āsīc chodhita-karaṇaḥ

This is how a silly grammarian with a narrow vision, who was lost in the study of grammar rules, was purified and exposed to the light by the disciples of Śaṅkara.

(33)
bhaja govindaṁ bhaja govindaṁ
govindaṁ bhaja mūḍha-mate
nāma-smaraṇādanyam upāyaṁ
nahi paśyāmo bhava-taraṇe

Worship Govinda! Worship Govinda! Worship Govinda! O fool! There is no other way to cross the ocean of life than to sing the names of the Lord.

iti śrimac-chaṅkarācārya-viracitaṁ
bhaja-govindaṁ sampūrṇam

Thus concludes the entire *Bhaja-govinda* hymn composed by Śrī Śaṅkarācārya.

Badrikāśram

After the encounter with the grammar scholar, Śaṅkara decided to retire to Badrikāśram (the Badrināth area) in the Himālayas and devote himself to writing commentaries on the scriptures. On the way to Badrikāśram, he and his disciples passed through several kingdoms, including the capital city Jyotirdhām, where he was respectfully welcomed by the king. He stayed in Badrikāśram for four years. It was there that Śaṅkara rescued and reinstalled the deity of Lord Nārāyaṇa of Nārada Kuṇḍa that had been thrown in the Alakanandā River by Buddhist priests. Here, at the age of sixteen, he wrote commentaries on the *Viṣṇu-sahasra-nāma*, the *Prasthāna-trayī* (Upanishads, *Vedānta Sūtra,* and Bhagavad Gita), and the *Sanāt-sujātīya* (a philosophical section of the *Mahābhārata*). These commentaries are of great importance because they establish the basis and foundations of Advaita Vedanta. Śaṅkara wrote profusely and he also continued to teach Vedanta to both his disciples and the general public.

The great sage Vyāsa visited Śaṅkara, disguised as an old man, and challenged him to debate and defend his teachings of non-duality.

The intense debate between them lasted four days. It was interrupted only by the intervention of Pādmapāda, who declared that as long as Śiva and Viṣṇu were arguing, there could be no peace in the world. When Vyāsa realized that his true identity had been discovered, he blessed Śaṅkara and granted him sixteen additional years of life. Finally, he expressed his desire to see him spreading his non-dual message throughout India.

Kumārila Bhaṭṭa

Kumārila Bhaṭṭa was a great sage from Assam, in northeastern India. He was a recognized scholar of *mīmāṁsā* and a ritualist. According to tradition, he was an incarnation of Subrahmaṇya, son of Śiva and Pārvatī. His purpose was to restore the Vedic religion and counteract the expansion of Buddhism. He was famous for his texts on *mīmāṁsā* such as the *Mīmāṁsā-śloka-vārttika.* In his teachings, he emphasized the superiority of ritualism over knowledge. His message differed from Advaita since it supported the existence of a personal God and did not deal with transcendental reality. He studied Buddhism in order to counteract it and establish the superiority of *Sanātana-dharma*. He hid his Brahmanic origin and disguised himself as a monk in order to enter a Buddhist monastery and be accepted as a disciple of Dharmakīrti. However, he was found out. The monks conspired to kill him by throwing him from a tower, to prevent him from leaving the monastery with their philosophical secrets. When he learned about their plot, Kumārila thought that if the Vedas were really a divine revelation, he would surely be saved from death. He was indeed thrown from a high tower, but only one of his eyes was hurt. It is said that the cause of this injury was from questioning the infallibility of the Vedas. From that day on, Kumārila dedicated his life to fighting Buddhism in philosophical debates.

In time, he recognized that he had committed two great sins: first, he had deceived his Buddhist guru, and second, he had denied the existence of God. In order to atone for his sins, he decided to burn himself alive. When Śaṅkara arrived at Prayag, he was informed that the great sage of Assām was about to immolate himself. Śaṅkara reached the place when Kumārila had already begun to burn. From the lit pyre, he told him that the conditions of the meeting obviously did not allow for a philosophical debate. Instead, he invited Śaṅkara to debate with his disciple Maṇḍana Miśra, also known as Viśvarūpa. At the request of Kumārila, Śaṅkara recited the *tāraka-mantra* (liberating mantra: *śrī rāma jaya rāma jaya jaya rāma*) while the great scholar of *mīmāṁsā* left his body. This scene presents an interesting symbol: a great adept of ritualism committing suicide and being consumed by the flames of his own ritual.

Maṇḍana Miśra

Maṇḍana Miśra lived in Māhiṣmatī-pura, a city on the banks of the Narmadā River in what is now Madhya Pradesh. Śaṅkara and his disciples made a long journey to Māhiṣmatī in order to meet Maṇḍana Miśra. Kumārila's disciple was very well educated by his master and had attained the highest level of erudition. He married Ubhaya Bhāratī and settled down in Māhiṣmatī. His wife was equally scholarly, and both led exemplary lives that strictly adhered to the rules and regulations of the sacred scriptures. Ubhaya Bhāratī was considered to be an incarnation of Sarasvatī, the goddess of knowledge, and Maṇḍana Miśra an incarnation of Lord Brahmā. Like his master Kumārila, Maṇḍana Miśra was a scholar of the *mīmāṁsā* school, which comes directly from the *karma-kāṇḍa* part of the Vedas and emphasizes the ritualistic aspect of the scriptures.

When Śaṅkara arrived at Maṇḍana Miśra's house, the door was locked because he was performing the *śraddhā* ceremony. According to the scriptures, a renounced monk is not allowed to enter the closed house of a householder. However, using his mystic powers, Śaṅkara entered the house through the locked door. Maṇḍana was enraged because he thought it was disrespectful that Śaṅkara was present during a ritual to honor his deceased father. But Śaṅkara was determined to free Maṇḍana Miśra from his fanatic dedication to dogmatic ritualism, which had made him deeply hostile toward renunciate monks. Since he had always thought that people took *sannyās* in order to escape the Vedic regulations, Śaṅkara's visit did not please him at all.

Since Maṇḍana behaved with such animosity, Vyāsa and Jaimini, as well as the *brāhmaṇas* present at the ritual, advised him to invite Śaṅkara and treat him with hospitality. Maṇḍana realized his mistake and invited Śaṅkara to participate in the *śraddhā*. However, Śaṅkara rejected the invitation, saying that he did not come to participate in rituals but to engage Maṇḍana in a philosophical debate. Maṇḍana accepted the challenge but asked to start the debate the following day when the ritual was over.

The place for the debate was the town of Maṇḍleśvar, near Maheśvar. The ancient temple of Gupteśvar Mahadev is believed to be the exact place of the encounter. Maṇḍana, being older than Śaṅkara, gave him the right to choose the arbitrator of the debate. Śaṅkara appreciated this and praised his opponent's courtesy. He chose Maṇḍana's wife, Ubhaya Bhāratī, to act as the judge.

They agreed that if Maṇḍana was defeated, he would adopt *sannyāsa* and become a follower of Vedanta, and if Śaṅkara was defeated, he would leave the *sannyāsa* order and become a follower of ritualism. Ubhaya Bhāratī asked both participants to put on a garland of flowers, saying that the one that withered first would indicate who had lost. The debate focused on the interpretation of the Vedas. Śaṅkara presented the Advaitic interpretation and Maṇḍana, that of the *mīmāṁsā*. The debate lasted several months. Many scholars gathered around to hear the elevated discussion. As time went by, it was becoming clear that Maṇḍana Miśra was losing. His garland was noticeably wilting. His brilliant intellect and great scholarship failed to overcome Śaṅkara's direct realization of ultimate reality. Maṇḍana was about to accept defeat when his wife Ubhaya Bhāratī declared that in order to defeat a married man, the opponent must also defeat his wife. Śaṅkara accepted and faced Ubhaya Bhāratī. She told him that although he had perfect knowledge of all the issues in question, being a *sannyāsī*, he was still ignorant about married life, or *kāma-śāstras*. Śaṅkara was given a month to research and study the science of conjugal love.

It is said that Śaṅkara used his yogic powers to enter the body of the recently deceased King Amaruka. In the body of the king, he was able to learn about married life as an observer.

When he returned to the body, Śaṅkara resumed the debate, but Maṇḍana Miśra gave up in the end. As stipulated, Maṇḍana Miśra became one of Śaṅkara's four most important disciples and received the name of Sureśvarācārya. Eventually, he was named the first leader of the Śṛṅgeri Maṭhā monastic order. His name was later changed to Vārttikakāra (the commentator) because of the commentaries he wrote on Śaṅkara, especially on the *Bṛhad-āraṇyaka* and *Taittirīya Upanishads*.

His wife followed her husband's lead and joined the Śaṅkara group.

The funeral of his mother

Upon learning that his mother was very ill and that her departure seemed imminent, Śaṅkara left for Kālaḍi, his homeland. He wished to fulfill the promise he had made and take care of her funeral. Using his supernatural powers, Śaṅkara quickly reached his native Kālaḍi. Although she was very ill, his mother was happy to see him after so long. When Śaṅkara sang the *Śiva-bhujaṅga* in honor of Lord Śiva, the *śiva-dūtas,* the servants of Śiva, immediately appeared to escort Āryāmbā on her final path. However, Āryāmbā, who was a devotee of Kṛṣṇa, was frightened of them. Then Śaṅkara sang the hymn *Viṣṇu-bhujaṅga*, glorifying Lord Viṣṇu. Immediately, the beautiful *viṣṇu-dūtas* appeared to escort Śaṅkara's devoted mother to Vaikuṇṭha, the abode of Lord Viṣṇu.

When his mother died, none of the relatives attended the funeral or helped with the last rites. The family was strongly opposed to Śaṅkara performing the funeral rites because of his *sannyāsī* status. Although etiquette dictated that a renounced monk should not perform funeral rites for a relative, Śaṅkara had made a promise to his mother. Without any help, he transported his mother's body to the funeral pyre and thus fulfilled his promise.

His missionary work

Śaṅkara continued to travel throughout India, spreading his teachings with great enthusiasm to all who were interested. This earned him not only devotees and followers but also detractors. However, he knew how to defeat them with his brilliant and profound wisdom. At a time when orthodoxy was unable to defend religious principles, Śaṅkara destroyed superstition and protected the Vedic tradition with Upanishadic wisdom. Clearly, Śaṅkarācārya never saw dualism as an enemy of his Advaitic message. He never intended to eliminate or destroy dualist schools whose teachings differed from his own, nor did he consider dualist schools to be rivals of Advaita Vedanta. His mission was to restore the message of non-duality and emphasize the similarities of the different Vedic systems.

Various biographies have differences and inaccuracies in their description of the route Śaṅkara followed during his missionary work. However, everyone agrees that the great *ācarya* visited all the most important pilgrimage sites.

Throughout his travels, Śaṅkara had innumerable discussions and debates with many scholars, leaders, and followers of diverse sects and philosophical schools. Thanks to his direct experience of ultimate reality, his clear vision of Truth allowed him to convince others of his Advaitic message.

In Rameśvaram, he debated with *Śaiva* scholars, in Ujjayinī with *Kāpālikas*, in Ananta-śayanam with *Vaiṣṇavas*, in Subrahmaṇya-sthala with the followers of the cult of Hiraṇya-garbha, in Tulajā-bhavānī Puram with *Śāktas*, in Kuvalaya Puram with the worshippers of Mahālakṣmī, and in Puraṅgavaram with the devotees of Lord Gaṇeśa.

Another miracle occurred in the state of Tamil Nadu in Tiruvidaimarudur, which is one of the three most sacred sites for worshipping Śiva. Śaṅkara prayed to Lord Śiva, asking that the *mahā-liṅga* in the temple openly and publicly declare the authenticity of Advaita. In response to his prayer, Śiva manifested from the *mahā-liṅga*, raised his right hand, and proclaimed: *satyam advaitam, satyam advaitam, satyam advaitam,* or "Advaita is truth." All present were amazed at this spectacular miracle and accepted Śaṅkara as their master and his message as true.

The debate with the *Kāpālikas*

The Mallikārjuna temple is one of the twelve sacred *jyotir-liṅga* temples of Lord Śiva. This temple is located on Śrī Sailam mountain, on the banks of the Pātāla-gaṅgā, Kṛṣṇa River, in the southern state of Andhra Pradesh. Śrī Śailam was a real fortress of followers of the *Kāpālika* sect. Śaṅkara arrived, accompanied by a group of disciples. After exchanging a few words, the *Kāpālikas* realized that they would be unable to defeat Śaṅkara in a debate. Therefore, they devised a plan to kill him. They chose a moment when the great *ācārya* was alone and sent a messenger who told him that they needed the head of a king or a great sage in order to propitiate Lord Śiva and since they could not get the head of a king, they asked for his head, which would be perfect for this purpose. When the *Kāpālika* messenger asked Śaṅkara to grant his head for the sacrifice, Śaṅkara immediately agreed but told the messenger that he should behead him in the absence of his disciples while he was in deep meditation. The *Kāpālika* did exactly what he was told and returned when Śaṅkara was alone and meditating.

When Pādmapāda went to take his daily sacred bath that day, he had a premonition that Śaṅkara was in great danger. Alarmed, he prayed to Lord Nṛsiṁhadeva, his *Iṣṭa-devatā,* imploring him to protect his beloved master. The blessed Lord Nṛsiṁhadeva, half man and half lion, possessed him and made him arrive at the scene just in time to save his teacher. When Śaṅkara was about to be beheaded, Nṛsiṁhadeva appeared and killed the assassin.

Gokarṇa

From Śrī Śailam, Śaṅkara traveled to Gokarṇa, the location of the sacred temple of Gokarṇa and the abode of the *Ātma-liṅgam* Mahābaleśvar, one of the seven *mukti-sthalas* of Karnataka widely revered by the Tamil saints, or *nayanārs,* in their hymns. Gokarṇa was an important pilgrimage center on the west coast of India. In this temple, Śaṅkara composed a hymn and worshipped Lord Śiva. There were many *Śaiva* followers whose spiritual master was Nīlakaṇṭha. A great debate was held there and at the end of the debate all the *Śaivas* became Śaṅkara's disciples.

Hariharapura

From Gokarṇa, Śaṅkara went to the village of Hariharapura. There, on the banks of the Tuṅga river, there is a temple dedicated to the goddess Śāradāmbā. From there, he proceeded to Mūkambikā, in Kollur in the Udupi district, where there is a temple dedicated to Mūkambikā Devī. It was there that Śaṅkara found a couple crying inconsolably over the death of their son. Their despair deeply moved Śaṅkara, who implored the Goddess Mūkambikā to resurrect the child. How great was the happiness of his parents to see the child open his eyes and return to life!

Śaṅkara arrived at a village called Śrī Bali, today called Śivalli. This village was the home to a very devout *brāhmaṇa* called Prābhakara, whose thirteen-year-old son seemed to have been born mute. Since he had never said a word in his life, his family, neighbors, and friends considered him mentally retarded and treated him as such. When Prābhakara learned of Śaṅkara's visit, he approached the great master and begged him to see his son. In his heart, he had faith and hope that by the grace of the sage his son would speak. Śaṅkara gladly agreed and when he saw the boy, he realized that he was in front of a great soul and asked him, "Why don't you speak?" The child replied, "It is useless to speak, since the reality of what is cannot be expressed in words." Śaṅkara asked, "Who are you?" The child's response was a dozen brilliant verses on the nature of the Self. His words have been preserved for future generations and were later commented on by Śaṅkara himself in a text called *Hastāmalakīya-bhaṣya*. With the due consent of his family, the boy was accepted and initiated as a disciple with the name Hastāmalaka, which means "one whose wisdom is as clear as a fruit in the palm of your hand." This was the third of Śaṅkara's close disciples. Later, Hastāmalaka was made the leader of the Dvārakā monastery and wrote important texts, some of which his master commented on.

Śṛṅgeri

Next, Ādi Śaṅkara went to Śṛṅgeri, a city and a central *tālūka* (an administrative division) located in the Cikkamagalūru district. Śṛṅgeri is located on the banks of the Tuṅgā River, where the first *maṭha*, called Śṛṅgeri Śāradā-pīṭha, was later established. Śaṅkara recalled, perhaps with nostalgia, how he had stopped there a decade prior as he searched for his spiritual master.

Śaṅkara and his disciples remained in Śṛṅgeri for several months. When King Ādityavarma learned that the great *ācārya* was there, he took care of all his needs. A group of wealthy devotees and King Sudhanvā, who reigned in Ujjainī, went to visit him. Pādmapāda and a group of other disciples began to plan the founding of a great *maṭha* in Śṛṅgeri. However, their master asked them to be prudent and not start complicated projects. Instead, he suggested opening a small temple to Śāradā Devī. With the help and contributions of devotees and followers, they built a temple and installed a beautiful deity of the Goddess. Śaṅkara himself worshipped the deity and composed hymns to Śāradā Devī.

Ādi Śaṅkarācārya taught that bhakti should never be abandoned or underestimated, even after accepting the renounced order of life. During this time, the great master wrote some of his most important works.

There was a boy in Śṛṅgeri named Giri, although others called him Kalānātha, who enjoyed serving Śaṅkara directly. Under the name of Toṭaka, this child became another of Śaṅkara's most prominent disciples. His main virtues were not scholarly achievements or intellectual brilliance, but total surrender and dedication to fulfilling the master's personal needs.

One day, Śaṅkara wanted to give a lecture to his disciples but was waiting for Giri, who had gone to the river to wash his teacher's clothes. Many disciples were impatient to listen to Śaṅkara and perhaps somewhat upset about Giri's delay. Tired of waiting and referring to Giri's intellectual abilities, Pādmapāda said: "Why wait for someone who is like a wall?" The master was clearly displeased with these words and decided to bless Giri with the knowledge of all the sacred Vedic writings. When Giri returned from his service, he looked ecstatic and blissful. In front of his master, he sang a beautiful hymn glorifying the *ācārya* in a complex *toṭaka* metric. This brilliant hymn was known as *Toṭakāṣṭaka*. From then on, Giri was known as Toṭakācārya, in honor of the hymn and its *toṭaka* poetic meter. Later, he would be appointed as the first *jagad-guru* of *Jyotir-maṭha pīṭha*, the northern *maṭha* founded by Śaṅkarācārya near Badrināth. His works also include the *Śruti-sāra-samuddharaṇam*, a synthesis of the Upanishadic wisdom composed in the *toṭaka-candas* (poetic meter).

Kashmir

The last chapter of the *Mādhavīya Śaṅkara-vijaya* describes Śaṅkara's visit to the altar of Śāradā in Kashmir. The temple is located in the village of Śāradā in Kashmir Azad, on the banks of the Nīlam river. The temple is located at an altitude of 11,000 feet above sea level and is about 70 miles from Śrīnagar. Before being forced to convert to Islam, the local people were very devout Hindus. At the time, Kashmir was an important center for Vedic studies. In honor of this temple, Kashmir was called Śāradā Deśa. Śāradā Devī was also called Kashmir Pura-vāsinī, or "resident of Kashmir." Śaṅkara learned that the temple had four doors and a throne of omniscience, *sarva-jña-pīṭha*. Only someone who was omniscient could sit on the throne. Upon hearing this, Śaṅkara felt that it was his divine mandate to go to the temple and sit on the throne to establish the absolute superiority of Advaita Vedanta. When Śaṅkara reached the southern door, he saw a group of scholars from different schools and beliefs. They stopped him and initiated a debate, refusing to accept the superiority of Śaṅkara's message. Finally, everyone had to agree that Śaṅkara was very well versed in all the various schools they represented. Then the door of Śāradā's altar opened. Śaṅkara was about to sit on the throne when he heard the voice of the goddess Śāradā. She declared that in order to be worthy of sitting on the throne, one must be omniscient as well as pure. It was clear that Śaṅkara could not claim purity after spending time in King Amaruka's palace. However, Śaṅkara replied that although he had indeed stayed in King Amaruka's palace, he had not done so with his own body. The goddess accepted Śaṅkara's response. Only then, after passing this final test, did Śaṅkara proceed to sit on the sacred *sarva-jña-pīṭha*. The *ācārya* glorified the goddess Śāradā Devī in the first verse of *Prapañca-sāra*.

There are those who claim that while in Kashmir, Śaṅkarācārya met with the great master Abhinavagupta, but it is not clear if this is the same person as the famous *Trika* master called Abhinavagupta. Others claim that Śaṅkarācārya wrote the *Saundarya-Laharī* while in Kashmir.

Departure

From Badrikāśram, Śaṅkara and his disciples went to Kedārnāth. He was thirty-two years old and knew that the final moment was approaching, so he chose the sacred place of Kedārnāth to leave the world. The great master told his disciples to ask him all the questions they deemed necessary. He wished to leave no room for doubt or confusion in his teachings. Pādmapāda only asked him what they should do after his departure. King Sudhanvā suggested that the master should appoint four disciples to establish four *maṭhas* in the four corners of India to preserve and spread his teachings through disciplic succession. Śaṅkara chose Pādmapāda, Sureśvara, Hastāmalaka, and Toṭaka to establish the four *maṭhas*. These *maṭhas* were based in the south: Śāradā Pīṭha (in Śṛṅgeri, Karṇātaka); in the east: Govardhāna Maṭha (in Pūrī, Orissa); in the west:

Kālikā Pīṭha (in Dvārakā, Gujarāt); and in the north: Jyotir Maṭha (in Joṣīmath, Uttar Pradeś).

Śaṅkara dictated a book of rules and regulations to be followed in the *maṭhas*. This text is called the *Mahānuśāsana*. King Sudhanvā asked Śaṅkara to explain the essence of Vedanta. Śaṅkara repeated the *Daśa-ślokī*, the same ten verses that he had recited in his first meeting with his master. Śaṅkara told them that those who meditated on the meaning of these verses could find the essence of all the wisdom of Advaita Vedanta. Everyone there entered a deep meditation. Śaṅkarācārya entered *mahā-samādhi* and through his power, dissolved his body into five elements and disappeared from the sight of mortals.

Śaṅkarācārya established the basis for future *Smārtas*, who give him the highest authority. He was both the orthodox defender of eternal religion and the rebel *Smārta* who broke the rules and regulations of the renounced order of life to fulfill the promise made to his mother.

Sanskrit
PRONUNCIATION GUIDE

The Sanskrit alphabet vowels

अ *a* आ *ā* इ *i* ई *ī* उ *u* ऊ *ū*

ऋ *ṛ* ॠ *ṝ* ऌ *ḷ* ए *e* ऐ *ai* ओ *o* औ *au* अं *aṁ* अः *aḥ*

Consonants

Gutturals	क *ka*	ख *kha*	ग *ga*	घ *gha*	ङ *ṅa*
Palatals	च *ca*	छ *cha*	ज *ja*	झ *jha*	ञ *ña*
Cerebrals	ट *ṭa*	ठ *ṭha*	ड *ḍa*	ढ *ḍha*	ण *ṇa*
Dentals	त *ta*	थ *tha*	द *da*	ध *dha*	न *na*
Labials	प *pa*	फ *pha*	ब *ba*	भ *bha*	म *ma*
Semivowels	य *ya*	र *ra*	ल *la*	व *va*	
Sibilants	श *śa*	ष *ṣa*	स *sa*		
Aspirates	ह *ha*				

Pronunciation

Vowels

Sanskrit letter	Transliteration	Sounds like
अ	*a*	b**u**t
आ	*ā*	f**a**ther
इ	*i*	f**i**t, **i**f, l**i**ly
ई	*ī*	f**ee**, pol**i**ce
उ	*u*	p**u**t
ऊ	*ū*	b**oo**t, r**u**le, r**u**de
ऋ	*ṛ*	(between ri and ru, as in K**ri**shna)
ॠ	*ṝ*	(between ri and ru) c**ru**cial
ऌ	*ḷ*	(similar to lr)
ए	*e*	m**a**de
ऐ	*ai*	b**i**te, **ai**sle
ओ	*o*	**o**h
औ	*au*	f**ou**nd, h**ou**se

Consonants

Gutturals

(back of the throat)

Sanskrit letter	Transliteration	Sounds like
क	*ka*	**k**ill, see**k**, **k**ite
ख	*kha*	Ec**kha**rt
ग	*ga*	**g**et, do**g**, **g**ive
घ	*gha*	lo**g-h**ut
ङ	*ṅa*	si**ng**, ki**ng**, si**nk**

Palatals

(tip of the tongue touches the roof of the mouth)

Sanskrit letter	Transliteration	Sounds like
च	*ca*	**ch**icken
छ	*cha*	cat**ch h**im
ज	*ja*	**j**oy, **j**ump
झ	*jha*	he**dgeh**og
ञ	*ña*	ca**ny**on

Cerebrals

(tip of the tongue against the front part of the roof of the mouth)

Sanskrit letter	Transliteration	Sounds like
ट	*ṭa*	**t**rue, **t**ub
ठ	*ṭha*	an**th**ill
ड	*ḍa*	**d**ove, **d**rum, **d**octor
ढ	*ḍha*	re**d-h**ot
ण	*ṇa*	u**n**der

Dentals

(tip of the tongue against the teeth)

Sanskrit letter	Transliteration	Sounds like
त	*ta*	**t**able
थ	*tha*	ligh**th**earted
द	*da*	**d**esk
ध	*dha*	a**dh**ere
न	*na*	**n**ot, **n**ut

Labials

(lips together, the tongue is not used)

Sanskrit letter	Transliteration	Sounds like
प	*pa*	**p**ine, **p**ut, si**p**
फ	*pha*	u**ph**ill
ब	*ba*	**b**ird, **b**ear, ru**b**
भ	*bha*	a**bh**or
म	*ma*	**m**other, **m**ap

Semivowels

Sanskrit letter	Transliteration	Sounds like
य	*ya*	**y**et, lo**y**al, **y**es
र	*ra*	**r**ed, **y**ear
ल	*la*	**l**ull, **l**ead
व	*va*	(between v and w) i**v**y, **v**ine

Sibilants

Sanskrit letter	Transliteration	Sounds like
श	*śa*	**s**ure
ष	*ṣa*	**sh**rink, bu**sh**, **sh**ow
स	*sa*	**s**aint, **s**in, hi**ss**

Aspirate

Sanskrit letter	Transliteration	Sounds like
ह	*ha*	**h**ear, **h**it, **h**ome

Additional Sounds

Anusvāra

(A nasal sound, written as a dot above and to the right of a Sanskrit letter)

Sanskrit letter	Transliteration	Sounds like
·	*ṁ*	hu**m**, te**m**pt, pu**mp**

Visarga

(A final aspirate sound, written as two dots after a Sanskrit letter)

Sanskrit letter	Transliteration	Sounds like
:	*ḥ*	Echoing the last vowel: ha, hi, hu, he, ho
तः	*taḥ*	'ta-ha'
तीः	*tīḥ*	'tee-hi'
नेः	*neḥ*	'ne-he'
धूः	*dhūḥ*	'dhuu-hu'
		etc.

Prabhuji

H.H. Avadhūta Śrī Bhaktivedānta Yogācārya
Ramakrishnananda Bābājī Mahārāja

About Prabhuji

Prabhuji is a writer, painter, an *avadhūta*, the creator of Retroprogressive Yoga, and a realized spiritual master. In 2011, he chose to retire from society and lead the life of a hermit. Since then, his days have been spent in solitude, praying, writing, painting, and meditating in silence and contemplation.

Prabhuji is the sole disciple of H.D.G. Avadhūta Śrī Brahmānanda Bābājī Mahārāja, who in turn is one of the closest and most intimate disciples of H.D.G. Avadhūta Śrī Mastarāma Bābājī Mahārāja.

Prabhuji was appointed as the successor of the lineage by his master, who conferred upon him the responsibility of continuing the sacred *paramparā* of *avadhūtas*, officially appointing him as guru and ordering him to serve as Ācārya successor under the name H.H. Avadhūta Śrī Bhaktivedānta Yogācārya Ramakrishnananda Bābājī Mahārāja.

Prabhuji is also a disciple of H.D.G. Bhakti-kavi Atulānanda Ācārya Mahārāja, who is a direct disciple of H.D.G. A.C. Bhaktivedānta Swami Prabhupāda.

Prabhuji's Hinduism is so broad, universal, and pluralistic that at times, while living up to his title of *avadhūta*, his lively and fresh teachings transcend the boundaries of all philosophies and religions, even his own. His teachings promote critical thinking and lead us to question statements that are usually accepted as true. They do not defend absolute truths but invite us to evaluate and question our own convictions. The essence of his syncretic vision, Retroprogressive Yoga, is self-awareness and the recognition of consciousness. For him, awakening at the level of consciousness, or the transcendence of the egoic phenomenon, is the next step in humanity's evolution.

Prabhuji was born on March 21, 1958, in Santiago, the capital of the Republic of Chile. When he was eight years old, he had a mystical experience that motivated his search for the Truth, or the Ultimate Reality. This transformed his life into an authentic inner and outer pilgrimage. He has completely devoted his life to deepening the early transformative experience that marked the beginning of his process of retroevolution. He has dedicated more than fifty years to the exploration and practice of different religions, philosophies, paths of liberation, and spiritual disciplines. He has absorbed the teachings of great yogis, pastors, rabbis, monks, gurus, philosophers, sages, and saints whom he personally visited during years of searching. He has lived in many places and traveled the world thirsting for Truth.

From an early age, Prabhuji noticed that the educational system prevented him from devoting himself to what was really important: learning about himself. Despite his parents' insistence, he stopped attending conventional school at the age of 11 and engaged in autodidactic formation. Over time, he would become a serious critic of the current educational system.

Prabhuji is a recognized authority on Eastern wisdom. He is known for his erudition in the *Vaidika* and *Tāntrika* aspects of Hinduism and all branches of yoga (*jñāna*, *karma*, *bhakti*, *haṭha*, *rāja*, *kuṇḍalinī*, *tantra*, *mantra*, and others). He has an inclusive attitude toward all religions and is intimately familiar with Judaism, Christianity, Buddhism, Sufism, Taoism, Sikhism, Jainism, Shintoism, Bahaism, and the Mapuche religion, among others. He learned about the Druze religion directly from the scholars Salach Abbas and Kamil Shchadi.

Prabhuji studied Christian theology in depth with H.H. Monsignor Iván Larraín Eyzaguirre at the Veracruz Church in Santiago de Chile and with Mr. Héctor Muñoz, who holds a degree in theology from the Universidad Católica de la Santísima Concepción.

His curiosity for Western thought led him to venture into the field of philosophy in all its different branches. He specialized in Transcendental Phenomenology and the Phenomenology of Religion. He had the privilege of studying intensively for several years with his uncle Jorge Balazs, philosopher, researcher, writer, and author of *The Golden Deer.* He studied privately for a few years with Dr. Jonathan Ramos, a renowned philosopher, historian, and university professor graduated from the Catholic University of Salta, Argentina. He also studied with Dr. Alejandro Cavallazzi Sánchez, who holds an undergraduate degree in philosophy from the Universidad Panamericana, a master's degree in philosophy from the Universidad Iberoamericana, and a doctorate in philosophy from the Universidad Nacional Autónoma de México (UNAM).

Prabhuji holds a doctorate in Vaishnava philosophy from the respected Jiva Institute in Vrindavana, India, and a doctorate in yogic philosophy from the Yoga Samskrutum University.

His profound studies, his masters' blessings, his research into the sacred scriptures, and his vast teaching experience have earned him international recognition in the field of religion and spirituality.

His spiritual search led him to study with masters of diverse traditions and travel far from his native Chile to places as distant as Israel, India, and the USA. Prabhuji studied Hebrew and Sanskrit to deepen his understanding of the holy scriptures. He also studied Pali at the Oxford Centre for Buddhist Studies. Furthermore, he learned ancient Latin and Greek from Javier Álvarez, who holds a degree in Classical Philology from the Sevilla University.

His father, Yosef Har-Zion ZT"L, grew up under strict discipline because he was the son of a senior police sergeant. As a reaction to this upbringing, Yosef decided to raise his own children with complete freedom and unconditional love. Prabhuji grew up without any pressure. During his early years, his father showed his son the same love regardless of his successes or failures at school. When Prabhuji decided to drop out of school to devote himself to his inner quest, his family accepted his decision with deep respect. From the time his son was ten years old, Yosef talked to him about Hebrew spirituality and Western philosophy. They engaged in conversations about philosophy and religion for days on end and late into the night. Yosef supported him in whatever he wanted to do in his life and his search for Truth. Prabhuji was the authentic project of freedom and unconditional love of his father.

At an early age and on his own initiative, Prabhuji began to practice karate and study philosophy and religion. During his adolescence, no one interfered with his decisions. At the age of 15, he established a deep, intimate, and long friendship with the famous Uruguayan writer and poet Blanca Luz Brum, who was his neighbor on Merced Street in Santiago de Chile. He traveled throughout Chile in search of wise and interesting people to learn from. In southern Chile, he met machis who taught him about the rich Mapuche spirituality and shamanism.

Two great masters contributed to Prabhuji's retroprogressive process. In 1976, he met his first guru, H.D.G Bhakti-kavi Atulānanda Ācārya Swami, whom he would call Gurudeva. In those days, Gurudeva was a young *brahmacārī* who held the position of president of the ISKCON temple at Eyzaguirre 2404, Puente Alto, Santiago, Chile. Years later, he gave Prabhuji first initiation, Brahminical initiation, and finally, he initiated Prabhuji into the sacred order of renunciation called *sannyāsa* within the Brahma Gauḍīya Saṁpradāya. Gurudeva connected him to the devotion to Kṛṣṇa. He imparted to him the wisdom of bhakti yoga and instructed him in the practice of the *māhā-mantra* and the study of the holy scriptures.

In 1996, Prabhuji met his second guru, H.D.G. Avadhūta Śrī Brahmānanda Bābājī Mahārāja, in Rishikesh, India. Guru Mahārāja, as Prabhuji called him, revealed that his own master, H.D.G. Avadhūta Śrī Mastarāma Bābājī Mahārāja, had told him years before he died that a person would come from the West and request to be his disciple. He commanded him to accept only that particular seeker. When he asked how he would identify this person, Mastarāma Bābājī replied, "You will recognize him by his eyes. You must accept him because he will be the continuation of the lineage."

From his first meeting with young Prabhuji, Guru Mahārāja recognized him and officially initiated him into the *māhā-mantra*. For Prabhuji, this initiation marked the beginning of the most intense and mature stage of his retroprogressive process. Under the guidance of Guru Mahārāja, he studied Advaita Vedanta and deepened his meditation.

Guru Mahārāja guided Prabhuji on his first steps toward the sacred level of *avadhūta*. In March 2011, H.D.G. Avadhūta Śrī Brahmānanda Bābājī Mahārāja ordered Prabhuji, on behalf of his own master, to accept the responsibility of continuing the lineage of *avadhūtas*. With this title, Prabhuji is the official representative of the line of this disciplic succession for the present generation. Besides his *dikṣā-gurus*, Prabhuji studied with important spiritual and religious personalities, such as H.H. Swami Dayananda Sarasvatī, H.H. Swami Viṣṇu Devānanda Sarasvatī, H.H. Swami Jyotirmayānanda Sarasvatī, H.H. Swami Pratyagbodhānanda, H.H. Swami Swahananda of the Ramakrishna Mission, and H.H. Swami Viditātmānanda of the Arsha Vidya Gurukulam. The wisdom of tantra was awakened in Prabhuji by H.G. Mātājī Rīnā Śarmā in India.

Prabhuji wanted to confirm his *sannyāsa* initiation in an Advaita Vedanta lineage. His *sannyāsa-dīkṣā* was confirmed by H.H. Swami Jyotirmayānanda Sarasvatī, founder of the Yoga Research Foundation and disciple of H.H. Swami Śivānanda Sarasvatī of Rishikesh.

In 1984, he learned and began to practice Maharishi Mahesh Yogi's Transcendental Meditation technique. In 1988, he took the *kriyā-yoga* course on Paramahaṁsa Yogananda. After two years, he was officially initiated into the technique of *kriyā-yoga* by the Self-Realization Fellowship.

In Vrindavana, studied the bhakti yoga path in depth with H.H. Narahari Dāsa Bābājī Mahārāja, disciple of H.H. Nityananda Dāsa Bābājī Mahārāja of Vraja.

He also studied bhakti yoga with various disciples of His Divine Grace A.C. Bhaktivedānta Swami Prabhupāda: H.H. Kapīndra Swami, H.H. Paramadvaiti Mahārāja, H.H. Jagajīvana Dāsa, H.H. Tamāla Kṛṣṇa Gosvāmī, H.H. Bhagavān Dāsa Mahārāja, and H.H. Kīrtanānanda Swami, among others.

Prabhuji has been honored with various titles and diplomas by many leaders of prestigious religious and spiritual institutions in India. He was given the honorable title *Kṛṣṇa Bhakta* by H.H. Swami Viṣṇu Devānanda (the only title of Bhakti Yoga given by Swami Viṣṇu), disciple of H.H. Swami Śivānanda Sarasvatī and the founder of the Sivananda Organization. He was given the title *Bhaktivedānta* by H.H. B.A. Paramadvaiti Mahārāja, the founder of Vrinda. He was given the title *Yogācārya* by H.H. Swami Viṣṇu Devānanda, the Paramanand Institute of Yoga Sciences and Research of Indore, India, the International Yoga Federation, the Indian Association of Yoga, and the Shri Shankarananda Yogashram of Mysore, India. He received the respectable title *Śrī Śrī Rādhā Śyam Sunder Pāda-Padma Bhakta Śiromaṇi* directly from H.H. Satyanārāyaṇa Dāsa Bābājī Mahant of the Chatu Vaiṣṇava Saṁpradāya.

Prabhuji spent more than forty years studying hatha yoga with prestigious masters in classical and traditional yoga, such as H.H. Bapuji, H.H. Swami Viṣṇu Devānanda Sarasvatī, H.H. Swami Jyotirmayānanda Sarasvatī, H.H. Swami Satchidananda Sarasvatī, H.H. Swami Vignanananda Sarasvatī, and Śrī Madana-mohana.

He attended several systematic hatha yoga teacher training courses at prestigious institutions until he achieved the level of Master Ācārya. He has completed studies at the following institutions: the Sivananda Yoga Vedanta, the Ananda Ashram, the Yoga Research Foundation, the Integral Yoga Academy, the Patanjala Yoga Kendra, the Ma Yoga Shakti International Mission, the Prana Yoga Organization, the Rishikesh Yoga Peeth, the Swami Sivananda Yoga Research Center, and the Swami Sivananda Yogasana Research Center.

Prabhuji is a member of the Indian Association of Yoga, Yoga Alliance ERYT 500 and YACEP, the International Association of Yoga Therapists, and the International Yoga Federation. In 2014, the International Yoga Federation honored him with the position of Honorary Member of the World Yoga Council.

His interest in the complex anatomy of the human body led him to study chiropractic at the prestigious Institute of Health of the Back and Extremities in Tel Aviv, Israel. In 1993, he received a diploma from Dr. Sheinerman, the founder and director of the institute. Later, he earned a massage therapy diploma at the Academy of Western Galilee. The knowledge he acquired in this field deepened his understanding of hatha yoga and contributed to the creation of his own method.

Retroprogressive Hatha Yoga is the result of Prabhuji's efforts to improve his practice and teaching methods. It is a system based especially on the teachings of his gurus and the sacred scriptures. Prabhuji has systematized various traditional yoga techniques to create a methodology suitable for Western audiences. Retroprogressive Yoga aims to experience our true nature. It promotes balance, health, and flexibility through proper diet, cleansing techniques, preparations (*āyojanas*), sequences (*vinyāsas*), postures (*asanas*), breathing exercises (*prāṇayama*), relaxation (*śavāsana*), meditation (*dhyāna*), and exercises with locks (*bandhas*) and seals (*mudras*) to direct and empower *prāṇa*.

Since his childhood and throughout his life, Prabhuji has been an enthusiastic admirer, student, and practitioner of classic karate-do. From the age of 13, he studied different styles in Chile, such as kenpo and kung-fu, but specialized in the most traditional Japanese style of shotokan. He received the rank of black belt (third dan) from Shihan Kenneth Funakoshi (ninth dan). He also learned from Sensei Takahashi (seventh dan) and practiced Shorin Ryu style with Sensei Enrique

Daniel Welcher (seventh dan), who granted him the rank of black belt (second dan). Through karate-do, he delved into Buddhism and gained additional knowledge about the physics of motion. Prabhuji is a member of Funakoshi's Shotokan Karate Association.

Prabhuji grew up in an artistic environment and his love of painting began to develop in his childhood. His father, the renowned Chilean painter Yosef Har-Zion ZT"L, motivated him to devote himself to art. He learned with the famous Chilean painter Marcelo Cuevas. Prabhuji's abstract paintings reflect the depths of the spirit.

Since he was a young boy, Prabhuji has been especially drawn to postal stamps, postcards, mailboxes, postal transportation systems, and all mail-related activities. He has taken every opportunity to visit post offices in different cities and countries. He has delved into the study of philately, the field of collecting, sorting, and studying postage stamps. This passion led him to become a professional philatelist, a stamp distributor authorized by the American Philatelic Society, and a member of the following societies: the Royal Philatelic Society London, the Royal Philatelic Society of Victoria, the United States Stamp Society, the Great Britain Philatelic Society, the American Philatelic Society, the Society of Israel Philatelists, the Society for Hungarian Philately, the National Philatelic Society UK, the Fort Orange Stamp Club, the American Stamp Dealers Association, the US Philatelic Classics Society, Filabras – Associação dos Filatelistas Brasileiros, and the Collectors Club of NYC.

Based on his extensive knowledge of philately, theology, and Eastern philosophy, Prabhuji created "Meditative Philately" or "Philatelic Yoga," a spiritual practice that uses philately as the basis for practicing attention, concentration, observation, and meditation. Meditative Philately is inspired by the ancient Hindu *maṇḍala* meditation and it can lead the practitioner to elevated states of consciousness, deep relaxation, and concentration that fosters the recognition of consciousness. Prabhuji wrote his thesis on this new type of yoga, "Meditative Philately," attracting the interest of the Indian academic community due to its innovative way of connecting meditation with different hobbies and activities. For this thesis, he was honored with a PhD in Yogic Philosophy from Yoga-Samskrutum University.

Prabhuji lived in Israel for many years, where he furthered his studies of Judaism. One of his main teachers and sources of inspiration was Rabbi Shalom Dov Lifshitz ZT"L, whom he met in 1997. This great saint guided him for several years on the intricate paths of the Torah and Chassidism. The two developed a very intimate relationship. Prabhuji studied the Talmud with Rabbi Raphael Rapaport Shlit"a (Ponovich), Chassidism with Rabbi Israel Lifshitz Shlit"a, and the Torah with Rabbi Daniel Sandler Shlit"a. Prabhuji is a great devotee of Rabbi Mordechai Eliyahu ZT"L, who personally blessed him.

Prabhuji visited the United States in 2000 and during his stay in New York, he realized that it was the most appropriate place to found a religious organization. He was particularly attracted by the pluralism and respectful attitude of American society toward freedom of religion. He was impressed by the deep respect of both the public and the government for religious minorities. After consulting his masters and requesting their blessings, Prabhuji relocated to the United States. In 2003, the Prabhuji Mission was born, a Hindu church aimed at preserving Prabhuji's universal and pluralistic vision of Hinduism and his Retroprogressive Yoga.

Although he did not seek to attract followers, for 15 years (1995–2010), Prabhuji considered the requests of a few people who approached him asking to become his monastic disciples. Those who chose to see Prabhuji as their spiritual master voluntarily accepted vows of poverty and life-long dedication to spiritual practice (*sadhāna*), religious devotion (*bhakti*), and selfless service (*seva*). Although Prabhuji no longer accepts new disciples, he continues to guide the small group of monastic disciples of the Ramakrishnananda Monastic Order that he founded.

In 2011, Prabhuji founded the Avadhutashram (monastery) in the Catskills Mountains in upstate New York, USA. The Avadhutashram is the headquarters of the Prabhuji Mission, his hermitage, and the residence of the monastic disciples of the Ramakrishnananda Monastic Order. The ashram organizes humanitarian projects such as the Prabhuji Food Distribution Program and the Prabhuji Toy Distribution Program. Prabhuji operates various humanitarian projects, inspired in his experience that serving the part is serving the Whole.

In January 2012, Prabhuji's health forced him to officially renounce managing the mission. Since then, he has lived in solitude, completely away from the public, writing and absorbed in contemplation. His message does not promote collective spirituality, but individual inner search.

Prabhuji has delegated the choice to his disciples between keeping his teachings exclusively within the monastic order or spreading his message for the public benefit. Upon the explicit request of his disciples, Prabhuji has agreed to have his books published and his lectures disseminated, as long as this does not compromise his privacy and his life as a hermit.

In 2022, Prabhuji founded the Institute of Retroprogressive Yoga. Here, his most senior disciples can systematically share Prabhuji's teachings and message through video conferences. The institute offers support and help for a deeper understanding of Prabhuji's teachings.

Prabhuji is a respected member of the American Philosophical Association, the American Association of Philosophy Teachers, the American Association of University Professors, the Southwestern Philosophical Society, the Authors Guild, the National Writers Union, PEN America, the International Writers Association, the National Association of Independent Writers and Editors, the National Writers Association, the Alliance Independent Authors, and the Independent Book Publishers Association.

Prabhuji's vast literary contribution includes books in Spanish, English, and Hebrew, for example, *Kundalini Yoga: The Power is in you*, *What is, as it is*, *Bhakti-Yoga: The Path of Love*, *Tantra: Liberation in the World*, *Experimenting with the Truth*, *Advaita Vedanta: Be the Self*, commentaries on the *Īśāvāsya Upanishad* and the *Diamond Sūtra*.

About the Prabhuji Mission

Prabhuji, H.H. Avadhūta Śrī Bhaktivedānta Yogācārya Ramakrishnananda Bābājī Mahārāja, founded the Prabhuji Mission in 2003, a Hindu church aimed at preserving his universal and pluralistic vision of Hinduism.

The main purpose of the mission is to preserve Prabhuji's teachings of Pūrvavyāpi-pragatiśīlaḥ Yoga, or Retroprogressive Yoga, which advocates for a global awakening of consciousness as the radical solution to humanity's problems.

The Prabhuji Mission operates a Hindu temple called Śrī Śrī Radha-Śyāmasundara Mandir, which offers worship and religious ceremonies to parishioners. The extensive library of the Retroprogressive Yoga Institute provides its teachers with abundant study materials to research the various theologies and philosophies explored by Prabhuji in his books and lectures. The Avadhutashram monastery educates monastic disciples on various aspects of Prabhuji's approach to Hinduism and offers them the opportunity to express devotion to God through devotional service by selflessly contributing their skills and training to the Mission's programs, such as the Prabhuji Food Distribution program, a weekly event in which dozens of families in need from Upstate New York receive fresh and nutritious food

Service and glorification of the guru are fundamental spiritual principles in Hinduism. The Prabhuji Mission, as a traditional Hindu church, practices the millenary *guru-bhakti* tradition of reverence to the master. Some disciples and friends of the Prabhuji Mission, on their own initiative, help to preserve Prabhuji's legacy and his interfaith teachings for future generations by disseminating his books, videos of his internal talks, and websites.

About the Avadhutashram

The Avadhutashram (monastery) was founded by Prabhuji in the Catskills Mountains in upstate New York, USA. It is the headquarters of the Prabhuji Mission and the hermitage of H.H. Śrī Avadhūta Bhaktivedānta Yogācārya Ramakrishnananda Bābājī Mahārāja and his monastic disciples of the Ramakrishnananda Monastic Order.

The ideals of the Avadhutashram are love and selfless service, based on the universal vision that God is in everything and everyone. Its mission is to distribute spiritual books and organize humanitarian projects such as the Prabhuji Food Distribution Program and the Prabhuji Toy Distribution Program.

The Avadhutashram is not commercial and operates without soliciting donations. Its activities are funded by Prabhuji's Gifts, a non-profit company founded by Prabhuji, which sells esoteric items from different traditions that Prabhuji himself has used for spiritual practices during his evolutionary process. Its mission is to preserve and disseminate traditional religious, mystical, and ancestral crafts.

Avadhutashram
Round Top, NY, USA

The Retroprogressive Path

The Retroprogressive Path does not require you to be part of a group or a member of an organization, institution, society, congregation, club, or exclusive community. Living in a temple, monastery, or *āśram* is not mandatory, because it is not about a change of residence, but of consciousness. It does not urge you to believe, but to doubt. It does not demand you to accept something, but to explore, investigate, examine, inquire, and question everything. It does not suggest being what you should be but being what you really are.

The Retroprogressive Path supports freedom of expression but not proselytizing. This route does not promise answers to our questions but induces us to question our answers. It does not promise to be what we are not or to attain what we have not already achieved. It is a retro-evolutionary path of self-discovery that leads us from what we think we are to what we really are. It is not the only way, nor the best, the simplest, or the most direct. It is an involutionary process par excellence that shows what is obvious and undeniable but usually goes unnoticed: that which is simple, innocent, and natural. It is a path that begins and ends in you.

The Retroprogressive Path is a continuous revelation that expands eternally. It delves into consciousness from an ontological perspective, transcending all religion and spiritual paths. It is the discovery of diversity as a unique and inclusive reality. It is the encounter of consciousness with itself, aware of itself and its own reality. In fact, this path is a simple invitation to dance in the now, to love the present moment, and to celebrate our authenticity. It is an unconditional proposal to stop living as a victim of circumstance and to live as a passionate adventurer. It is a call to return to the place we have never left, without offering us anything we do not already possess or teaching us anything we do not already know. It is a call for an inner revolution and to enter the fire of life that only consumes dreams, illusions, and fantasies but does not touch what we are. It does not help us reach our desired goal, but instead prepares us for the unexpected miracle.

This path was nurtured over a lifetime dedicated to the search for Truth. It is a grateful offering to existence for what I have received. But remember, do not look for me. Look for yourself. It is not me you need, because you are the only one who really matters. This life is just a wonderful parenthesis in eternity to know and love. What you yearn for lies in you, here and now, as what you really are.

Your unconditional well-wisher,
Prabhuji

Prabhuji today

Prabhuji is retired from public life

Prabhuji is the sole disciple of H.D.G. Avadhūta Śrī Brahmānanda Bābājī Mahārāja, who is himself one of the closest and most intimate disciples of H.D.G. Avadhūta Śrī Mastarāma Bābājī Mahārāja.

Prabhuji was appointed as the successor of the lineage by his master, who conferred upon him the responsibility of continuing the sacred *paramparā* of *avadhūtas*, officially appointing him as guru and ordering him to serve as Ācārya successor under the name H.H. Avadhūta Śrī Bhaktivedānta Yogācārya Ramakrishnananda Bābājī Mahārāja.

Prabhuji is also a disciple of H.D.G. Bhakti-kavi Atulānanda Ācārya Mahārāja, who is a direct disciple of H.D.G. A.C. Bhaktivedānta Swami Prabhupāda.

In 2011, he chose to retire from society and lead the life of a hermit. Since then, his days have been spent in solitude, praying, writing, painting, and meditating in silence and contemplation. He no longer participates in *sat-saṅgs*, lectures, gatherings, meetings, retreats, seminars, study groups, or courses. We ask everyone to respect his privacy and do not try to contact him by any means for gatherings, meetings, interviews, blessings, *śaktipāta*, initiations, or personal visits.

Prabhuji's teachings

As an *avadhūta* and a realized master, Prabhuji has always appreciated the essence and wisdom of a wide variety of religious practices from around the world. He does not consider himself a member or representative of any particular religion. Although many see him as an enlightened being, Prabhuji has no intention of presenting himself as a preacher, guide, coach, content creator, influencer, preceptor, mentor, counselor, consultant, monitor, tutor, teacher, instructor, educator, enlightener, pedagogue, evangelist, rabbi, *posek halacha*, healer, therapist, satsangist, pointer, psychic, leader, medium, savior, or guru. In fact, Prabhuji believes that the quest for the Self is individual, solitary, personal, private, and intimate. It is not a collective endeavor to be undertaken through social, organized, institutional, or community religiosity.

To that end, Prabhuji does not proselytize or preach, nor does he try to persuade, convince, or make anyone change their perspective, philosophy, or religion. Others may find his insights valuable and apply them wholly or in part to their own development, but Prabhuji's teachings should not be interpreted as personal advice, counseling, guidance, self-help methods, or techniques for spiritual, physical, emotional, or psychological development. The proposed teachings do not aspire to be definitive solutions for life's spiritual, material, financial, psychological, emotional, romantic, family, social, or physical problems. Prabhuji does not offer miracles, mystical experiences, astral journeys, healings, connections with spirits, supernatural powers, or spiritual salvation.

Although he did not seek to attract followers, for 15 years (1995–2010), Prabhuji considered the requests of a few people who approached him asking to become his monastic disciples Those who chose to see Prabhuji as their spiritual master voluntarily accepted vows of poverty and life-long dedication to spiritual practice (*sādhanā*), religious devotion (*bhakti*), and selfless service (*seva*). Prabhuji no longer accepts new disciples, but he continues to guide the small group of veteran disciples of the Ramakrishnananda Monastic Order that he founded.

Public services

Even though the monastery does not accept new residents, volunteers, donations, collaborations, or sponsorships, the public is invited to participate in daily religious services and devotional festivals at the Śrī Śrī Radha-Śyāmasundara temple.

Titles by Prabhuji

What is, as it is: Satsangs with Prabhuji (English)
ISBN-13: 978-1-945894-26-8
Lo que es, tal como es: Satsangas con Prabhuji (Spanish)
ISBN-13: 978-1-945894-27-5
Russian: ISBN-13: 978-1-945894-18-3

Kundalini yoga: The power is in you (English)
ISBN-13: 978-1-945894-30-5
Kundalini yoga: El poder está en ti (Spanish)
ISBN-13: 978-1-945894-31-2

Bhakti yoga: The path of love (English)
ISBN-13: 978-1-945894-28-2
Bhakti-yoga: El sendero del amor (Spanish)
ISBN-13: 978-1-945894-29-9

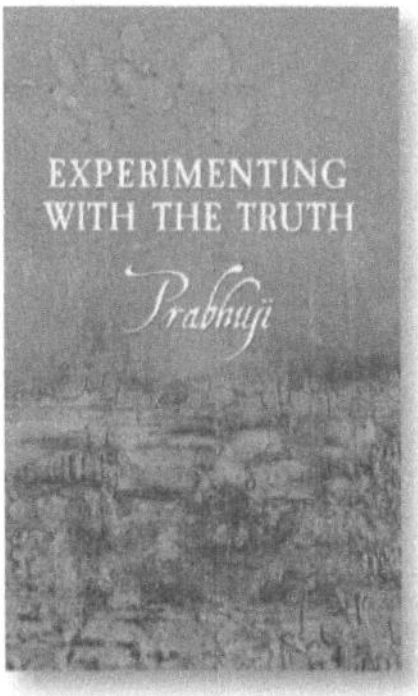

Experimenting with the Truth (English)
ISBN-13: 978-1-945894-32-9
Experimentando con la Verdad (Spanish)
ISBN-13: 978-1-945894-33-6

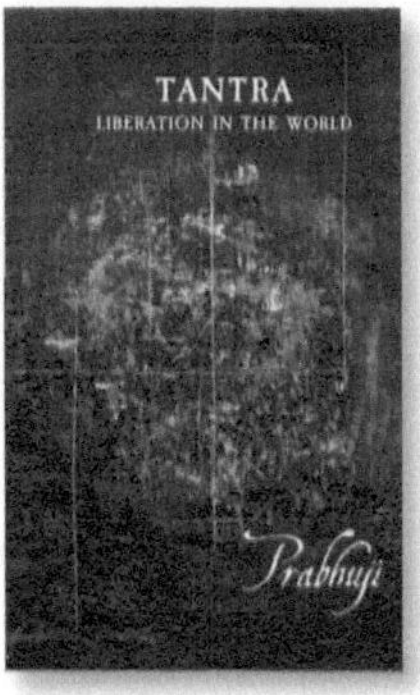

Tantra: Liberation in the world (English)
ISBN-13: 978-1-945894-36-7
Tantra: La liberación en el mundo (Spanish)
ISBN-13: 978-1-945894-37-4

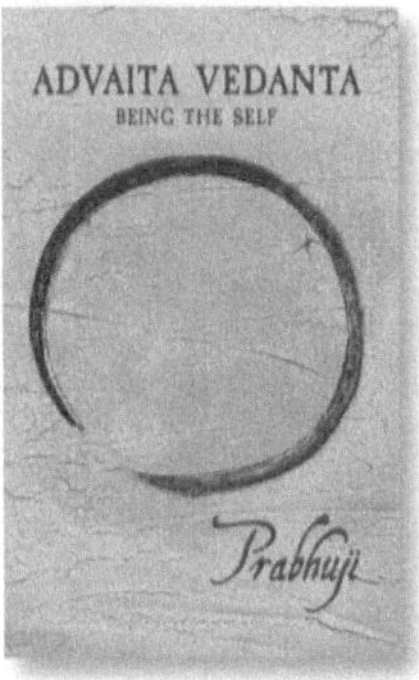

Advaita Vedanta: Being the Self (English)
ISBN-13: 978-1-945894-34-3
Advaita Vedanta: Ser el Ser (Spanish)
ISBN-13: 978-1-945894-35-0

Īśāvāsya Upanishad
commented by Prabhuji
(**English**)
ISBN-13: 978-1-945894-38-1
Īśāvāsya Upaniṣad
comentado por Prabhuji
(**Spanish**)
ISBN-13: 978-1-945894-40-4

The Diamond Sūtra
commented by Prabhuji
(**English**)
ISBN-13: 978-1-945894-51-0
El Sūtra del Diamante
comentado por Prabhuji
(**Spanish**)
ISBN-13: 978-1-945894-54-1

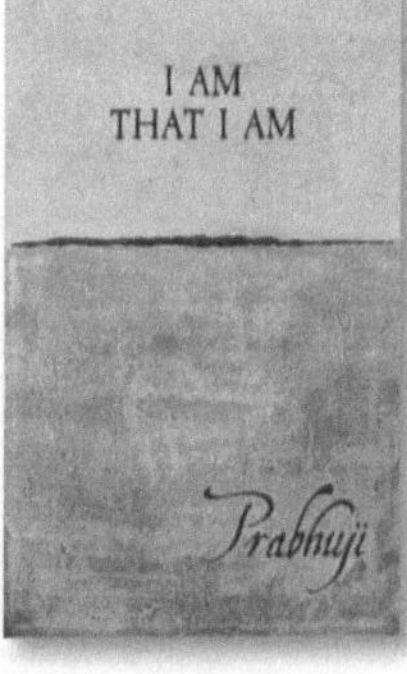

I am that I am
(**English**)
ISBN-13: 978-1-945894-45-9
Soy el que soy
(**Spanish**)
ISBN-13: 978-1-945894-48-0

www.ingramcontent.com/pod-product-compliance
Lightning Source LLC
Chambersburg PA
CBHW030145100526
44592CB00009B/128
* 9 7 8 1 9 4 5 8 9 4 2 0 6 *